# THE MEANING AND USES OF

# POLISH HISTORY

WITHDRAWN

## ADAM BROMKE

EAST EUROPEAN MONOGRAPHS, BOULDER

DISTRIBUTED BY COLUMBIA UNIVERSITY PRESS, NEW YORK

1987

To the memory of
Staszek, Kazik, Julek, Wiesio, Misio
and many other of my young friends
who fell in the Warsaw uprising.

# Table of Contents

# INTRODUCTION

This book is composed of two parts. The first is an essay of my own, reviewing the unique role which the study of history occupies in Poland. It is my contention that since most of the contemporary political programs are influenced by the Poles' perception of their past, history serves for them as a sort of *sui generis* national ideology. The significance of this phenomenon, its advantages as well as its shortcomings, is examined. To that end an extensive, although by no means complete, review of major works on Poland's recent history is also undertaken. Special attention is given to the role of the Polish studies in the west.

My next contention is that in order to perform better its role as *magistra vitae*, Polish history should be studied in a more systematic fashion. Above all, some regularities in it should be ascertained. Again I underline a special role which the western scholars, the historians as well as the social scientists, could play in such as intellectual endeavor. In this context I restate my own model of Poland's recent history which I first presented in my *Poland's Politics, Idealism vs. Realism* in 1967; and I re-examine it in the light of the events of the last two decades.

I am the first to admit that my essay is a contentious one. It is deliberately submitted in this form in order to stimulate a debate on the relationship between history and politics in Poland which, I believe, is badly needed. As such the essay is also a highly personal one. It reflects not only many years of my study of the subject, but also my own encounters with various episodes in Polish recent history.

The second part of this volume consists of selected writings from the Polish political thought of the 20th century, and especially the last thirty years. The excerpts concentrate upon three major themes which I also underline in my own essay, namely: the dichotomy between idealism and realism in Polish politics, the nature of modern Polish nationalism, and the role of Catholicism in Poland. I believe that none of these writings have been available in English before. I have selected the translated all of them myself. In doing so, I have tried to convey the gist of the author's arguments and to present them in English prose that is as simple as possible.

I should like to express gratitude to many friends, the Poles and the interested westerners, scholars and persons from many other walks of life, who in the endless discussions helped me to understand better the meanders of Polish history and politics. The specific intellectual debts are acknowledged in the text. I am also obliged to my critics — those who by engaging with me in honest polemics have assisted me in clarifying my thoughts, and those who in their vociferous attacks revealed to me the confusion of their own political thinking.

I am grateful to Laurie Miller, my collaborator and friend for many years, for his valuable editorial assistance in both improving my own text and in translating the appendices.

A.B.
Dundas, Ontario
July
1986

# I

# HISTORY AND POLITICS

The Poles are passionately involved in their history. For a nation which during the last two centuries has desperately struggled not only for independence but for its very survival as a separate entity, this is only natural. The Poles search history for the errors which brought their defeats and miseries; and even more often, they turn to the past glory of their state for encouragement and inspiration in their repeated efforts to regain their freedom, and they revere their predecessors who — even if vanquished — have fallen in the battle.

Under foreign rule in the nineteenth century, Adam Mickiewicz's epic *Pan Tadeusz* and Henryk Sienkiewicz's Trilogy, as well as the historical paintings of Artur Grottger and Jan Matejko, played important roles in keeping Polish nationalism alive. At the turn of the century Stanislaw Wyspianski's play *Liberation* and Stefan Zeromski's lyrical *Dream of the Sword* stirred the Poles toward striving once again to regain their independence with arms. And the historians proper then regarded it as their patriotic duty to counter the Russian and German historiography that denigrated Poland's past. This in itself provided their works with political connotations, but they did not stop there, and went beyond just searching for truth.

Historiographic debates have repeatedly been a convenient guise for contemporary political arguments. Couched in an Aesopian narrative of distant events, they have evaded the watchful eye of foreign censors, while the true meaning can easily have been detected by the Poles, so well versed in their history. The Cracow historians' critique in the late 1860s of the decline of the Polish state in the 18th century, which they attributed to the lack of statescraft on the part of the Poles,

1

and in the course of which, in particular, they blamed the uprising of 1794 for the partitions, was largely aimed at denouncing the foolhardy insurrectionist tradition which, in their opinion, had led to the disastrous uprising of 1863. In turn, the repudiation of their views by the Warsaw historians early in the 20th century was undertaken in the name of scholarly objectivity, but was also directed at rehabilitating the program of military struggle for Poland's freedom.

In the short-lived independent Polish state, naturally, critical interpretation of the past was dismissed, and the Warsaw school remained ascendant. As one of its prominent spokesmen, Waclaw Sobieski, put it: "When we were chained in slavery, we dwelt upon the vices of our forefathers, which had allegedly brought about the dismemberment of Poland.... Today the times have changed. Having our own state, we look at the past in a different light".[1] In the inter-war period, then, the Poles' dominant view of their history was both linear and romantic — the restoration of the state after over a century of subjugation was regarded as the natural culmination of the heroic deeds and sacrifices of their predecessors. It was this same view which inspired the Poles in their relentless efforts to regain their freedom during World War II.

After the war the Poles once again sought refuge in their history. New heroes, who had fallen in the many battles of 1939-1945, were now added to the national pantheon; the cemetery of the many young Warsaw insurgents of 1944 became revered as another Polish shrine. During the dark night of Stalinism Warsaw's Old City, where the worst fighting took place during the uprising, was painstakingly restored from the wartime ruins. Wladyslaw Gomulka resisted rebuilding the Royal Castle, which he saw as a symbol of the *ancien regime,* but Edward Gierek, gaining much popularity, consented to rebuilding this too. And the historians reverted to their traditional task of protecting the national past by correcting its distortions in foreign, and particularly Soviet, historiography.

To bypass the Communist censorship the Aesopian language was not only revived, but elaborated. Even some quite esoteric — though nevertheless clear to the Poles — historical episodes were evoked. In the mid-1960s a debate stirred by Andrzej Wajda's film based on Zeromski's novel *The Ashes,* depicting the Poles' military exploits during the Napoleonic Wars, was conducted in this fashion.[2] In fact, the debate had little to do with either Zeromski or Napoleon — it simply served as a convenient guise for discussing the Poles' experience of fighting on the side of the Western powers and, in turn, counting upon their assistance, during World War II.*

A similar debate took place in the late 1970s over Tomasz Lubienski's book under the significant title, *To Fight or Not to Fight?*, reviewing the Polish uprisings against the Russians in 1794, 1830 and 1863.[3] But by that time the resorting to allegories in the official press was hardly necessary. For by then historical writings issued in the many *samizdat* papers, and calling a spade a spade, abounded. And soon afterwards the Solidarity press devoted a great deal of space to a review — with strong anti-Soviet overtones — of recent history.

The searching in the past for guidance as to what to do today, still goes on in Poland. Immediately after the introduction of martial law in December 1981 comparisons were drawn (either because the authors really believed in the historical analogy, or just as a means to bypass the censorship) with the defeat of the uprising in 1863.[4] The merely temporary character of these two historical reversals (although after 1863 it took the Poles more than half a century to regain their independence) was underlined. Furthermore, the lasting accomplishments of the insurgents of 1863, and, by implication, the Solidarity followers, were highly praised. This way new vanquished heroes, whose example nevertheless ought to be followed, were added to the already long list of Polish martyrs.

The perennial political role of the study of history was emphasized in the leaflet announcing the XIII Congress of Polish historians in September 1984. "In our country", it asserted, "knowledge of the past has a special meaning. During the captivity it gave heart to and laid the foundations of national consciousness. It also protected, and still protects today, especially important social values: dignity, liberty, democracy, tolerance and the striving for truth".[5] And in an opening address at the Congress Professor Andrzej Zahorski emphasized the tasks of the Polish historians. Invoking the Helsinki Final Act he asserted that: "Aspiring to truth and freedom is an inalienable human right of each one of us".[6]

---

*The Communist censors, being Polish, were, of course, not unaware of the contemporary implications of the historical debates. Yet, since these did not challenge the official dogmas outright, the censors were evidently ready to overlook them. Indeed, it seems the censors regarded such discussions as a useful "safety valve", i.e., a substitute for genuine political polemics. The Polish censors, in turn, may have hoped that this form of political polemics — precisely because of their esoteric nature — would escape the attention of their own Soviet overseers.

The tendency to use history for didactic purposes, of course, is not unique to Poland. It has been part of historiography ever since Herodotus and Thucidides depicted the heroic deeds of the ancient Greeks. Yet, there seems little doubt that in Poland it has acquired exceptional significance. "The foreigners", observed one Polish historian, "speak of us as obsessed with our past. Even if they somewhat exaggerate, we ourselves tacitly admit to a slight infatuation with Clio, particularly when she is clothed in white and red. History is an important and serious concern among us — it is a presence in the everyday life of the people and the citizens, the society and the nation. [It] is everywhere in our country and it pulses with authentic life."[7] The past, thus, continues to be venerated by the Poles and serves as an inspiration in their modern endeavors. It is for them a veritable *magistrae vitae* — a sort of *sui generis* nationalist idealogy.

\* \* \*

In the post-war period the dominant approach to the study of Polish history, of course, has been the Marxist one. It also has taken a linear view of Poland's past, but a different one from that of traditional Polish historiography. The past, especially since the appearance of the Marxist movement in the 1880s, has been interpreted as logically leading to the emergence of the workers' state: the People's Poland closely aligned with the USSR. During the climax of Stalinism in the early 1950s no views of history other than those closely toeing the official line were tolerated, and the Polish Historical Society went into eclipse.

After 1956 the political controls over historiography were somewhat relaxed and the activities of the Polish Historical Society were resumed. Still, the Marxist version of Poland's past remained the official one and works deviating from it were either rigorously censored, or altogether banned from publication. Writing in 1975 a popular Catholic writer, Stefan Kisielewski, painted a bleak picture of the situation in Polish historiography. For all practical intents and purposes, he argued:

> the study of Polish history is non-existent. In its place there is a one-sided compiliation artificially put together...geared to official propaganda, and exclusively serving to mold the minds of the students in a way desired by the Communist party. The specialty of our system, as Orwell envisaged, is history in the service of politics, adjusted and projected backward.[8]

Particularly strict political control was exercised over the study of the history — from its very inception until the latest events — of the Communist movement itself. One could say very little, Kisielewski observed ironically, about Bierut, Ochab or Gomulka. The same applied to Poland's relations with the USSR, or indeed, to Poland's more distant relations with the Tsarist Russia where no criticism whatsoever was permitted. A disillusioned veteran Communist, Wladyslaw Bienkowski, even claimed that the Soviet ambassador himself assumed the role of chief censor of such writings. "Under his pressure...in historical works entire sections are deleted, even when they deal with long-ago Polish-Russian relations — as if the Soviet authorities identified themselves with the policies of the Russian Tsars."[9]

Yet, despite all the obstacles, in the 1960s and the 1970s the presentation of a more objective picture of Polish history was also advanced. The tedious efforts on the part of the historians in this regard were well depicted by one of the leading figures among them, Stefan Kieniewicz. "For over thirty years", he asserted, "many of us honestly and patiently drudged to recreate the national past in a manner that was, as much as possible, complete, accurate and true, and to overcome the many prejudices and limitations which stood in the way of our doing so."[10]

The study of distant events, of course, was politically less controversial and many historians sought refuge in these relatively "safe" subjects. Except for Polish-Russian relations, their works dealing with the period prior to the late 19th century were generally quite objective. However, some interesting books dealing with more recent times also appeared.[11] In addition, many articles, some even occasionally quite controversial, appeared in the popular weeklies, and especially in the Communist but fairly liberal *Polityka,* the Catholic but pro-regime *Kierunki,* and the independent Catholic *Tygodnik Powszechny.* These were, as ever, eagerly received by the history-conscious Polish readers.

The Polish historians found different ways to overcome the political restrictions. On the one hand they used the obligatory Marxist version of history and reinterpreted it in a more subtle fashion — in a way somewhat akin to the French *Annales* — focusing upon economic and social developments. The works of Henryk Wereszycki, and even more so those of Stefan Kieniewicz, on Polish history during the partitions, fruitfully followed this approach. On the other hand many writers turned to historicism, in the tradition of Leopold von Ranke, and concentrated on producing relatively narrow monographs avoiding any broader political implications.

Despite all the political obstacles, research into various recent episodes in the Polish history led to many valuable books and articles appearing in print. Janusz Pajewski and Wlodzimierz T. Kowalski wrote about the restoration of the Polish state in 1918. Andrzej Garlicki produced several books on the Pilsudskiite movement in the inter-war period; and Halina and Tadeusz Jedruszczak dealt with the last years of the existence of independent Poland. Jacek K. Majchrowski addressed himself to the activities of the Christian Democrats and Jerzy Janusz Terej to those of the national democrats before and during World War II. A Catholic author, Andrzej Micewski, covered a broad range of subjects, including the programs of the main political movements, and especially the Pilsudskiites, in the II Republic, and he published a comprehensive biography of the national democratic leader, Roman Dmowski (although in the last case, for the book to be released by the censors, he had to add several highly critical pages).

Polish history during World War II was also given considerable attention. Olgierd Terlecki and Roman Wojnicki each wrote biographies of General Wladyslaw Sikorski (although the complete text of Terlecki's study could appear only in the West). Kowalski wrote widely about the role of Poland in the wartime diplomacy (in 1978, together with a Party Secretary, Ryszard Frelek, he even produced a popular TV serial on Polish foreign policy before World War II). A Catholic historian, Wladyslaw Bartoszewski, covered in considerable detail the struggle against the German occupants by the non-Communist Polish underground.

Micewski, in fact, went beyond wartime and produced a history of the major developments in Polish politics in 1945-76. It focused upon the activities of the Catholic political groups "Pax" and "Znak", but as a background it also presented a remarkably candid picture of the major developments in the Communist party.[12] Since the author was personally involved in these events — he was at first a member of "Pax", and, then, of "Znak" — his account was not devoid of personal overtones, but as a whole he managed to maintain objectivity (his book appeared in the West, but it has been quite widely read in Poland). In the 1960s and the 1970s, thus, although somewhat unevenly, Polish historiography made considerable progress.*

---

*The list of the authors and works mentioned above, as well as in the following pages, does not pretend to be comprehensive. It reflects this author's own research interests, and, as such, undoubtedly has many omissions.

Yet, there remained glaring lacunae deeply hurtful to the Poles' national pride. The one-sided treatment of Polish history under Communism produced a strong reaction in the late 1970s and the early 1980s. The subjects which hitherto had been taboo — including the most sensitive episodes in Polish-Soviet relations — were explored with particular glee, at first in the *samizdat* publications issued by the democratic opposition, and, subsequently, in the Solidarity papers.

In opposing the Marxist approach, however, many writers fell victims of another linear view of history. They went back to the belief of the Warsaw school — which seemed to fit so well Poland's situation in 1980-81 — that, ultimately, the Poles' efforts and sacrifices are bound to be rewarded by restoration of their independence. This conviction has not been abandoned even after the introduction of martial law in December 1981. It inspired the rise of Solidarity underground and it still permeates many clandestine papers. It also found an echo at the Congress of the Polish historians in 1984. The Chairman of the State Council, a former professional historian himself, Henryk Jablonski, was conspicuously missing from that gathering, while several dissident historians who had been just released from custody, were feted there.

Yet, both linear views of Polish history: the Marxist as well as that of the Warsaw school, are erroneous. Neither did the II Republic prove to be durable and now capable of easy restoration; nor is the People's Poland the final, and immutable, outcome of the inevitable march of historical forces. The linear view of history is itself simply a myth; history is full of surprises and has often produced strange hybrids. The Polish history has by no means been exclusively motivated by the class struggle; at times — as the Communists painfully learned in 1920, 1945, and most recently in 1980-81 — the Poles have displayed remarkable solidarity in upholding their right to independence. Yet, there have also been periods in their history — notably in the 1870s, in the 1950s, and even in the early 1970s when the Poles have abandoned an all-out struggle for independence and have tried to improve their lot by seeking reconciliation with foreign rulers.

\* \* \*

Since World War II at least as important work in Polish history has been carried out in the West as at home. Poland's role during the war was discussed in the memoirs of various western statesmen, notably Winston Churchill's, and in the major historical studies covering wartime diplomacy. The Communist takeover in Poland was described in the personal recollections of the two American Ambassadors: Arthur Bliss-Lane and Stanton Griffis. Hugh Seton-Watson covered the developments in Poland in some detail in his seminal work on the Communist revolutions in Eastern Europe,[13] and his example was followed by many western scholars — historians as well as political scientists. Courses on Polish history and politics (although normally treated in a broader context of the study of Eastern European governments) were gradually added to the curricula at numerous western universities, and especially in the United States.

Yet, in the immediate post-war years the knowledge of recent Polish history in the West remained limited. A bibliography issued in 1969 pointed out substantial gaps.[14] In the English-speaking world the only historian of major stature specializing in Poland was William John Rose. A Canadian by Birth, he studied at Oxford and during World War I was stranded in Silesia where he learned Polish. After the war he returned to Poland to complete his doctorate at the Jagiellonian University in Cracow. Subsequently, he became director of the School of Slavonic and East European Studies in London (where, during World War II, he kept closely in touch with the Polish exiles there). He returned to Canada in 1950. His *The Rise of Polish Democracy,* published in 1944, and his other numerous writings stood out as the main source of scholarly information about the developments in Poland in 1863-1939.* The only other comprehensive work in English, covering the events until 1935, was *The Cambridge History of Poland.*

After World War II the study of Poland in the West received a powerful stimulus from the presence of a large number of Polish exiles. Some half a million of the Poles stranded at the end of the war, mostly in Western Europe, declined to return to their Communist-ruled homeland. Among them were many prominent political figures and leading intellectuals, including some historians. And in time a younger generation of scholars, who supplemented their education in the West,

---

*Rose liked the Poles and enjoyed their company — on social occasions he would proudly quote from memory entire passages from *Pan Tadeusz;* yet, he also found their way of political reasoning exasperating. In 1960 he told this author that he totally failed to understand how the Poles could demand the return of their pre-war eastern territories, and at the same time insist that they retain the provinces they obtained from Germany at the end of the war. For an account of Rose's academic career and complete bibliography of his writings see *Canadian Slavonic Papers* (University of Toronto Press, Vol. V, 1959).

emerged from their ranks. The main emigré centers were London (which had been the seat of the wartime Polish Government-in-Exile) and Paris, but many of the emigrés, and especially the younger ones, moved on to the United States and Canada (where sizeable Polish communities had long been in existence). Some of them undertook university teaching and conducted research into Polish affairs, especially in history and politics.

The reasons for the emigrés' keen interest in history were threefold. First, after their defeat they wanted to vindicate their political program by writing down their recollections and gathering documents to counteract the Communists' arguments. Second, they felt that access to historical truth, at least as they saw it, would be helpful for the younger Poles to withstand the onslaught of the Marxist ideology. Their publications in Polish — which filtered into Poland in considerable numbers — were chiefly aimed to serve this purpose. And, third, the emigrés considered it their duty to spread their views in the West from which they expected assistance in liberating their country from the Soviet domination, an eventuality that would also enable them to return home and perhaps to regain political power there. To that end they strove to disseminate their publications by translating them into the major western languages; while those emigrés who were able to do so (although relatively few managed it successfully), turned to writing in foreign languages, and especially in English.

In the emigrés' historical writings, thus, the search for truth and political expediency became inseparably linked. Naturally, they subscribed to the traditional linear view of history which asserted that sooner or later the trend of events is bound to lead to the restoration of Poland's independence. And anybody who dared to question this approach was regarded as a traitor to the Polish cause. When in 1953 Samuel L. Sharp, in his *Poland, White Eagle on a Red Shield*, voiced pessimism about Poland's chances of freeing itself soon from Soviet suzeranity, a veritable campaign of vilification was launched against him in the emigré press. The Paris monthly *Kultura* — apparently hoping to find a sympathetic echo in the United States where Senator McCarthy's campaign was under way — even denounced Sharp for "un-American" activities.[15] Thus, in their efforts to vindicate what they believed to be the true version of history, driven by as much malice as despair, the emigrés resorted to methods similar to those used by their Marxist counterparts at home.

The emigrés nevertheless have made a significant contribution to the study of recent Polish history. Above all, they have collected a wealth of information about it. The Sikorski Institute and the Center for the Study of the Polish Underground in London, the Pilsudski Insititute in New York, the Dmowski Institute in Chicago, and some other similar institutions have collected rich archives, surpassing in the fields of their specialization the best library collections not only in the West, but even in Poland. And these have been of great help to professional historians. Some of the documents, moreover, for instance, the two-volume collection on Polish-Soviet relations during World War II, have been published in English translation.

Of great value too has been the publication of memoirs of many former politicians, diplomats and soldiers who participated in various historical episodes. These are scattered throughout the various emigré periodicals such as *Kultura, Wiadomosci* or *Mysl Polska*. An especially rich collection of such writings is available in the series of *Zeszyty Historyczne* issued since 1961 by the Literary Institute in Paris, which by now exceeds seventy substantial volumes. The texts included, incidentally, have been written not only by emigrés, but also by authors at home whose manuscripts have been smuggled abroad.

Many memoirs by former Polish leaders have also appeared in book form, and some have been translated into English. The fact that more often than not they are openly partisan does not detract, and in a way even enhances — by capturing the spirit of the times — their value. For instance, the recollections by the last pre-war Polish Premier, General Felicjan Slawoj-Skladkowski, both reveal a considerable literary talent in the author, and eloquently testify to his utter incompetence as a statesman.

Among particularly valuable memoirs covering the early stages of the 20th century are those by Aleksandra Pilsudska, who was at Pilsudski's side, first as his mistress, and then second wife, from 1906 until 1935; as well as those by Wincenty Witos, thrice premier in the years 1920-1926. There are also the recollections of Dmowski, both as a politician and a man, by his successor as a national democratic leader, Tadeusz Bielecki, and by his close friend, Izabella Lutoslawska-Wolikowska. The inter-war Polish diplomacy is described in his "final report" by Jozef Beck, the Polish Foreign Minister in 1931-39, and in the diary of his deputy, Jan Szembek. The activities of General Sikorski both before World War II and as Premier of the Polish Government-in-Exile in 1939-1943 are described by three of his collaborators: the Christian Democratic leader, Karol Popiel, General Marian Kukiel and Colonel Leon Mitkiewicz.

The World War II diplomacy is covered by the Polish ambassadors in Washington and London, Jan Ciechanowski and Edward Raczynski, respectively (the first book was originally written in English and the

second was translated into that language), as well as by the Polish
Ambassador in Kuibyshev, Jan Kot. The collection of speeches and
writings by General Kazimierz Sosnkowski, who was Commander-
in-Chief of the Polish armed forces in 1943-44 (supplemented by the
recollections of his aide, Witold Babinski); and the memoirs of General
Wladyslaw Anders, who commanded the Polish troops in the USSR
and then in Italy, described the Polish war exploits against a broad
background of international events. Generals Stanislaw Kopanski,
Stanislaw Maczek and others address themselves to the specific cam-
paigns in which the Polish units fighting on the western side participated.

General Tadeusz Bor-Komorowski, the Home Army Commander
in 1943-44, and many of his subordinates, notably the two emissaries
to the West, Jan Karski and Jan Nowak, depict the struggle of the
Polish underground. The memoirs of a Peasant Party leader, Stefan
Korbonski, and those by a national democrat, Zbigniew Stypulkowski,
throw light on political aspects of the clandestine activities. And Jozef
Mackiewicz probed deeply into the murder of the Polish officers in
Katyn who were captured by the Soviets in 1939.

Some of the emigrés also turned to writing historical works *par
excellence*. Marian Kukiel, who, in addition to being a general, was
also a professional historian, authored a valuable volume on Poland's
history during the partitions (although toward the end, where he
describes the events in which he himself participated as a young man,
he tends to be somewhat less objective). Adam and Lidia Ciolkosz
covered the history of early socialist movement in Poland, and
Zygmunt Zaremba sketched the entire history of the Polish Socialist
Party. Stanislaw Kozicki's seminal work on the National League,
written in Poland, was also published in the West. And the restoration of the Polish state at the end of World War II was dealt with
by Tytus Komarnicki in English and Tadeusz Piszczkowski in Polish.

The inter-war developments were first described in a journalistic
fashion by Stanislaw Mackiewicz, and, in a more scholarly manner,
in English, focusing primarily on economics, by Ferdinand Zweig.
These were followed by a three-volume work, which also covered
the wartime, by Wladyslaw Pobog-Malinowski. It offers an un-
abashedly pro-Pilsudskiite interpretation of events, but it does contain
a wealth of detailed information. Pobog-Malinowski also prepared
a comprehensive biography of Pilsudski, and Waclaw Jedrzejewicz
painstakingly put together a calendar of the late Marshal's activities.
In contrast, a leading national democrat, Jedrzej Giertych, wrote a
highly critical account of Pilsudski's political activities. And a former

diplomat, Roman Debicki, published in English a concise volume on Poland's foreign policy in 1919-39.

\* \* \*

The emigrés' efforts to record Poland's history, of course, did not stop at 1945. The works on the events during World War II were supplemented by accounts of the new developments as these unfolded. They included the publication in Polish (and often in English too), of the most important political documents, writings by opposition leaders, memoirs by the new exiles, as well as analyses of the events at home prepared by the emigrés. These works of course were even more political in their nature than the books about more distant happenings. They not only subscribed to the view of history as inevitably leading toward the restoration of Poland's independence, but they also directly challenged the Marxist interpretation of the situation.

The recollections by the people who left Poland were scattered throughout various emigré papers, and some also appeared as books. The Communist takeover was well documented by in the memoirs written, after he left the country in 1947, by the Polish Peasant Party leader, Stanislaw Mikolajczyk, and his collaborator at that time, Stefan Korbonski. Zbigniew Stypulkowski recorded in some detail the trial of the Polish underground leaders in Moscow in 1945 in which he was one of the defendants (all of these works appeared in English and some other western languages). Czeslaw Milosz and Marek Korowicz depicted the situation existing in Poland during the climax of Stalinism, and Alcja Zawadzka-Wert and George J. Flemming that in the early Gomulka era.

In 1952 *Kultura* published a three-volume analysis of the developments in Poland during the immediate post-war years; and then it started issuing a systematic series documenting major events at home, particularly the more dramatic ones, such as those in 1956, 1968 and 1970. Similar efforts were undertaken in the mid-1950s by the Polish Section of the Free Europe Press in New York, and in the 1960s by the Institute for the Study of Home Affairs in London. *Kultura* also published the writings on some prominent dissidents — among its early authors were Wladyslaw Bienkowski, Jacek Kuron and Karol Modzelewski.

In the 1970s, and particularly with the rise of the democratic opposition in Poland after 1976, more and more works by writers at home appeared in the West. In addition to *Kultura,* these were issued by the Polonia Publishing Fund and "Odnowa" in London. In time new publishing houses were founded: "Libella" in Paris, "Aneks" in London and Polonia Publishers in Chicago. Among the authors from Poland whose writings were popularized this way were well known dissidents, such as Adam Michnik and Marek Turbacz, Catholic writers Stefan Kisielewski, Andrzej Micewski and Janusz Zablocki, and sociologists Jan Szczepanski and Marek Tarniewski. In 1979 an expanded edition of a Polish history of the period 1784-1918 by Henryk Wereszycki, which has been banned at home, appeared in the West.

The osmosis between historical and political thought in Poland and in the emigration worked both ways. On the one hand the works of the writers at home were published in the West; and on the other hand the western publications filtered back home and had a profound impact there. As Adam Michnik put it: "The emigration returned to the home-land. Its books were increasingly smuggled across the border, they were passed from person to person and hidden from the vigilant eyes of the police. The emigration brought knowledge about the world, the truth about national history, the leading works of contemporary literature and non-censored reflections about Polish hopes and hope-lessness."[16] The influence of the emigrés' writings was also evident in historiography. Works by the historians abroad more and more frequently were included in the bibliographies and footnotes, and occasionally even cited in the historical texts at home.

After the suppression of Solidarity, paradoxical as it may appear, some of the western historical studies were still permitted to appear at home in Poland. Popiel's biography of General Sikorski, and Ciechanowski's book on the Warsaw uprising (the latter becoming an instant bestseller) were published in Poland in 1984. And articles by a Polish historian living in the United States, Piotr Wandycz, as well by this author, were published in the Catholic weeklies: *Tygodnik Powszechny* and *Lad* respectively. They dealt mostly with approaches to historiography, but their contemporary implications, no doubt, were apparent to the Polish readers.*

---

*This does not mean that Wandycz's and my views are similar; in fact, our articles articulated very different approaches to the uses of history (see Ch. II). Still, it was entirely novel that polemics between two professors of Polish origin, who had taught in North America for over thirty years, were permitted (and without either article in any way being censored) to appear in the official Polish press.

At the same time a new wave of Polish emigrés — many of them former activists of the democratic opposition and of Solidarity — appeared in the West. They brought with them a wealth of detailed information about the latest political developments in Poland and a firm commitment to continue the struggle for their country's independence. Many of the newcomers have already written their recollections of the dramatic events in which they participated and have helped to publish those by their colleagues who stayed at home. This way the life of the Polish political emigration has been effectively extended for another generation. Among the new refugees there are also some professional historians and political scientists, who will certainly endeavor to continue, as best as they can, their work abroad.

The emigrés, then, won the battle against the Marxists hands down. The Marxists, of course, worked against heavy odds. They were generally regarded as apologists for the unpopular, and foreign imposed, Communist system; in fact, they were often no less resented than the German or the Russian writers who had denigrated Poland's history during the partitions. The Marxists, however, have generously contributed to their own defeat. They have made singularly little effort to fit their interpretation of history into the specific Polish conditions and, instead, have simply parroted the Soviet line. Their linear version of Poland's past, seen exclusively in terms of a class struggle which culminated in the emergence of People's Poland, was easy to demolish. It flew, moreover, in the face of the repeated political crises in the country.

By the early 1980s, then, under the impact of developments at home and the influence of the emigrés, by and large the younger Poles have reverted to the traditional view of the country's history seen primarily as a continuous struggle for freedom which through their efforts and sacrifices sooner or later is bound to lead to the restoration of their independence. The political triumph of the Warsaw school of historiography over the Marxist one, thus, is undeniable — whether or not this has brought the Poles closer to historical truth, however, is another matter.

*  *  *

As to the emigrés' third objective, namely, the spreading of their views of Polish history in the West, they have been partially, but only partially, successful. Various factors here have played into their hands. First of all the Marxist interpretation of Poland's past has made little headway in the West — not only because of its political content, but also because of its low intellectual quality. In the 1940s and the 1950s, moreover, the impact of the inter-war Polish historiography among the western scholars was still strong. The picture of the foolhardy Poles struggling for their independence against all odds — militarily brave, but politically often naive people — was only re-affirmed by the westerners' contacts with them during World War II. It was well summed up by Harold MacMillan in depicting the spirit of the Polish troops fighting alongside the British troops in Italy. ''It was an extraordinary sense of romance; not gaiety exactly, but chivalry, poetry, adventure. It was more than a military formation. It was a crusade.''[17]

Last but not least, the osmosis with the Polish emigrés affected not only the historians in Poland, but those in the West as well. Some of the emigrés themselves became professional historians and took up teaching posts at various western universities, especially in the English-speaking world. In the immediate post-war years the towering figure among them in the United States was Oskar Halecki. An inspiring lecturer, and a prolific and erudite writer, he helped to educate the new generation of American historians specializing in Poland. Before the war Halecki was one of the leading exponents of the Warsaw school — his major area of interest being the Jagiellonian period. He tended to see Poland's contemporary role as somewhat analogous to that which it played in the 16th century: as a bulwark of western civilization in Eastern Europe. In 1956 he edited the first major volume in English on the developments in the country after World War II. Many younger western historians became influenced by the views of Halecki and, consciously or unconsciously, subscribed to the Warsaw school's linear view of Polish history.

And those younger historians who found the prevailing view of Poland's past in the West unsatisfactory, tended to seek refuge in historicism in the tradition of von Ranke. Their works avoided any broader syntheses and focused on description of specific events, usually in the form of fairly narrow monographs — in other works they abstained from drawing any contemporary conclusions from the past and just wrote *histoire événementalle*. And in doing so — although for different reasons — they converged with the concurrent trends amoung the historians in Poland.

In the 1960s and the 1970s the study of Polish history in the West, and especially in the English-speaking countries, made substantial progress. A bibliography published in 1977 testified that many past gaps had been filled;[18] and in the following years many new valuable works appeared. The literature on Poland's history in English now ranks next only to that in Polish. Indeed, some studies by the western scholars are unrivalled by anything available in Poland. And the literature in English has been strengthened by translations into it of major works from other western languages (as, for instance, an excellent volume, covering the period 1914-1965, by Hans Ross, which was originally written in German).

Among the works on the partitions' period Wandycz's study stands out. The volume edited by R. F. Leslie covers the events for 1864 to the present, although the part from prior to 1914 (written by himself) is rather sketchy. M. Kamil Dziewanowski wrote about Poland in the 20th century, and Norman Davies dealt in some detail with the events in the 19th and the 20th centuries in his comprehensive study of the entire Polish history. Peter Brock wrote about the rise of modern Polish nationalism, and the early stages of the peasant movement. Anthony Polonsky prepared a substantial volume on the independent Polish state and a part of Leslie's volume on the same subject (including World War I). Joseph Rothschild addressed himself to the Pilsudskiites' coup d'etat in 1926; and Edward D. Wynot came out with an interesting study of Poland in 1935-39, with special attention to the Pilsudskiites' political program.

Thaddeus Gromada edited a volume on the inter-war Polish diplomacy and Anna Cieciala wrote about Beck's foreign policy in 1938-39. Davies covered the Polish-Russian War, Wandycz Polish-Soviet relations in 1917-1921, and Bohdan Budurowicz those in 1932-39. Dziewanowski authored a study of Pilsudski's federalist plans in the east, and Peter J. Potychnyj edited a general volume on Polish-Ukrainian relations. Harald von Riekhoff addressed himself to Polish-German relations in 1918-1933, and Wandycz to the Franco-Polish alliance in 1919-1925. Finally Jan Karski has recently come out with a comprehensive study of the great powers' policies toward Poland in 1919-1945 — from Versailles to Yalta.

Poland's struggle during World War II was given a great deal of attention by the western historians. Jan Ciechanowski prepared a section on wartime history for Leslie's volume in addition to his book on the Warsaw uprising. Janusz Zawodny wrote about the Warsaw uprising too and about the murder of the Polish officers at Katyn. Jan T. Gross described the fate of the Polish society under the German occupation.

Edward J. Rozek came out with a general work on Poland's role in the allied wartime diplomacy, while Polonsky issued a collection of major documents pertaining to this subject, George V. Kacewicz probed into Polish-British relations in 1939-1945, and Richard C.

Lukas examined Polish-American relations in 1941-45; while Wandycz in his comprehensive study on Poland and the United States also covered the post-war developments. The same prolific author prepared a monograph on the plans for post-war Polish-Czechoslovak federation. Sarah Meiklejohn Terry explored Sikorski's designs to move Poland's boundary westward at the end of the World War II, and Elisabeth Wiskeman described how this actually happened.

Surprisingly, the story of the Marxist movement in Poland received relatively little attention among the western historians. The best history of pre-war Polish Communism is undoubtedly Dziewanowski's *The Communist Party of Poland*, originally issued in 1959.[19] The establishment of the Communist rule in Poland is also covered in a volume by Polonsky and Boleslaw Drukier, which includes a valuable selection of pertinent documents. Some other writers offered interesting insights into this subject in the introductory chapters of their books addressed to more contemporary events.

* * *

The post-war developments have been mainly the domain of the political scientists and the journalists. Nevertheless a few professional historians have covered them too. Dziewanowski discussed the situation at home quite extensively, both in his second edition of the history of Polish Communism and in his work on Poland in the 20th century; and Wandycz reviewed in some detail the developments in the last part of his volume on Polish-American relations since 1945. The most incisive presentation of post-war Polish history, however, was written by a political scientist, Zbigniew A. Pelczynski, as a concluding section in Leslie's book.

Valuable contributions to the study of the early stages of People's Poland were included in some works dealing with Eastern Europe as a whole. In his book on the original Yugoslav-Soviet dispute, Adam B. Ulam offered a detailed discussion of the crisis in the Polish Communist party in 1948-49. Zbigniew K. Brzezinski covered at some length the developments in Poland in the 1940s and the 1950s in his penetrating study of the Soviet bloc published in 1960 (although when he returned to the discussion of the Polish events in his 1965 book on Europe he was less successful). And Paul E. Zinner prepared a valuable collection of documents on the Polish crisis in 1956.

The outcome of the events in Poland in 1956 surprised the western observers and aroused their curiosity. Especially in contrast with the uprising in Hungary in the same year, Poland's "peaceful revolution" did not fit into the deeply entrenched western stereotypes of the Poles as the people ever ready to uphold their right to independence with arms and incapable of a policial compromise. A number of journalistic accounts probing into the seemingly contradicting nature of the "Polish October" — by Frank Gibney, Flora Lewis, Konrad Syrop and others — appeared in the late 1950s. It was largely to explain this apparent paradox — by pointing out that there was in Poland a long tradition of seeking compromise with powerful foreign rulers — that I wrote in the early 1960s my *Poland's Politics, Realism vs. Idealism.*

The early Gomulka period was dealt with in depth by Hansjakob Stehle (whose book was originally published in German), and Richard Hiscocks (although his account of early Marxism was somewhat confusing); while Nicholas Bethel produced a comprehensive biography of the Polish leader. Richard F. Staar, James Morrison, Jaroslaw Piekalkiewicz and Anthony Z. Kruszewski addressed themselves to the working of political institutions. Andrzej Korbonski systematically examined the Communist agricultural policies up to the 1960s. And Lucjan Blit produced a critical study of the Catholic "Pax" movement.

The early Gierek years were covered in a journalistic, but penetrating fashion by Geroge Blazynski and in a volume edited by John W. Strong and this author. Several interesting articles were written by A. Ross Johnson. By that time the authors living in Poland began to publish their writings in the West too. In 1970 Jan Szczepanski's *Polish Society* appeared in the United States.* And in the volume edited by Strong and myself several papers by well-known Polish writers — Communists and non-Communists alike — were included.

In addition to those of the political scientists, important contributions to the knowledge of post-war Poland have been made by other social scientists. A sociologist, Aleksander Gella examined the role of the Polish intelligentsia, and Aleksander Matejko that of the working class — both of them having left Poland in the late 1960s:** Joseph R.

---

*Significantly, Szczepanski's book was never published in Poland and, in fact, he ran into serious political difficulties for issuing it in the West. Had it not been for the fall of Gomulka at the end of 1970, not only Szczepanski's political, but even his academic career could have been in jeopardy.

**Since political science in Poland has mainly adhered to Marxism-Leninism, sociology, and in particular political sociology, has become a sort of substitute for it. It has attracted a large number of non-Marxist scholars who sought there a relatively unrestrained outlet for their creative energies.

Fiszman produced a study of the post-war educational system in Poland. And Thad P. Alton, John M. Montias, Michal Gamarnikow, Zbigniew Fallenbuchl, Bogdan Mieczkowski, George F. Feiwel, Leon Smolinski and others studied the Polish economy. In time they were joined by newcomers from Poland notably Janusz Zielinski, Stanislaw Gomulka and Wlodzimierz Brus.

The unfolding crisis in Poland after 1976 aroused new interest in the West. By that time a whole plethora of younger western social scientists made an appearance. Some of them came from Polish parentage and often had learned the language at home; others availed themselves of the programs existing at the western universities and the academic exchanges to spend some time in Poland. Jack Bielasiak, Maurice D. Simon and Jan de Weydenthal in the United States, Jean Woodall in Britain and John Besemeres in Australia traced the general political trends. Ray Taras addressed himself to the role of ideology, Sarah Meiklejohn Terry examined the working of the parliament, Jane Leftwich Curry the role of public media and Stefania Szlek Miller and André Liebich the position of the Catholic church. Alex Pravda and George Kolankiewicz focused on the changes in the working class. And Roger E. Kanet and George Schöpflin looked at Poland's position in the Communist bloc.

The younger western scholars were soon joined by newcomers from Poland, who managed to find for themselves teaching or research positions in the West. Jakub Karpinski analyzed the various political crises from 1956 to 1980; Barbara and Bronislaw Misztal examined the role of political elites, Aleksander Smolar inquired into the corruption in the higher echelons, while Maria Los investigated deficiencies in social policies.

In their political writings the new exiles naturally tended to embrace the traditional view of Polish history, conceived as a continuous struggle for freedom. Some of them, notably a prominent philosopher, Leszek Kolakowski, have made the full circle: from militant Marxists to a position close to that of the older emigrés. After 1976 the writings of other former Marxists who turned into leading dissidents, Edward Lipinski, Jacek Kuron, Adam Michnik and many others, were widely publicized in the West. Some of the western observers of the Polish scene followed in their footsteps. Their books, such as the one on oposition in Poland by Peter Raina (dedicated to Kuron and Michnik), or the volume on the rise of Solidarity edited by Abraham Brumberg, were largely political tracts with little pretence to scholarly objectivity.

During the Solidarity period Poland, of course, was in the center of world attention and the country was virtually opened to the western journalists. Scores of instant books on the Polish events then appeared in the West. As usual some of them were good and others less so. Generally, as reportages of what happened in 1980-81 they were valuable — indeed, no other episode in the Polish post-war history has been so well documented; but few of them offered profound analyses of these dramatic events. Most of the authors, moreover, carried away by the enthusiasm of the day, adopted an openly partisan, pro-Solidarity stance. Only more recently have the first more objective assessments of Solidarity by authors who participated in it, such as Jadwiga Sztaniskis or Aleksander Hall, become available in English.

\* \* \*

In the aftermath of Solidarity interest in the situation in Poland in the West has remained considerable. Indeed, never in the past — not even during World War II when the initial interest in the fate of the Polish nation in 1939 was soon overshadowed by other momentous events — has knowledge of that country in Western Europe and North America been as extensive as today. In western political circles there is a broad appreciation of Poland's strategic position in Eastern Europe and, consequently, its significance to Europe as a whole.

In the academic studies of the Communist states in Europe, Poland clearly occupies a place next only to the Soviet Union. The younger generation of western scholars who selected Poland as an area of specialization, has come of age. They will carry on their research well into the 21st century. And recently their ranks have been supplemented by many young Polish academics who have emigrated to the West and have found positions at the various universities there.

Among the politicians as well as the academics interested in Poland there is a strong tendency to sympathize with the Poles' endeavours for freedom. This is perfectly legitimate. There are very many unsatisfactory features of the political system existing in Poland. The recent crisis there — as the Communist party report issued in 1983 openly admitted[19] — was largely self-inflicted. And, in contrast, Solidarity espoused democratic values akin to those of the West. Yet the reasons for the instinctive sympathy on the part of the western scholars for the rebelling Poles go even deeper than that. The Solidarity period evoked in the West the traditional image of Polish history — apparently still deeply entrenched — as basically a perennial struggle for independence. This, it seems is the main reason why some of the western writings came dangerously close to embracing the linear view of the developments in Poland as inevitably leading toward a shaking off by the Poles of foreign suzeranity.

Yet, for the western scholars to adopt virtually the same position as the Polish emigrés would be wrong. While rightly refuting as erroneous the Marxist linear view of history, they should not fall into the opposite trap of embracing its nationalist mirror image, which is equally fallacious. For the fact is that during the last two centuries a truly independent Polish state has existed only for twenty years and during the remaining time the Poles, *nolens volens,* have lived under foreign rule and tried to cope with their lot the best they could. And, at least in the immediate future, the prospects of Poland freeing itself from foreign suzeranity, unfortunately, are not good. The odds are that the Poles at least for some time to come will have to put up with the dependence upon their eastern neighbor.

Recognizing Poland's predicament has nothing to do with abandoning one's personal preferences. The western scholars can openly sympathize with the legitimate aspirations of the Poles toward independence.* Yet, in their writings they should not confuse their wishes with the existing realities. Even if the cause of Polish freedom is right, it does not follow that it will be accomplished soon. And by not presenting the facts as they are — even when they are discouraging — the western scholars would not be faithful in their calling, which is to present the truth.

---

*I have stated my own personal preferences as to the future of Poland in the introduction to my *Poland, The Protracted Crisis* (Oakville, Ont., 1983), where I wrote: "I shall not conceal that my sympathies, although tempered by the awareness of the reality of the country's geopolitical position, have always been on the side of the Polish nation in its legitimate aspirations towards greater freedom".

*NOTES*

1. Quoted by Konstanty Wojciechowski, *Dzieje literatury polskiej* (Hanower, 1946). P. 226.
2. For the account of the debate stirred by Wajda's film see my: "History and Politics in Poland", *Problems of Communism*, No. 5, Vol. XV, Sept.-Oct. 1966.
3. Tomasz Lubienski, *Bic sie czy nie bic?* (Krakow, 1978). For more detailed review of this book see Chapter IV.
4. Notably by a prominent Polish historian, Henryk Wereszycki: "Znaczenie powstania styczniowego w dziejach narodu polskiego", *Tygodnik Powszechny*, May 30, 1982. For more on this subject see Chapter III.
5. *Tygodnik Powszechny*, August 9, 1984.
6. *Committee in Support of Solidarity REPORTS* (New York), No. 28, October 28, 1984.
7. Tadeusz Lepkowski, "Historia i spoleczenstwo. Przed zjazdem historykow polskich", *Tygodnik Powszechny*, August 19, 1984.
8. *Zeszyty historyczne* (Paris), No. 34, 1975. P. 231.
9. *Kultura* (Paris), April 1976. P. 104.
10. Quoted in Maciej Kozlowski, "Historyk i publicysta", *Tygodnik Powszechny*, July 9, 1984.
11. For an encouraging view of the state of Polish historiography in the 1970s see: Tadeusz Piszczkowski, "Sytuacja i rola historykow krajowych", *Mysl Polska* (London), May 1, 1979.
12. Andrzej Micewski, *Wspolrzadzic czy nie klamac ? Pax i Znak w Polsce 1945-1976* (Paris, 1978).
13. Hugh Seton-Watson, *The East European Revolution* (London, 1956).
14. Paul L. Horecky (ed.), *East Central Europe, A Guide to Basic Publications* (Chicago, 1960). The part on Polish history until 1945 was prepared by Piotr S. Wandycz, and the one covering the events after World War II by myself.
15. "Antyamerykanski pisarz - Professor Sharp", *Kultura*, January-February 1954. Pp. 106-114.
16. Andrzej Zagozda (pseudonym of Adam Michnik), "Czy emigrowac ?", *Kultura*, June 1982, Pp. 68-9.
17. Harold MacMillan in the introduction to Wladyslaw Anders, *An Army in Exile* (London, 1949). p. xiv.
18. Norman Davies, *Poland Past and Present, A Select Bibliography of Works in English* (Newtonville, 1977). This is the most comprehensive, but still far from complete, bibliography of works on Poland; it would be useful to prepare an updated edition, where many missing items would be incorporated.
19. Its second edition published in 1976 was updated to cover the events in the 1960s and the early 1970s, but unfortunately the earlier part was not expanded to include the materials on the early history of the Marxist movement which had come to light since 1959.
20. The relevant portions of the report are included as Appendix I in my *Eastern Europe in the Aftermath of Solidarity* (Boulder, Co., 1985).

# II

## IDEALISM vs. REALISM

In the post-war period, seeking broader historical generations has not been popular in Poland. In trying to escape from the sweeping vistas of official Marxism, the historians have tended to seek refuge in narrow historicism in the von Ranke tradition. The more modern western approaches, exemplified by the *Annales* — borrowing the methodologies used in social sciences and striving at some broader syntheses — have not been fashionable among the Polish historians. This may well be due to the fact that the social scientists in Poland — and especially the political scientists, who have been predominantly Marxists — have had little to offer to the historians. Anyway, there has been little cooperation between the two sides. As Stefan Kieniewicz observed in 1977: "Any historian who undertakes a so-called inter-disciplinary study will be battered from both sides, and so far no change in this situation is in sight."[1]

Yet, in the early 1980s, as the new political climate emerged in the country, new trends also appeared in Polish historiography. An appeal for closer cooperation between the historians and the social scientists came from a well known political scientist, Remigiusz Bierzanek, who was respected for his independent views. In a penetrating article on the role of history in the study of international relations, published in 1980, he advocated closing the distance between the two disciplines. "In order to advance research in international relations", he wrote, "it is important to establish":

> a dialogue between the historians and political scientists which can have a very useful, stimulating effect on both disciplines.... In view of the

23

developments in political science in the last decade it would be desirable if the historians concerned with political history were familiar with its studies and accomplishments — and in the same fashion the political scientists who try to derive some generalizations from the historical experiences ought to be in some degree historians.[2]

Bierzanek scolded those historians who, while claiming that their discipline is *magistra vitae,* yet confine themselves just to examining narrow, past events. "The task of making generalizations and discovering regularities based on past experiences," he argued, "should not be the exclusive domain of the social sciences."[3] And referring explicitly to similar approaches in the West, Bierzanek called upon the Polish historians to look at their discipline not just as the development of knowledge of the past, but rather as a study of man conceived in time.*

A historian, Antoni Maczak, admitted in 1983 that in the past his colleagues have shied away from the approach recommended by Bierzanek. A historian, he wrote:

from the first day of his studies is taught — and rightly so — that he must not commit anachronisms. The fear of sinning this way deprives him of the ability to compare in time. He is afraid to draw analogies and to transgress the boundaries of periodization which he himself has erected. As a result he escapes into the sphere of literature or into such difficult and imprecise concepts as social consciousness or national character.[4]

Maczak acknowledged an important didactic role for history. The task of the historians, he asserted, is "to study the past in order to arrive at the truth about it, as well as to offer society a rational basis for overcoming its present adversity."[5] And another writer, Henryk Samsonowicz, went even further and warned the historians — clearly with the political crisis of 1980-81 in mind — against addressing themselves exclusively to distant, "safe" events. The duty of a historian,

---

*As an example of insufficiencies in the Polish historiography Bierzanek singled out the fact that in the extensive literature on the uprising of 1863, the historians do not provide an answer — which could be quite instructive — to the question, why did the insurrection not take place during the Crimean War, when the chances of Poland's obtaining western assistance would have been much better.

he argued, "is not just cognition, but also assessment. And one has to assess what happened even only yesterday, even though the time perspective may not be really sufficient to do so properly"[6].

In bringing history and social sciences together the western students of Poland could make an important contribution. Indeed, in several respects they are uniquely equipped to do so. They are, of course, free from the constraints imposed by the official Marxist ideology. They also have easier access to the current trends in western historiography which has been more receptive than that in Poland to incorporating the various modern approaches and methodologies from social sciences. And, last but not least, many important sources in Polish history — especially since 1939 — are readily available in the West. Thus, the efforts of the western historians to use their knowledge of the past in order to interpret the present events should be encouraged. At the same time the social scientists should not confine themselves to just analyzing current events, but ought to try placing them in a broader historical perspective — relating them to their precedents.

There are, however, also dangers facing the western students of Poland who attempt to follow an inter-disciplinary approach. On the one hand the historians are rarely sufficiently familiar with the contemporary Polish scene to undertake broad generalizations reaching beyond the period of their specialization. They may also shy away from controversy and, instead, seek confort in monographs interpreting more distant but politically safe events. The study of Polish history in the West, thus, could profit by an expansion of its horizons, and greater courage on the part of its practitioners. On the other hand the western political scientists frequently lack the good grasp of Polish history which to their counterparts in Poland comes almost instinctively. They may fall, then, into the trap that often swallowed the behavioralists of the 1960s and 1970s, who constructed broad historical models not supported by solid evidence. While delving into history the social scientist should select their facts and evolve their theories with utmost care. And whenever in doubt they should appropriately qualify their findings.

* * *

Recently two important works on Polish history have appeared in the United States. These are: *Realism in Polish Politics: Warsaw Positivism and National Survival in the Nineteenth Century Poland* by Stanislaus A. Blejwas (Yale Russian and East European Publications,

1984); and: *Roman Dmowski, Party, Tactics, Ideology* by Alvin Marcus Fountain II (East European Monographs, Boulder, Co. 1980). Fountains' study received surprisingly little attention, probably because its appearance coincided with the rise of Solidarity and so it was overshadowed by the many books reviewing these dramatic events.[7] Blejwas' study still awaits its reviews and it is to be hoped that it will arouse the broad interest which it deserves.

Both books are meticuously researched, well organized and written. While both authors demonstrate sympathy with the objects of their study, this does not detract from their scholarly objectivity. Together they cover the years 1863-1907, but in fact they go beyond that. Blejwas' opening part deals in a comprehensive fashion with the precursors of Warsaw positivism — the early exponents of "organic work" — which takes him back to the third partition of Poland in 1795. And in his final part (which to some extent overlaps Fountains' volume) he depicts the rise of the positivists' successors: the socialists and the national democrats. Fountain, in turn, after reviewing in depth the rise of national democracy in 1895-1907, sketches its fortunes in the remaining years before World War I, and even reaches beyond into the inter-war period. There again he links with Blejwas, who in the Afterword tries to evaluate the impact of the 19th century positivism on post-war People's Poland.

Both authors are well aware that they have moved into largely uncharted territory. For the histories of both positivism and national democracy — since they do not fit into either the class conflict or the struggle for independence versions of Polish history — were given little attention in the past. To the Marxists, the positivists and the national democrats represented dispised bourgeois movements; and the latter, moreover, in 1905 clashed head on with the socialists. And to the traditional historians the renunciation by the positivists and the national democrats of armed struggle as the only means to regain independence, made them contemptible conciliationists if not outright traitors. Furthermore the fact that in the inter-war period the national democrats were also the main political rivals of the Pilsudskiites, did not enhance their prestige in the eyes of the Warsaw historians either.

Strangely enough these important chapters in Polish history are also little known in the West (the last writer who really gave them their due was Rose). For the programs of both the positivists and the early national democrats come closer to western political thought than those of any other Polish political movements. The positivists were influenced by the philosophic ideas of August Comte (indeed, their very name was derived from his concept of perceiving reality), the scientific theories of Charles Darwin and Henry Thomas Buckle, and the social teachings of John Stuart Mill and Herbert Spencer. And Dmowski, in turn, was under the spell of the political thought of Edmund Burke and Ernest Renan. The young national democratic leader, in fact, was such an ardent admirer of England that (as Fountain notes) even Sir Bernard Pares was surprised.

Blejwas and Fountain have succeeded admirably in closing this gap in our knowledge of Polish history. Blejwas' work on positivism is the best available in English, and it compares favorably with anything published on this subject in Polish. And Fountain's study — if only because the literature on national democracy is so scarce — is outstanding in both languages. Indeed, both of these volumes deserve to be translated as soon as possible into Polish.

The main significance of Fountain's and Blejwas' works is in their demolishing once and for all the traditional version of Polish history as consisting of virtually uninterrupted struggle for independence. They demonstrate that for half a century — from 1864 until 1914 — the Poles tried to improve their lot, not just by armed insurrections, but by seeking accommodation with the foreign rulers. Their efforts met with mixed success — only in Galicia did they actually win substantial political autonomy. But the Poles in other provinces also made important strides, especially in the economic, social and cultural spheres. These achievements helped the Polish society to consolidate its strength — indeed, it was during that period that a truly modern Polish nation, permeating all social classes, came into existence — and to regain its independence when an opportunity to do so presented itself in 1918.

The two American authors, moreover, dispose of the view widely subscribed to by the traditional historians that the efforts at reconciliation with foreign rulers amounted to the abandonment of the goal of Poland's independence. True, there were some individuals — such as Stanislaw, Szczesny Potocki after 1795, or Kazimierz Krzywicki after 1863 — who, driven by opportunism, or, perhaps even more by dispair, advocated that the Poles should forsake their separate national identity. For the positivist, and even more, for the national democrats, reconciliation with foreign rulers was merely a political tactic, aimed at strengthening the country internally in anticipation of an opportunity to restore its independence in the future. Indeed, they believed that protecting the Polish nation from losses that repeated insurrections would cause, was the most effective way to bring nearer this cherished goal.

Blejwas disputes the views expounded by the traditional historians and argues persuasively that the positivists, and notably Aleksander Swietochowski, never renounced Poland's independence as their ultimate objective. And Fountain demonstrates conclusively that to the national democrats the programs of "organic work" and the restoration of the Polish state were entirely complimentary and they consciously pursued them side by side. True, Dmowski was aware of the tactical incompatibility of openly advocating Poland's autonomy in the Tsarist Empire, and at the same time proclaiming the goal of its independence, but there is no question that for an ardent nationalist such as he was, freedom of the Polish nation from foreign rule was the uppermost value. And it should be added that when the opportunity to restore an independent Polish state came during World War I, the national democratic leader did not refrain from promoting it by military force too.

The two books are also significant in providing a clear periodization of the events which they discuss. Blejwas regards 1863 as a watershed between what he calls (borrowing the terminology adopted in my *Poland's Politics*) the idealist and the realist periods in Polish history. At that time, under the impact of a shattering military defeat at the hands of the Russians, and the disillusionment with the West which had offered no assistance in their struggle, the Poles abandoned the romantic program and embraced positivism. Yet, after the 1880s with the revival of the nation's internal strength and the rise of a young generation free from the defeatist memories of 1863, the Poles moved once again toward idealism. The positivists were challenged by the socialists and the national democrats who — as Fountain points out — at first worked closely together, but, then, as their respective ideologies crystallized, split apart. And on the eve of World War I, from the socialists' ranks there emerged the Pulsudskiite movement (significantly joined by several sessesionist groups from the national democratic ranks), which openly reverted to the romantic program of armed struggle for independence. The two authors, thus, demonstrate that at least in 1795-1914 there was a clearcut cycle in Polish history: a movement from idealism to realism and back to idealism.

The question then arises — which Blejwas poses directly in the Afterword — whether similar periodization can be discovered in the subsequent stages of Polish history. To what extent did the Warsaw uprising in 1944 and its abandonment in defeat by Poland's western allies produce traumatic effects among the Poles like those in 1863, resulting in the rise of what Stanislaw Stomma labelled in the 1950s as "neopositivism"?[8] And, in turn, how far did revival of political aspirations among the Poles in the 1970s — epitomized by the critique of Stomma's concepts by a young historian, Adam Michnik, in 1976[9] — parallel the political trends from the turn of the century? And this evokes additional questions as to what extent the transformation from one period into another coincided with the generational turnover, and, similarly, to what extent the younger people consciously reverted to the example, skipping the experiences of their fathers, of the generation which had moved in the same direction at the turn of the century? In short, has there been a persistent cycle in Polish history over the last two centuries manifested in the repeated shifts between idealism and realism?

Those are not idle questions. At the least they can provide us with a map for systematic historical research. Rather than groping in the dark from one episode to another — ending with enlightening, but narrow monographs — the historians should be able to select their areas of research in a systematic fashion and offer us some broader generalizations about Poland's past. And at the best, finding answers to the above questions could make the study of Polish history a better *magistra vitae*. By tracing the regularities in the past the historians, as well as the social scientists, could contribute to our better understanding of the present, and perhaps even anticipate what will happen in the future.

* * *

I should like to believe that in constructing my historical model of Polish politics I have lived up to the above listed requirements. I presented it first in my *Poland's Politics,* published in 1967. The volume's main goal was to analyze the postwar developments in the country (and especially the crisis in 1956), but these were presented against a broad historical background going back to the era of partitions. Subsequently, I myself characterized the book "as an attempt at systematic inquiry into the nature of Poland's politics viewed as a cycle between idealism and realism".[10] I returned to his subject — testing my model against the passage of time — in two articles published in the *Canadian Slavonic Papers* in 1978 and 1982. In the first I summed up my findings in the following fashion:

> The division between idealists and realists is not, of course, unique to Poland; to a lesser or greater extent it is present in the political life of

all nations. What is exceptional about Poland, however, is the significance which this split has acquired in that country. This is the result of the fact that for the past two centuries Polish politics has been characterized by *Primat der Aussenpolitik* — the primacy of foreign over internal politics ...''

Under these circumstances it is only natural that the split between the idealists and the realists became central to Poland's politics...The division came into prominence toward the end of the 18th century and persisted throughout the entire era of partitions. The idealist, or 'romantic', school of political thought gave first priority to the restoration of Poland's independence. The idealists advocated a relentless struggle against the occupying powers, especially Russia, and looked to [the West] for assistance. To advance their goals they were prepared to undergo great sacrifices. In contrast, the realist, or 'positivist' school became reconciled with the necessity of a limited national autonomy. The realists did not abandon the ultimate goal of Poland's freedom from foreign rule, but they repudiated striving for it at any costs. Their first concern was to protect the nation from repeated and futile losses and, instead, to secure for it as normal an internal development as possible.

At various stages of history the two programmes underwent substantial modifications to fit the changing external as well internal, circumstances. Yet, over the last two hundred years they have also retained a basic continuity in their respective assumptions.[12]

The division between the idealists and the realists continues in today's Poland. In an article published in the Winter 1985 issue of *Slavic Review* on the current debates among Polish historians Elisabeth Kridl Valkenier observed that overarching the contending arguments is "the eternal query: What is *the* historical tradition that has guided and should guide the Poles in time of adversity? Is it the romantic spirit of revolt and intransingence or the realistic spirit of accommodation and slow organic work?''

The model of Polish politics as a dichotomy between positivism and romanticism is, of course, by no means novel. In elaborating it I profited from the historical works on the 19th century by Wilhelm Feldman and Henryk Wereszycki[13] as well as the early political thought of Roman Dmowski. Among contemporary writers I was influenced by Stanislaw Stomma and Jan Szczepanski. I should like to think, however, that I managed to introduce into this traditional Polish controversy — if only by injecting into it some contemporary western concepts — somewhat greater rigor.

The model which I contructed in the 1960s, I believe, has served me well in my subsequent research and writings on Poland. It has also been acknowledged as a source of inspiration by some other scholars.* Last but not least it has stirred up a good deal of fruitful (although at times acrimonious) debate.

I have been criticized from four different corners: two of them political, and two methodological. Since my model did not fit into the vision of history conceived exclusively as a class struggle, *Poland's Politics* was not well received by the Marxists. For several years it was treated by them as "non-book" and deliberately ignored. At the same time I was quite regularly denounced in Poland for some of my other writings. In 1968 I was labelled (along with Walt W. Rostow and William B. Griffith) as one of the brains responsible for formulating the political line of Paris *Kultura* (sic!).[14]

It was only in 1975 that my book was first mentioned in the Polish press. In an article in *Polityka* under the significant title: "Realism, but what realism?", a well known Polish sociologist, Jerzy J. Wiatr, acknowledged its scholarly merits, but argued that rather than embracing the true realism, which, of course, is expressed in the Communist program, I advocated (along with Zbigniew K. Brzezinski) the changing of the political system in Poland through its gradual evolution.[15] And only in the fall of 1980, when freedom of the media in Poland was virtually complete, and the dichotomy between idealism and realism was particularly relevant, was an interview with me about *Poland's Politics* shown on a popular program on Polish television. Subsequently, *Poland, The Protracted Crisis*, published in 1983, was reviewed in several Communist as well as Catholic papers.[16] Yet, I was still denounced by the hardline Communist weekly, *Argumenty*, as striving to replace the early socialists Warynski and Marchlewski as the Polish national heroes, with bourgeois politicians, such as Swietochowski and Dmowski.[17]

Since it did not fit into their version of history seen as an incessant struggle for independence, *Poland's Politics* was also not welcomed among the Polish emigrés. There were few direct attacks against it,

---

*Meanwhile, of course, some other writers have arrived at conclusions somewhat similar to those of mine on their own. Particularly valuable is a monograph by Leszek Kaminski, (supplementing well the works of Blejwas and Fountain) discussing the impact of the 19th Century romanticism upon Polish political thought, especially that of the Pilsudskiites, in the inter-war period. *Romantyzm a ideologia. Glowne ugrupowania polityczne Drugiej Rzeczpospolitej wobec tradycji romantycznej* (Warsaw, 1980).

but rather — as in the official Polish press — it was discreetly passed over in silence. And with the emigrés views gaining upper hand at home, my approach became unpopular with the opposition circles there. A talk on this subject which I gave to the leading Polish dissidents during a visit to Warsaw in 1978, was received by them in a distinctly reserved manner.[18] The reviews of *Poland, The Protracted Crisis* in the official Polish press, moreover, served as an occasion for new attacks against my approach by the emigrés. In 1984 the Paris *Kultura* suggested that I should assume the chair of Marxism-Leninism in Warsaw (sic!).[19] Such arguments, coming from the exponents of either the Marxist or the traditional nationalist, linear versions of Polish history, did not bother me. On the contrary, I found them interesting for they confirmed that evidently I have touched upon particularly sensitive nerves in the advocates of both of these erroneous approaches.

In contrast, in western scholarly circles my writings have been generally well received, although there have been some reservations too. Yet they have been concerned not so much with the substance of my argument, but rather my methodology.

These I have welcomed for they have focused on the conceptually weak aspects of my model, and, this way, have helped me to elaborate on it. Since my approach adhered to the traditionalist school of international relations, the behavioralists did not approve of it. They criticized *Poland's Politics* as being in its historical part an old-fashioned work, and in its modern part just political journalism. From the behavioralists' peculiar vantage, I must admit, there are valid reasons to see it this way. Their problem was, however, that their own approach did not prove to be any more illuminating. Their valiant attempts to apply the systems analysis or the decision-making approach to the study of Polish, or, for that matter to Communist politics in general, have not been particularly rewarding. If the so-called "scientific" approach is to be vindicated, at least in the case of Poland, it still awaits its seminal work.

The traditional historians — busy with writing their narrow monographs — were more reticent about entering into a debate. They duly registered their objections to my interpretation of some specific events — usually confined within the period in which they specialized — but as a whole they abstained from discussing the broader methodological questions which I had raised. It was only in 1983 that a senior Polish-American historian, Piotr Wandycz — provoked by the application of my model to the events in 1980-81 — locked horns with me.[20] And next year he returned to the subject of the relationship between history and politics (although no longer directly polemicizing with me).[21]

Wandycz's argument was largely a restatement of the approach to the study of history in the tradition of von Ranke. It can be summarized in four points. First, Wandycz finds the terms idealism and realism, or, for that matter, romanticism and positivism, imprecise. Second, although he does not altogether reject searching for some broader historical regularities, he is sceptical about the prospect of success in such endeavors; to him history is basically a succession of unique events. Third, he is particularly wary of drawing analogies between the position of Poland in the 19th century and the situation today, which he considers as fundamentally different. And, fourth, Wandycz warns about the danger of such analogies being exploited for political purposes. These are legitimate reservations voiced by a traditional historian, but, in turn, each one of them invites criticism.

\* \* \*

I was already well aware of the problems inherent in my model when I was writing *Poland's Politics,* and I have openly admitted to their existence in my subsequent writings. To begin with I was not entirely satisfied with the terminology which I adopted, for I knew that it was open to confusion. I replaced the Polish terms: "romanticism" and "positivism" with "idealism" and "realism" primarily in order to make these concepts more readily accessible to the western readers. But as an early critic of mine not without some justification observed: "realism and romanticism properly belong to literature; and positivism and idealism to philosophy", and they are of little help in explaining political phenomena.[22]

Idealism and realism, moreover, imply certain psychological predispositions on the part of individuals participating in the historical events. The realists tend to be by temperament more down to earth and more cautious, while the idealists are more emotional and prone to euphoria or despair. These innate traits, moreover, can be accentuated by the influence of the environment. And this has been evident in the Polish history too. During the partitions the western Poles — exposed to the more practical German way of thinking — tended to be more realistic; and in contrast, the eastern Poles — influenced by the Russian proclivity toward extremism and even nihilism — were more romantic.*

---

*For an analysis of the Polish national character along those lines see: Jan Szczepanski, Appendix 6.

As Fountain rightly observes, Dmowski, although he came from the Russian part of Poland, was a realist by temperament and felt a close affinity with the Poles in the western provinces, and it was there that the national democrats, their appeal enhanced by their anti-German line, made their most important political inroads. In contrast, Pilsudski, who came from the eastern borderlands, all his anti-Russianism notwithstanding, was an easterner *par excellance.** And this psychological divide — somewhat akin to the split between the westerners and the Slavophiles in Russia — persists in Poland until today.

The alternative to adopting the terms of "idealism" and "realism" would have been to label the two perennial tendencies in Polish politics — as Norman Davies does[23] — as "insurrectionist" and "concilia-tionist" (and in my description of idealism and realism I use these terms in a similar sense). Yet, this would have not avoided the central conceptual difficulty. For, as Davies correctly observes, both the "insurrectionists" and the "conciliationists" enjoyed only brief moments of complete control, and most of the time the political situation in the country was more complex than that, reflecting a changing amalgam of both programs. The co-existence of the positivist and romantic ideas even during the climax of a realist period, after the uprising of 1863, was well captured in an epic by Maria Dabrowska:

> Daniel Ostrzenski's friends were the young students or recent graduates: lawyers, physicians and teachers, botanists, historians and mathematicians... Together they read the works of Buckle and Huxley, discussed the evolutionary theory of Darwin, played Chopin's revolutionary etude ... and sang Mickiewicz's ballads...[24]

Indeed, there were some strange hybrids of idealism and realism. The Warsaw positivists, as Blejwas reminds us, at the same time professed loyalism to the Russian throne and engaged in modest conspiratorial activity. And Pilsudski, in order to prepare the military force with which he planned to regain Poland's independence, cooperated with the Austrian authorities in Galicia.

No matter how labelled, then, whether idealism and realism or insurrectionism and conciliationism, these represent only the two

---

*Tadeusz Bielecki once told me that Dmowski was well aware of this paradoxical difference — the westerner willing to cooperate with Russia, and the easterner being against it — between himself and Pilsudski.

political extremes between which the actual programs of various political movements spread on a broad spectrum. The difficulty of classification along those lines, moreover, is compounded by the fact that during the era of partitions realism and idealism may have been more strongly accentuated — reflecting the local opportunities for cooperation with the occupying powers or the lack of them — in one part of Poland than another. In the long run, however, these local differences tended to level off, providing for the emergence of a dominant political trend throughout all of the Polish lands. And in all the territories and at all times the presence of the two opposed poles of idealism and realism — even if just in the Weberian sense of ideal types — could be detected.

The existence of the two extremes of idealism and realism enables us to undertake a typology of political programs — depending on where they fit on the continuum — at any given time. This, in turn, allows us to compare them in time, and by doing so to trace their lineage. This, however, has to be done in accordance with a clearly defined set of classificatory criteria. It seems to me that there are four major features which constantly reappear in the programs of various Polish political movements over time and which help us to classify them as either idealist or realist. Reduced to their bare essentials these distinguishing traits are as follows:

| *Idealists* | *Realists* |
|---|---|
| an armed struggle for independence | acceptance of autonomy |
| underground activity | organic work |
| strong anti-Russian sentiments | greater awareness of the danger from Germany (occasionally combined with an ideology common with the Russians) |
| expectations of West assistance | disillusionment with the West |

\* \* \*

It is probably because both idealism and realism rarely appeared in their pure forms that the adherents to historicism deny the existence of any uniform pattern in Polish history. They reject the cyclical theory in the same fashion as they repudiate, and rightly, the linear view of history. Yet, there are basic differences between the two. The linear theory posits that history inexorably moves toward some rationally predetermined goal, which makes it both mechanistic and ideological in its nature. In contrast the cyclical theory is purely empirical in character, in that it is based upon merely the observing of a repetition of two situations where similarities are more pronounced than differences.* It does not deny, moreover, the existence of new elements in each new phase, nor does it claim that the cycle must necessarily be constantly repeated.** Indeed, should its roots be eliminated and an entirely new situation emerge, the cycle will end too.

The existence of a cycle in 19th century Polish history, as has been re-affirmed by Blejwas and Fountain, is indisputable. With the restoration of the Polish state in 1918 it seemed that an entirely new situation had emerged, an, thus, that the old cycle would also have come to an end. Yet, due to Poland's vulnerable position in the international sphere, the pattern re-emerged with a vengeance during World War II. Evidently the principle of *Primat der Aussenpolitik* was still valid, and, consequently, the oscillation between idealism and realism was still the only course for the Poles to follow.

Wandycz does not completely deny that some phenomena are repeated in Polish history. He tends to attribute this, however, to the steadfast national character of the Poles. Yet, this is hardly a satisfactory explanation, for, as any political scientist knows, the notion of national character is an elusive one; and, moreover, it is changeable over times, so clearly it is not determined just by tradition, but by some other forces. One, then, should search for the specific historical determinants which have shaped the attitudes of the Poles in such a special way.

My answer to this is that the roots of the cycle in Polish history can be found in the vulnerability of the Polish nation in the international sphere and the persistent primacy of external over internal developments in Polish politics, which has left the Poles with basically two

---

*The cyclical theory, incidentally, is widely used in some branches of history, notably in describing economic fluctuations or the shifts from the left to the right, or *vice versa,* in politics. In the international sphere it underlies the theory of balance of power.

**Rudolf Jaworski put this well: "History does not repeat itself. This, however, does not exclude the possibility that it can generate a kind of compulsion for repetition. By this we mean repeated efforts to achieve a certain goal in whatever constellation". *East European Quarterly.* "History and Tradition in Contemporary Poland", Vol. XIX, No. 3, September 1985, p. 359.

options: either struggle for independence or adopt a conciliatory policy toward the foreign rulers.

In *Poland's Politics,* using the above listed four classificatory criteria to delineate the difference between idealism and realism, I described in some detail the rise in the immediate post-war years of neo-positivism; and in the two articles in the *Canadian Slavonic Papers* I analyzed a shift on the part of the Poles in the 1970s back to political romanticism.* I believe, thus, that my model has withstood the test of time, and, as long as the primacy of foreign over internal affairs continues to prevail in Polish politics, the Poles will continue to move back and forth on a "continuum between the two extremes of foolhardy idealism and thoroughgoing realism".[12]

\* \* \*

The oscillation between idealism and realism, moreover, has often coincided with a generational turnover, marked by the presence or absence of defeatist memories among the young Poles. Many insurgents from 1863 and 1944 subsequently embraced realism, and, in turn, their sons, no longer remembering the lost battles, raised the banner of idealism once again.

An important *caveat,* however, must be inserted here. The external developments and the internal changes in Poland have not always been complimentary; at times they have worked at crosspurposes and even have ended in a national catastrophe. During World War I the aspirations of the Poles toward independence coincided with the emergence of a favorable situation in Europe; in 1831, 1863, and again in 1944, however, the Polish uprisings were not carefully enough synchronized with the international developments and turned into disasters. In order to arrive in each specific situation at the proper political decisions, thus, the correct relationship between the international external and domestic internal factors must be carefully determined.

It follows, then, that the cycle in Polish history has not worked in a purely deterministic fashion. There has been in it a strong influence of outside elements, but Poland has not been — as Davies seems to suggest in the title of his book — just "God's Playground". Although restricted, the element of free choice by the Poles has also been there. They could have either continued against all odds in their struggle for independence, or they could have tried to improve their lot by

---

*More detailed discussion of this subject is included in Ch. III.

accommodation with the foreign rulers. Or, they could have consciously sought the optimum of freedom attainable at the given time through a combination of both idealism and realism.

Seen in this fashion, as I put it in 1978:

> Neither idealism nor realism is an end in itself. They are merely alternative means to advance Poland's national interests. Depending on the circumstances, either one or the other should be followed. In their moderate forms both are useful. As Edward Carr aptly observed, idealism without realism is naive, and realism without idealism is sterile.[25] In their extreme forms, however, both are harmful. Idealism, which, in the name of national independence, exposes the nation to the peril of extinction, and realism, which, in order to preserve the biological survival of the people, exposes them to the danger of losing their own identity, are both self-contradictory. The avoidance of these extremes and the choice of a proper synthesis of idealism and realism — aimed at attaining an optimum of the national interests available at any given time — represents the essence of good statemanship.

> The art of politics — moving on a continuum between idealism and realism, at times embracing one and at times the other — was aptly practiced by the Poles during the era of the partitions. After the Congress of Vienna the Polish generals who had served under Napoleon joined the Polish army under the command of the Russian tsar. Following the uprising of 1830 Prince Adam Czartoryski, a former Foreign Minister under Alexander I, became a leader of the Polish emigrés in France. Margrave Aleksander Wielopolski, who in 1830 was an emissary seeking assistance from France and Britain to the Polish insurrection, in the early 1860s emerged as a leading proponent of cooperation with Russia. Adam Asnyk, who played a major role in the uprising of 1863, later assumed the role of an ardent advocate of positivism. And Roman Dmowski, a former chairman of the Polish faction in the Russian Duma, during World War I formed Polish units in France.[26]

Dmowski's example serves here as the best illustration. The realist program is not always synonymous with rationalism. It would have been irrational for the Poles during World War I — when a favorable international situation developed for the restoration of their independent state, to cling to the realist program of mere reconciliation with the foreign rulers. Such a convoluted realism would have amounted to surrender, and in effect, treason. This was precisely why at that time Dmowski abandoned his former realist stance, and embraced an idealist position *par excellance,* promoting Poland's independence — as did the Napoleonic generals a century before — through a Polish military struggle on the side of the West.

By the same token the attempts by the advocates of idealism to present their program as the only rational course available to the Poles — when no opportunities whatsoever to restore an independent Polish state has existed — have been wrong. Such a distorted idealism, leading to the continuation of futile and costly military struggle, which often has degenerated into just a cult of martyrdom, has also amounted to a betrayal of the Polish national interests. Through repeated defeats it has not advanced, but has worsened the condition of the Poles.

Dmowski understood the interdependence between the two and consciously rejected both extreme idealism and extreme realism. In the opinion of some people, he argued, "our political thought is doomed to shift from one extreme to the other. Either revolution, conspiracy and the seeking of independence through military uprising ... or the abandonment of all aspirations to independent existence, the complete acceptance of fate, the unconditional surrender. There is thesis and antithesis, but there is no attempt to seek a synthesis".[27]

* * *

Arriving at consensus over Poland's external relations at any given time has been complicated by the divisions among various political movements over domestic issues. For if since 1795 the struggle for the country's independence has been the dominant aspect of Polish politics, it has not been, of course, the sole one. Like all other nations, the Poles have also been concerned with the internal progress of their society: its modernization and reform.* The political movements, thus, have divided not only along horizontal, but also along vertical lines, ranging from the conservatives who have upheld the existing social

_____

*Looking at it in retrospect I am inclined to believe that the major weakness of *Poland's Politics* was insufficient emphasis on the internal divisions among the Poles. I touched upon this, especially in reviewing the Communist political program, but basically my model was a two-dimensional one focusing upon the divisions over foreign policy. I am still convinced that in Poland's position the external aspects take precedence over internal ones, but a complete model of Polish politics should take into account the horizontal as well as the vertical divisions, as presented in the following pages.

*status quo* to the revolutionaries who have striven to overthrow the existing system by force.*

The relationship between horizontal and vertical divisions has not always been simple. To the movements which subscribed to the organic notion of a society and its evolutionary change — such as the positivists, the national democrats, or the Pilsudskiites in the inter-war period, the goals of national independence and social progress have been largely complimentary. To them organic work, and later, the internal strengthening of the Polish state, also served the goal of winning or upholding national independence. And, conversely, freedom from foreign rule was regarded as conducive to carrying out domestic reforms in a way most beneficial to the country.

For the revolutionary movements, however, the problem has often been more complex. The socialists have traditionally split between those who have given priority to Poland's independence and those who have been preoccupied with carrying out a social revolution. The main body of the Polish Socialist Party subscribed to the former program, while its left wing, as well as the Proletariat, and, later the Social Democracy of the Kingdom of Poland, supported the latter. The populist movement likewise has repeatedly split between its reformist and radical wings. It has generally subscribed to the program of independence, but — except during World War II, and especially in 1945-47 when it emerged as the main opposition force against the Communists — the Peasant Party has not developed a distinct foreign policy platform of its own.

The divisions along horizontal and vertical lines have produced some strange political phenomena. In advocating the program of Polish autonomy in the Habsburg Empire the Galician conservatives were also motivated by a desire to maintain their privileged social status there. In contrast, Pilsudski and many of his followers joined the socialist movement, not because they were particularly attracted to Marxism, but because they believed the revolutionary road to be the

---

*It should be added that there was a third important issue in Polish politics, namely, the relationship between the Poles and the various other nationalities living with them, especially in the borderlands. However, since this problem has always had a strong external aspect, i.e. it was linked to the determination of Poland's frontiers; as well as an internal one, i.e. the extent of freedom to be granted to the national minority groups — it can be subsumed into the horizontal-vertical political divisions. In any case, since 1945, when Poland emerged as ethnically one of the most homogenous nations in the world, the problem has lost its former significance.

surest way to restore Poland's independence. And the social democrats consistently advocated Poland's union with Russia, which, paradoxically — insofar as the horizontal division was concerned — brought them close to the position of the conservatives; except, of course, that the latter stood for cooperation with the actual Tsarist government, while the former looked forward toward cooperation with a future Russian government which was yet to emerge after the revolution.

Yet, taking into account both the horizontal and vertical divisons, a fairly clear distribution of the major Polish political movements at any given time could be drawn. And by applying the same criteria over time their lineage also could be traced. In the years 1863 until World War I this could be presented in the following diagramatic fashion:

RIGHT

| | |
|---|---|
| Wielopolski<br>the Galician conservatives<br>the positivists | Zamoyski |
| the Whites | the realists |
| the national democrats | the Pilsudskiites |
| the activists | the passivists |
| CONCILIATION ———————— | ———————— INSURRECTION |
| | the Reds |
| the socialists (left) | the socialists |
| Proletariat<br>the social deomocrats | |

LEFT

(The movements which stayed in existence over a long time often changed their position. Thus, the national democrats moved during World War I toward openly advocating Poland's independence, while at the same time the Pilsudskiites largely abandoned their goal of social revolution).

After coming to power in 1944, the Polish Workers' Party, and since 1948 its successor the Polish United Workers' Party, has oscillated between utter dependence upon the Soviet Union and a blind copying of its system (as during the Stalinist period), and a concern for internal autonomy and social experimentation fitting more the country's own needs (as in 1945-47 and again after 1956). The programmatic debates among the Polish Communists over the exact meaning of "the Polish road to socialism", in fact, go on until this day.[28]

In the post-war years, thus, a new configuration of political movements emerged in Poland, and from the late 1940s until the rise of the democratic opposition in the late 1970s, it remained quite stable. In a diagramatic fashion it could be presented like this:

**RIGHT**

|  |  |
|---|---|
|  | the National Democracy |
|  | the Pilsudskiites |
|  | Christian Democracy |
|  |  |
|  | the democratic opposition right: |
| Znak | KPN |
| neo-Znak |  |
| CONCILIATION————————————+——————————INSURRECTION | |
|  | the Polish Peasant Party |
| Pax | the Polish Socialist Party |
| the Democratic Party |  |
| the United Peasant Party | the democratic opposition: left: |
|  | KOR |
| the Polish Socialist Party |  |
| (Left) |  |
| the Polish Worker's Party |  |
| the Polish United Workers' |  |
| Party |  |

LEFT

(All of the movements on the right were liquidated in the late 1940s, either by outright suppression, as were the National Democrats and the Pilsudskiites, or by splitting them and merging their left wings with the pro-Communist parties, like the Polish Peasant Party with the United Peasant Party and the Christian Democratic Party with the Democratic Party; while the Polish Socialist Party was merged directly with the Polish Workers' Party in 1948, assuming the name of the Polish United Workers' Party.

The small Catholic Znak group came into existence after 1956. At first it espoused the realist position but by the 1970s it had moved closer toward idealism. Although it retained its own organization it was replaced in the parliament by the neo-Znak group, which continued to adhere to the more realist program. The staunchly pro-regime Pax group during the Solidarity period also moved closer toward idealism, but after 1981 it promptly reverted to its traditional political position.)

In the inter-war period when an independent Polish state was restored and all the major political movements, of course, upheld its existence, the horizontal division in Polish politics lost its significance. The only exception was the Communist Party of Poland which stubbornly clung to the old social democratic program, and after the Bolshevik revolution in 1917 still continued to advocate Poland's union with Russia. This did not enhance the party's popularity among the Poles, and even led to its being treated as a virtual outcast in Polish politics. The Communist revolution in Russia also played havoc with the national democratic program. For geopolitical reasons the national democrats remained committed to Poland's cooperation with its eastern neighbor, but ideologically they were adamantly opposed to Communism. The ideological difference led the national democrats to embrace during World War II a strongly anti-Soviet position, paradoxically bringing them into cooperation with their traditional adversaries: the Pilsudskiites.

* * *

World War II revived the traditional horizontal divisions. All of the major pre-war political movements — regardless of their social programs — subscribed to the goal of restoring a truely independent Polish state. Yet, the Communists and their allies — the small splinter groups from the leftist political parties — continued to adhere to the program of both social revolution at home and close bonds with the Soviet Union. With the emergence of the Polish Workers' Party in 1942, however, learning from their past mistakes, the Communists modified both of these objectives. They endorsed the existence of a separate, although closely aligned with the USSR, Polish state, and the goal of a social revolution fitting Poland's own needs.

A comparison of the two diagrams illustrates a great deal of continuity in Polish politics for over a century. After 1945, as after 1963, the idealist movements were eliminated and replaced by the realist ones. The major difference was in the shift of the realists from the right to the left. Yet, in a different social context the Communists and their allies adopted all the major ingredients of the old realist program: acceptance of external dependence (although coupled with some internal autonomy) upon Russia, efforts at strengthening of the country through internal reform, distrust of the West and an emphasis upon continued danger to Poland from Germany. And as the years went on and the existing system ossified, the Communists, like the 19th century conservatives, also increasingly became the defenders of the social *status quo*.

The post-war system remained basically unchanged for almost thirty years. It was only with the rise of the democratic opposition, and, then, the birth of Solidarity in 1980, that new movements appeared on the Polish political scene. As the wounds of World War II healed and the young generation of Poles, free from the defeatist memories of their fathers, came of age, a new shift toward idealism got under way. The cyclical nature of Polish politics was working once again.

The above model of Polish politics, like all intellectual constructs, is only an approximation of reality. Wandycz, of course, is right in observing that no two historical situations are identical. In drawing historical analogies, thus, great care must be exercised to point out not only the similarities, but differences as well. Yet, drawing models of historical situations and comparing them over time should still perform a useful function. They provide a coherent analytical framework where otherwise unrelated events can be sorted out and their relationship systematically examined. And in this way any regular patterns in Polish politics can be discerned. Such an exercise, thus, can not only be a useful research tool to illuminate the past events, but it may also offer some helpful insights into the study of Polish history conceived as a contemporary *magistra vitae*.

NOTES

1. Stefan Kieniewicz, "Perspektywy dziejopisarstwa Polsce", *Polityka* October 25, 1977.

2. Remigiusz Bierzanek, "Doswiadczenie historyczne jako przedmiot badan nad stosunkami mi edzynarodowymi", *Studia Nauk Politycznych* No. 2 (44), 1980. P. 52.

3. *Ibid.*, P. 53.

4. Antoni Maczak, "Prawda i otucha", *Tygodnik Powszechny*, January 23, 1983.

5. *Ibid.*

6. Henryk Samsonowicz, "Czy nauczycielka zycia?", *Lad*, February 20, 1983.

7. Davies, for instance, totally ignores Fountain's work in his *God's Playground, A History of Poland* (Oxford, 1981), while he could certainly profit from it in his rather deferential treatment of Dmowski.

8. Stanislaw Stomma, *Mysli o polityce i kulturze* (Cracow, 1960). For excerpts see: Apendices IV and V.

9. Adam Michnik, "Le nouvel evolutionisme" in Pierre Kende and Krzysztof Pomian (eds.) 1956 *Varsovie-Budapest, La deuxieme revolution d'Octobre* (Paris, 1978). Pp. 205-7.

10. Paul L. Horecky (ed.) *East Central Europe, A Guide to Basic Publications* (Chicago, 1960). 671.

11. Adam Bromke, *Poland, The Protracted Crisis* (Oakville, Ont. 1983) P. 2.

12. *Ibid.* P. 1.

13. Wilhelm Feldman, *Dzieje polskiej mysli politycznej*, 2nd ed., (Warsaw, 1933); Henryk Wereszycki, *Historia polityczna Polski w dobie popowstaniowej 1864-1918* (Warsaw, 1948).

14. Witold Filler, *Teorie i praktyki paryskiej "Kultury"* (Warsaw, 1968). P. 25.

15. Jerzy J. Wiatr "Jaki realizm?", *Polityka*, November 27, 1976.

16. *Polityka*, September 24, 1983; *Tu i teraz*, September 28, 1983; *Lad*, November 13, 1983.

17. J.N., "Poetyzowanie polityki", *Argumenty*, July 31, 1983.

18. "U Walendowskich: spotkanie z profesorem Bromke", *Zapis*, July 1978. Mimeographed.

19. Jacek Berezin, "Professor Pimko", *Kultura*, July 1984. P. 140.

20. Piotr Wandycz. "Realizm, idealizm a historia", *Tygodnik Powszechny*, July 31, 1983; subsequently included in a collection of the author's writings: "Polska a zagranica", (Paris, 1986), pp. 129-135. Wandycz explored this subject again in: "Realizm a idealizm w dziejach Polski", *Trybuna* (London), No. 50/106-51/107, 1985. Pp. 38-42.

21. Piotr Wandycz, "O historycznych analogiach", *Kultura*, July-August, 1983; and "Magistra vitae", *Tygodnik Powszechny*, September 9, 1984.

22. "Keeping Poland on the Map", *The Times Literary Supplement*, August 31, 1967.

23. Davis, *op.cit.*, Vol. II. p. 46.
24. Maria Dabrowska, *Noce i dnie* (Warszawa, 1955), Vol. I. p. 11.
25. E. H. Carr, *The Twenty Years Crisis* 3rd ed., (New York, 1964). p. 14.
26. Bromke, *op. cit.*, pp. 4-5.
27. *Przeglad Wszechpolski*, August 1904, as quoted in Tadeusz Bielecki, "Wyprawa do Japonii", *Mysl Polska*, August 1, 1964.
28. For a review of those debates see my *Poland's Politics, Idealism vs. Realism* (Cambridge, Mass., 1967), Chs. 7 and 8; and my *Eastern Europe in the Aftermath of Solidarity* (Boulder, CO., 1985) Chs. 1-3.

# III

# THE DILEMMAS OF TODAY

Recent political developments — especially as dramatic as those in Poland during the last decade — are naturally more difficult to categorize precisely than are those from the past. The political crisis in the late 1970s and the rise of Solidarity in 1980-81 are exceptionally well documented, but objective analysis of them is hindered by the emotions evoked by these events, which are still intense.

Furthermore, even after the imposition of martial law in 1981 the situation in the country has remained fluid. The Communist party — reflecting internal struggles in its ranks — underwent major programmatic changes between its Congresses in 1980 and 1981, but even at the 1986 Congress it still showed no clear sense of direction. It restated the usual platitudes about overcoming the crisis in the country and making progress toward socialism — perhaps reassuring to the Soviets, but certainly not convincing to the Poles.

The programs of the different opposition groups have also been fragmentary and vague, and as the case of Solidarity itself, inconsistent and ephemeral. And as time goes on there has been no improvement. Early in 1986 the influential Warsaw Club of the Catholic Intelligentsia admitted this and urged the Polish society to try to evolve a practical and consistent program of action.[1] Apparently in present day Poland not only the government, but also the opposition is devoid of ideas for overcoming the country's crisis. Yet, as Samsonowicz rightly pointed out, none of the above obstacles should prevent the scholars from trying to evaluate the current happenings and to place them in a broader context of Polish history.

The Poles themselves are well aware of this need. In their programmatic discussions — seeking to cope with their dilemmas of today — they repeatedly seek inspiration in history. There is no question that valid parallels between the past and the current events exist. While reading Blejwas' and Fountain's books one finds an abundance of episodes from the partitions' era which look remarkably modern. Evidently, despite all the profound changes which have taken place since that time, an extraordinary degree of continuity has also been preserved in Polish history.

Yet, the historical analogies drawn by the Poles must not be accepted uncritically. For, all their passion for history notwithstanding, the Poles' actual knowledge of the past events, and especially that of the younger ones educated under Communism, is often superficial. It is colored by popular myths which focus on specific episodes and personalities that appeal to the emotions at a given moment. And some parallels are deliberately selected with little regard for historical truth just to underscore a political point.

The confusion concerning the use of history among the Poles for contemporary purposes is well illustrated by the lack of agreement as to which past events are really relevant today. To support their specific political programs various writers have used selected episodes from the last two hundred years in a random, and, indeed, at times mutually exclusive, fashion. The best examples of this have been the comparisons of the present situation in Poland to these which existed both *before* and *after* the uprising of 1863 — despite the fact that these two previous situations were diametrically different.

To avoid such confusion, in drawing historical analogies both the past and the present events should be examined in the light of the same classificatory criteria — which would illuminate both the similarities and the differences existing between them. Thus, by adopting as an analytical framework the spectrum between idealism and realism — and using the same four criteria as outlined in the previous chapter — an attempt at showing the distribution of the Polish political movements in the mid-1980s could be made.*

---

*Blejwas, in fact, makes such an attempt in the Afterword of his book, comparing the situation in Poland during the era of partitions with that under Communism, including the crisis in 1980-81. Yet, because he has not selected his classificatory criteria carefully enough the results of his analysis are not impressive. While he demonstrates an excellent grasp of 19th century Polish history, his knowledge of contemporary events is sketchy. Evidently, as a historian trained in von Ranke's tradition, he has found it difficult to move beyond his period of specialization.

This attempt must take into account not only the horizontal, but also the vertical divisions, for the realists, and even more the idealists, differ also along those lines. The vertical divisions reflect the traditional splits among the Communists, socialist, liberals, the Christian democrats and the national democrats. All of the groups opposing Communism adhere to the western type of democracy, but they differ over the desirable scope of individual freedom, the extent of government intervention in the economy, and the role which the Catholic church should occupy in the state.

Yet, all of the opposition groups recognize that at present it is the horizontal division which is of crucial significance. As long as the country is not independent the major divide among the Poles remains that between the idealists and the realists. This was explicitly noted in an article in the *samizdat* monthly *Independence:*

> The basic dividing line in the Polish opposition does not reflect the ideological differences, but cuts across them... The controversial issues among the social democrats, national democrats and liberal democrats concern specific problems in the post-Communist period. Today, however, questions of the strategy and tactics in the struggle against Communism should be paramount.[2]

Taking into account both the horizontal and vertical criteria, thus, the diagram of the Polish political movements would be:

RIGHT

Underground radicals (right wing)

Radical priests

The Episcopate
The Primate'e Lay Advisory Council

Open opposition (right wing)

CONCILIATION ———————————— INSURRECTION

The Catholic parliamentarians

Communist moderates

The Polish United Workers' Party and its allies (The Jaruzelski followers)

Communist conservatives

Open opposition (left wing)
The underground Solidarity

Underground radicals (left wing)

LEFT

* * *

The shift in Polish politics in the second half of the 1970s, culminating in the rise of Solidarity in 1980, followed several idealist precepts. First of all the Communist program of modernization and social reform — akin to the 19th century's organic work — proved to be a bitter disappointment for the Poles. After World War II, and even in the early Stalinist years, many of them enthusiastically responded to the government's appeal for the reconstruction and industrialization of the country; but by the mid-1950s it all ended in a major economic, and, subsequently, political, crisis. New and short-lived expectations of internal progress were aroused after Gomulka came to power in 1956, and again in the initial stages of Gierek's rule in the early 1970s. Yet, the major economic downturn in the late 1970s, bringing Poland to the verge of bankruptcy, dashed those hopes and led to the upheaval in 1980-81.

At the same time the Polish United Workers' Party lost its revolutionary élan. The older generation of ideologically motivated prewar Communists — never numerous and decimated in the Stalinist purges and during World War II — died or retired; with the ouster of Gomulka in 1970 virtually all of them were gone. And most of the leftist intellectuals who joined the party after the war — and, strangely enough, stayed with it during the climax of Stalinism — left its ranks in disillusionment after 1956, a good many of them even moving into open opposition in the 1970s.* During the Gierek years the ruling Communist elite became conspicuously, if not brazenly, transformed into a privileged "new class", deriving from its political position tangible economic benefits and often indulging in corrupt practices. The official revolutionary rhetoric was maintained, but it was an increasingly empty shell. If anything, the discrepancy between the Communist egalitarian pretences and their ossification into a privileged social class — apparent for everyone to see — only aggravated the popular resentment of the existing system.

Convinced that no economic or social progress could be achieved under Communism more and more Poles turned to active political opposition. In 1976 the Committee for Defence of the Workers was

_____

*The spurious reasons for many influential writers', academics' and journalists' joining the Communist party and their subsequent conversion into militant anti-Communism — often stemming from a guilt complex over their role during the Stalinist years — are clearly presented by Aleksander Hall in Appendix 14.

formed, followed by several other open oppositionist groups. They contributed to the growing ferment in the country, and after Solidarity was formed many of their leaders assumed key positions in that organization. By the end of 1981 the authority of the Polish United Workers' Party had sunk so low that in order to stay in power it had to take the step — unprecedented in any Communist state, and eloquently testifying to the gravity of the situation — of resorting to naked military rule.

Several international developments also encouraged the Poles to move from realism to idealism. The rise of the dissident movement in the USSR in the late 1960s and the early 1970s influenced both the activities and the program of the Polish opposition. The Poles followed the example of the Soviets in openly challenging the Communist system, and supplementing this by the issuance of illegal *samizdat* publications; and they hoped that the rise of opposition in the USSR would mark the beginning of a political evolution, or even a revolution, there.* Even though by the late 1970s the activities of the Soviet dissidents — exposed to stern persecution — had visibly declined, the Polish democratic opposition still hoped to establish cooperation with them. To that end KOR even sent an unofficial envoy, Zbigniew Romaszewski, to Moscow, who met there with Andrei Sacharov. And the Solidarity Congress in 1981 came out with an appeal to the Soviet workers to follow its example and to form free trade unions of their own.

The 1970 conclusion of the Polish-West German Treaty which upheld Poland's western boundary along the Oder-Neisse rivers, and the subsequent normalization of diplomatic relations between the two countries, diminished the Poles' apprehension of their western neighbor. At the same time the rise of East-West détente, the signing of the Helsinki Accords in 1975, and the Carter administration's stress on human rights legitimized in the eyes of many Poles their striving for greater independence from the USSR. And finally the 1980

---

*It was over the interpretation of the political trends in the USSR, as much as those in Poland, that in 1974 I clashed bitterly with Juliusz Mieroszewski. The chief political commentator in *Kultura* anticipated major changes in the Soviet Union, while I wrote: "There are no bases for believing that the Poles will soon find in Russia any other partners for negotiations than the present establishment and its successors." ("'Polska 'Ost-West Politik' "', *Kultura*, November, 1974. P. 37). Subsequent events have proved me right, but, meanwhile, Mieroszewski's views — precisely because they corresponded so closely to the Poles' wishes — undoubtedly had greater impact among them.

electoral victory of Ronald Reagan — with his more pronounced anti-Communist line — appeared to some of them to hold a promise of more decisive action on behalf of the Eastern European peoples by the United States.

After the imposition of martial law in December 1981 Solidarity was disbanded and several thousands of its activists were detained. The ensuing strikes and demonstrations were suppressed by special units of the riot police, the dreaded ZOMO. As a whole, however, force was used discriminately; the total number of dead during the next three years was less than 100.[3] Moreover, the military rule was gradually relaxed and by 1983 — although the government retained broad emergency powers — martial law was lifted and by next year an amnesty was declared for most of the political prisoners. The situation in the country became superficially normalized, yet the Jaruzelski regime hardly won the Poles to its side. If anything, its stern measures in 1981-83 antagonized the Polish society from the Communist government even more.

The open, although unorganized, opposition has continued in Poland even after martial law. The most visible in its ranks have been the former leaders of the democratic opposition and Solidarity, notably Lech Walesa, who, due to their public exposure, have enjoyed a measure of immunity. They have issued open letters to the Communist authorities and have given interviews to western correspondents (which are often beamed back to Poland by the western radio stations), critically assessing the developments in the country. There have been writers and journalists who have boycotted the official media and, instead, have published their articles and books in *samizdat* form or have distributed them as tapes. There have also been academics who have given lectures on the subjects not covered by the official universities' curricular to private audiences. Then there have been the artists who, in their theatrical performances, have underlined rousing political themes or in the cabarets have submitted the Communist system to subtle, but unmistakeable satire. And there have been the priests, like the hapless Father Jerzy Popieluszko — who was brutally murdered by vigilante security officers in the fall of 1984 — who have used the pulpit to expound their anti-Communist creed. And all of those manifestations of open opposition have had a strong romantic flavor. The grave of Rev. Popieluszko, by the church in Warsaw where he had used to preach, has been turned into still another national shrine.[4]

Even more importantly, since 1981 the Poles have embraced another idealist tenet: conspiratorial activity. In addition to the open opposition many clandestine groups have sprung into existence. The most important among them has been the underground Solidarity, which has developed an extensive network throughout the country led by the Temporary Coordinating Commission. The Polish conspirators have displayed a great deal of ingenuity and persistence. Evidently enjoying broad popular sympathy they have managed to outwit the police for years. It was only in the spring of 1986 that the head of the Temporary Coordinating Commission, Zbigniew Bujak, was arrested.

The example of the underground Solidarity has been followed by many local — and usually more radical — organizations. They have issued numerous *samizdat* publications in which they submit the Communist system to merciless criticisms, and search for ways to change, or even to overthrow it. Most of them have also advocated active resistance in the form of boycotts of some government activities, such as the elections, or occasional street demonstrations and strikes.

The Jaruzelski regime seems to have become reconciled to the continued existence of an opposition as long as it does not resort to violence. The most outspoken figures in the open opposition have been submitted to administrative chicaneries, and some of the leaders of the clandestine groups have been apprehended by the police and sentenced to various terms of imprisonment. As a whole, however, the repressive measures have stayed lenient. In 1984 all of the political prisoners were amnestied, although a year later their number once again grew to some 250.[5]

The restricted use of repression, however, has not been enough to close the gap between the Jaruzelski regime and the Polish people. Distrust and even hatred of the Communist authorities still permeate large segments of the Polish society. There is widespread disbelief that the present government will be able to carry out the reforms necessary to bring the country's economy out of its present morass.* Especially the young people see no prospects ahead of them. In despair some are leaving the country, while others turn to adamant opposition. In the eyes of many Poles the Communists just resemble the 19th century conservatives, whose loyalty to the foreign powers was

---

*Zbigniew M. Fallenbuchl summed up well the country's economic prospects: "There is a serious danger that the stabilization of the economy will take place at a very low level of stagnation. A very explosive social and political situation would, therefore, continue to exist." ("The Polish Economy under Martial Law", *Soviet Studies,* No. 4, Vol XXXVI, October 1984. P. 526).

motivated not only by the geopolitical reality, but also by a concern to perpetuate their privileged social status.

* * *

The shift from realism toward idealism in the last decade, however, has not been complete. Unlike their predecessors who on so many occasions in the past turned to armed struggle to attain Poland's independence, the contemporary Poles have abstained from following this romantic precept. In the late 1970s the democratic opposition encouraged exerting popular pressure upon the Communist government, but it did not advocate overthrowing the Communist system by force.* And the remarkable feature of Solidarity was that, while trying to carry out revolutionary changes in the country, it abstained from violence. When in December 1981 the Solidarity leaders called for free elections they must have been aware that implementing this would inevitably lead to the ouster of the Polish United Workers' Party from power. Yet, even then they did not call for an armed uprising, but hoped to bring about the change of the government through peaceful strikes and street demonstrations. In fact, the closest Solidarity came to turning to force was its planning, though never actually implementing, the formation of workers' detachments which would guard the leaders against molestation by the police.

The introduction of martial law, except for several isolated and limited episodes, was not countered with force; and the underground Solidarity has scrupulously adhered to the non-violent tactic. The sporadic street demonstrations have continued but the crowds have rarely resisted the police. And the plan to organize a general strike, initially contemplated by the Temporary Coordinating Commission — precisely because it could lead to large-scale violence — was at first shelved and then altogether abandoned. The Commission's tactic throughout has been to exert pressure upon the Jaruzelski regime in an entirely peaceful manner.

---

*In my discussion with the leaders of the democratic opposition in the spring of 1978 they strongly resented my observation that by turning to unofficial, oppositionist activities, in effect they had embraced the idealist program. In defending their course Jan Jozef Lipski even drew a parallel between them and the 19th century positivists, who also had engaged in modest conspiratorial ventures. The opposition leaders' insistence that they are realists seems to have been aimed at convincing me that their goals are rational, i.e. attainable, which, unfortunately, has not proved to be the case.

Yet, even in the Solidarity ranks some voices have been raised advocating a turn to force. Writing from internment in the spring of 1982, Jacek Kuron suggested forming a strong underground organization and warning the Communists that if necessary "...it will not refrain from violence".[6] And clandestine Solidarity leader, Wladyslaw Hradek, reported "... the existence, deep in the underground, of groups which are ready for anything — even the most desperate steps... They may resort to assassinations, destruction and sabotage.".[7]

Various smaller underground groups are more firmly wedded to the tenets of political idealism, including the possible use of force. An article in the monthly *Independence*, issued by the group of the same name, unequivocally rejected realism of all shades. It condemned outright the people whom it labelled as "conciliationists", including not only Jozef Cardinal Glemp and Loch Walesa, but also the members of the underground Solidarity Temporary Coordinating Commission. The conciliationists, the clandestine paper argued, do not believe that the regaining of Poland's independence is possible at present, and, consequently, they advocate compromise with the Communist government. They hope only to win from the Communist side some moderate concessions and they have even recognized as inevitable the suppression of Solidarity. The conciliationists, then, espouse the brand of realism which proposes "only such changes as the Communists could accept".[8]

In contrast, the people whom *Independence* labelled as "positivists", and who include several groups active in the underground, believe that Solidarity went too far and too fast and, this way, missed the opportunity to carry out substantial changes within the existing system, which contributed to its demise. The positivists recognize that in order to improve the situation in the country, the Communists must eventually be removed from power, but they do not see this happening in the near future. Yet, by taking this position the positivists, in fact, embrace the same program as the conciliationists for they fail to see that "...political realism which resorts to compromises ceases to be a conscious choice and becomes an end in itself.".[9]

The article in *Independence* went even further and turned the distinction between idealism and realism on its head. It argued that the struggle for independence is the only realist i.e. rational, course of action. No meaningful concessions can ever be won from the Communists. "Power can be taken away from the Communists, but they will never share it with anybody." Consequently, there is no other way to improve the situation in the country than by overthrowing Communism. And the inescapable implication of the article in *Independence* is that this goal is not only feasible, but that it can be attained in the near future.

The optimistic belief in the efficacy of their struggle against Communism on the part of the radical underground groups is supported by two other tenets taken from the traditional idealist program. First of all many participants in the political debates in the *samizdat* papers hope for the early weakening, or perhaps even collapse, of the Soviet Union. They display strong anti-Russian sentiments and see their efforts as part of broader struggle against Moscow-led international Communism. A survey of the programs of nine underground groups outside of the Solidarity structure indicated that five of them favor splitting the USSR into its national components.[10] "Independence" explicitly appealed for "a joint action of enslaved nations against Communism and Soviet imperialism",[11] while another group, named "Fighting Solidarity", issued leaflets addressed to the Russians and the Ukrainians (printed in their own languages), arousing them to participate in the common struggle until "the red thrones collapse".[12] The leaflets opened with the 19th century Polish romantic slogan "For our freedom and yours", and affirmed the authors' readiness "to sacrifice their blood, and, if need be their lives, to that end".

All of the programmatic manifestos emphasize Poland's traditionally strong ties to the West, which is intended to accentuate the West's obligation to come to its assistance.* At a minimum the underground radicals expect that through diplomatic and economic pressures the western powers will compel the Jaruzelski regime to restore Solidarity; and at a maximum they hope for western help in overthrowing Communism in Poland, and perhaps even in the Soviet Union.

The significance of the radical underground groups must not be exaggerated for, in fact, most of them are quite miniscule. Yet, their programmatic discussions — even when divorced from all political reality — are interesting for they reflect views held by broad segments of the Polish society, and especially the younger generation. And,

---

*In my recent discussions in Warsaw even the members of the moderate opposition turned to this subject over and over again. I have been repeatedly lectured on what the United States policy toward Eastern Europe should be — with a clear hope that I will convey this message to my American friends. And many of the recommendations in this regard, made by otherwise liberal-minded Poles, have been reminiscent of the extreme views of the American neo-conservatives [sic!].

in turn, the numerous *samizdat* nurture the romantic tendencies among the Poles. And spokesman for "Fighting Solidarity" made this propagandistic objective of his group quite clear. While admitting that the group does not enjoy a substantial popular following he added: "I do believe there are dreams enough and that there are certain parts of the social psyche into which Fighting Solidarity fits".

There is no doubt, then, that in the last decade a significant shift on the Polish political continuum — away from realism and closer to idealism — has taken place. Several ingredients of the traditional romantic program: the underground activity, the strong anti-Russian sentiments and the expectations of assistance from the West, have reappeared in Poland. If this trend continues it might lead the Poles to embrace the one missing idealist tenet, namely, the armed struggle to regain their independence. The fact that the preponderant power is on the Communist side will not necessarily prevent them from doing so. They may follow in the footsteps of the insurgents of 1863 whose song praised those "who marched unarmed into battle".*

In 1982 Henryk Wereszycki compared the suppression of Solidarity to the defeat of the uprising in 1863.[13] The distinguished historian probably wanted to enharten the Poles at the moment of their despair — by stressing the important role which the legend of the insurrection played in keeping alive Polish patriotism — yet in doing so he used the wrong analogy. For in contrast to the disastrous national losses in 1863, which made the Poles abandon political romanticism, the losses suffered during martial law were minimal and did not produce the same traumatic result. After 1981, thus, the Poles have continued to cling to political idealism. Indeed, Wereszycki's historical parallel is not only erroneous, but also dangerous for it implies that the worst is over. Yet, viewed in the context of a dichotomy between idealism and realism the present situation in Poland resembles more that which existed *before* rather than that *after* 1863. There is still a possibility that the trend away from realism toward idealism among the Poles will continue until it culminates in a violent explosion which will be put down by force and with considerable loss of life. Only then would the analogy between the suppression of Solidarity and the defeat of the uprising in 1863 come true.

---

*The situation was not much different during the uprising in 1944. At its start the platoon in which I served was equipped with 1 submachine gun, 7 pistols and a score of handgrenades. But we still confidently went into the battle for as our own song had it, "victory was certain to come after the shedding of a lot of blood and tears".

* * *

At the realist end of the political spectrum stands the Polish United Workers' Party. All of the Polish Communists are conciliationists in the sense that they are satisfied merely with Poland's autonomy from the USSR and do not seek the country's complete independence. They are also distrustful of the West and tend to play up the German danger, as they did once again in 1984 when the Christian Democratic government in Bonn appeared to condone the revisionist claims to the Polish western territories by the refugees' organizations. The Communists' major focus continues to be on internal progress, although since 1981 this has just amounted to efforts, and not even particularly successful ones at that, to resolve the dramatic economic crisis.

The Communist party has not yet fully recovered from the shock of the events of 1980-81. Since that time one third of its members have left its ranks and much of the remaining membership is still badly demoralized and divided. Over the major issues the party is split into at least three distinct factions, with the conservatives and the moderates placed at the two opposing wings, and Jaruzelski and his followers straddle the middle. To emphasize this in the fall of 1985 the government was reorganized in such a fashion that both the leading conservative and moderate figures were removed from it.

The party conservatives take a rigid ideological stand. They are determined to preserve Communism, and their privileged positions in it, intact. They would like to restore — either out of conviction or just as a legitimization of its staying in power — the revolutionary élan of the party. To that end they also pledge, although without much credibility, to eliminate corruption and social inequalities. The conservatives advocate resorting to stern measures in coping with the opposition, even if it increases the risks of a popular explosion and a Soviet intervention — indeed, they may welcome such a development as a means of gaining the upper hand in the party. They, of course, underline strongly Poland's close ties to the USSR and the necessity to follow closely its example.

The party moderates are more flexible over Communist ideology. They accept the need for at least some degree of reform, even if this would restrict their privileged social status in the existing system. They believe that this is the only way to avert a new confrontation in the country and advocate a dialogue with the more sober elements in the opposition. The party moderates naturally support Poland's alliance with the Soviet Union, but tend to emphasize not only its ideological, but also geopolitical aspects and Poland's different "road to socialism" from that of the USSR.

Jaruzelski has followed a middle course between the conservatives and the moderates, although — especially in his restrained use of repression — he has been closer to the latter. He has made it clear that he would deal sternly with any attempt at overthrowing the Communist system; at the same time, however, he has promised to undertake the necessary reforms, and in advancing them he has appealed for national reconciliation. His relations with the Catholic church have stayed entirely proper — as best evidenced by his courteous reception of John Paul II in Poland in 1983.[14] Jaruzelski's political program, however, has not been systematic or stemming from any well-considered premises; it has, rather, represented a series of *ad hoc* responses to the many urgent challenges with which the new Polish leader has had to cope since he came to power. His paramount objective has been to preserve a modicum of order in the country.

There is little evidence that Jaruzelski's policies have managed to overcome the political stalemate in Poland. He has failed to come out with any imaginative reforms which would take the country out of its economic morass. He has also made no real effort to enter into a dialogue with the opposition (although indirect contacts have been maintained through the good offices of the Catholic church). Jaruzelski himself may have come to the conclusion that, considering the profound chasm between the government and the opposition, the chances of finding common ground between them are remote; but, undoubtedly, he has been also held back from making such an attempt by the USSR.

Jaruzelski's middle course, moreover, has been repeatedly undercut by the party conservatives. The most direct challenge from them came when Father Popieluszko was murdered in the fall of 1984. The political objective of the security officers involved in this grisly affair was to stir up new unrest in the country, and this way to compel the party leader either to abandon his relatively lenient course toward the opposition or, after losing control over events, step down. It did not work out this way — Cardinal Glemp managed to calm the emotions of the Poles, preventing a new upheaval, and General Jaruzelski clamped down upon the perpetrators of the crime, tightening his control over the security apparatus. In fact, the party leader used this occasion to dismiss from the Politburo one of the leading conservatives — a former Minister of Internal Affairs — Miroslaw Milewski. The incident, however, was still significant in highlighting the fact that the conservatives will not abstain from the most drastic steps to advance their political goals. And in these efforts they naturally hope to find a sympathetic ear in Moscow.

So far, the Kremlin leaders have been supportive of Jaruzelski. Evidently, they appreciated his liquidation of Solidarity without the need to resort to direct Soviet intervention. This has given Jaruzelski some leeway vis-á-vis-Moscow, but there are limits beyond which he cannot go. One of them seems to be the entering into a dialogue with the opposition, which in the Soviets' eyes would amount to reverting to the situation in Poland from 1980-81. This was made quite explicit by an article in the fall of 1983 in the authoritative Soviet journal *Voprosy Filosofii* which scolded Jaruzelski's close ideological collaborator at that time, Jerzy Wiatr, for merely proposing to listen to the arguments of the opposition.[15]

Jaruzelski's scope of political maneouver, thus, remains seriously restricted. He is delicately poised between the pressures from his own society and those from the USSR. And, yet, he may not be able to continue his balancing act indefinitely. Should the economic situation take another dramatic downturn new workers' strikes — not even necessarily instigated by the underground, but stemming from sheer desperation — may erupt. And next time round they may not be so peaceful as in 1980.* This may require a direct Soviet intervention, which would also terminate Jaruzelski's usefulness to Moscow.

Jaruzelski's position has been compared to that of Margrave Wielopolski who, in the early 1860s, tried to defuse the explosive situation in the country by winning modest, but tangible concessions for Poland from Russia. His program, however, satisfied neither side, and after the uprising of 1863 he was repudiated by both.[16] There is a distinct possibility that in the end Jaruzelski may also fall between the two stools.

\* \* \*

On the realist side the Communists are joined by various non-Marxist political groups. Several of them follow the Polish United Workers' Party so closely that their programs are virtually undistinguishable. These include the United Peasant Party, the Democratic Party, and the two "progressive Catholic" groups: "Pax" and the

---

*Here, for once, I am in agreement with *Kultura* which in June 1985 observed that the worst in Poland is not over yet, and underlined the possibility of a new popular explosion. (Redakcja, "Obserwatorium", No. 6/453, 1985). Except that *Kultura* seems to welcome such a prospect, while I dread it.

Christian Social Association. In 1980-81 segments of these Communist satellite movements showed signs of independence and even sympathized with Solidarity; after 1981, however, they have been silenced, and all of these groups have fallen behind Jaruzelski's line. In 1983 they joined the Patriotic Movement of National Revival — an umbrella organization of all political movements supporting the Jaruzelski regime, chaired by "Pax" member and well-known writer Jan Dobraczynski, but clearly controlled by the Communists.

A different position was adopted by the Polish Catholic Social Union, led by Janusz Zablocki. This group, which came into existence in 1981, openly sympathized with the moderate wing of Solidarity; subsequently, its representatives in the parliament refused to support the introduction of martial law and opposed the disbanding of the free trade unions. The group joined the Patriotic Movement of National Revival, but maintained there its distinctly independent stance. This course was explained by its Chairman as an effort to advance reforms "... within the limits of the present system, exploiting all the legal opportunities existing in it".[17] In 1984, however, the group split, with Zablocki and his collaborators ostentatiously resigning, and the new leaders have fallen more closely behind the Communist line.

In the parliament of 1980-85 the Catholics were often joined in their opposing of various retrogressive government measures by some independent deputies. Among them the more prominent were well-known writers Edmund Osmanczyk and the late Karol Malcuzynski, former "Pax" leader Ryszard Reiff, and prominent sociologist Jan Szczepanski. Their criticisms, however, were increasingly muted and in 1985 they were all eliminated from the parliament.

Open opposition was also voiced by some professional associations, such as those of the journalists and the writers, but they were disbanded and replaced by new organizations more pliant to the government's wishes. Among the informal but influential groups, Experience and The Future has continued to issue reports proposing the minimum reforms which could be introduced even without restoring Solidarity.

A moderate realist program was also been advocated by the Primate's Advisory Council. Formed late in 1981, and was composed of prominent lay Catholic experts. Among them the best known were a historian, Andrzej Micewski, who has emerged as the key personal advisor to Cardinal Glemp, and Stanislaw Stomma, who had been one of the main exponents of neo-positivism in the late 1950s, then led the Znak parliamentary group until 1975, and was the Council's Chairman. Stomma elaborated on the Council's program early in 1982. Progress in Poland, he emphasized, is possible only through "an evolutionary transformation of socialism" and this requires a "strategy of small steps".[18]

Most importantly, the realist program is adhered to by the Episcopate of the Catholic church. Throughout all stages of the Polish crisis regular contacts between the religious leaders and the Communist officials — including frequent meetings between the Primate and the First Secretary — have been maintained. And during his visit to Poland in 1983 John Paul II held two private talks with General Jaruzelski. The church's first concern, of course, has been to preserve freedom of religion and it has effectively used its ongoing dialogue with the Communist authorities to that end. Even during martial law religious practices were not restricted in any way. The Sunday mass continued to be regularly broadcast by the state-owned radio network. Construction of several hundreds of new church buildings went ahead. Access to religious education was even expanded and the Catholic press proliferated. And the visit of the Pope to his homeland in 1983 served as an occasion for millions of Poles to openly demonstrate their firm attachment to their faith.

The strong position of the Catholic church in Poland, even when it is confined to purely spiritual functions, is of great political significance. The very existence of an organization completely independent of the Communist government offers the Poles a moral comfort and even a physical refuge in their time of trial. Yet, the church's role does not stop there. As a millenium-old institution it serves as a carrier of the Polish national traditions and a spokesman for aspirations of the Polish people. In his homilies in Poland — addressing millions of listerns — John Paul II in no uncertain terms restated the Poles' strivings for freedom and independence.

Following in the footsteps of his revered predecessor, Stefan Cardinal Wyszynski, whom he succeeded in mid-1981, Cardinal Glemp has also not refrained from direct involvement in politics. In the fall he desperately tried to avert an ultimate showdown between the Communist government and Solidarity by acting as a mediator between Jaruzelski and Walesa. And after martial law was imposed he steadfastly demanded its early lifting and the release of all detainees. He has repeatedly intervened on behalf of political prisoners, and in 1984 when Father Popieluszko was murdered — although the Primate clearly did not approve of the fiery priest's activities — he led a strong protest against it.

At the same time, however, Cardinal Glemp has distanced himself from the radical opposition as useless and even dangerous.* He has underlined that the underground, which adheres to the program of a frontal attack against the government, is devoid of realism. And he explicitly warned the Poles against turning to armed struggle. In a homily delivered at the Polish national shrine in Jasna Gora in 1982, he pointedly reminded his compatriots that the ill-fated uprising of 1863 brought about "... annihilation, depression, destruction and, even worse, long-lasting slavery".[19]

\* \* \*

The common denominator among the moderate non-Marxist realists is their conviction that an armed uprising would not improve, but worsen the plight of the Polish nation. None believes that an insurrection could succeed. It would be crushed by the preponderant military power on the Communist side, and, should this not suffice, by intervening Soviet forces. Such an outcome — as so many times in Poland's history — could lead to heavy losses in life among the young people and in all likelihood would be followed by even greater oppression. And the realists have no illusions that in such circumstances the West would be able to render Poland any effective assistance.\*\*

The fear of popular explosion is shared by the moderate Communists. It would be detrimental to their program of adopting internal

---

\*It was precisely this stand which among the radical underground groups, such as "Independence", has earned Cardinal Glemp the label of a "concilliationist", and his course has been deliberately contrasted with that of his predecessor.

Wyszynski's unique experience and the immense prestige which he gained during his many years as the Primate, and which was enhanced by his internment in 1953-56, of course, could not be immediately matched by his successor. Yet, the allegations that Glemp has abandoned Wyszynski's line are completely unfounded. In my last conversation with Cardinal Wyszynski on March 1, 1981 — only a few weeks before he died — I found him alarmed by the increasingly radical course of Solidarity, which he characterized as taking the country to the "verge of an abyss".

\*\*This is basically the position to which I have adhered in my writings on Poland. I have recently presented the reasons why I do not believe an uprising in Poland could be successful in my *Eastern Europe in the Aftermath of Solidarity* (Boulder, Co. 1985, especially Chs. III and V), so I shall not restate them here. A more detailed discussion of this subject is also included in several Appendices, notably those by Stomma, Zablocki and Hall.

reforms and expanding Poland's autonomy from the USSR. To a degree this view is adhered to by General Jaruzelski and his own followers in the Polish United Workers' Party too, for they realize that an armed uprising necessitating Soviet intervention would terminate their usefulness to Moscow and pave the way for their removal from power. In contrast, the party conservatives may welcome, and, in fact, may try to instigate, a new popular explosion in Poland, which could topple the Jaruzelski regime and lead to their taking over the government. Paradoxically, then, at least in the short run the positions of the Communist conservatives and the underground radicals are similar; yet, in the long run they differ diametrically, for once in power the party conservatives would not expand, but would restrict, both Poland's internal freedom and her external independence.

It is their common stand against the extremists at both ends of the political spectrum which brings the political movements in the center together. They are painfully aware of the limitations inherent in Poland's external position and the internal consequences thereof. This has led to the searching for compromises between the moderate Marxists and non-Marxists, and, above all, to the dialogue between the Communist government and the Catholic church. It is, however, a tenuous link, for avoiding an armed clash is merely a negative factor; while the two sides remain divided (an, indeed, subdivided in their own ranks) over their respective long term objectives, as well as over the tactics which should be followed to attain them.

The main difference between the moderates in the Communist ranks and those in open opposition is that the former consider Poland's autonomy from the USSR as an end in itself, while the latter continue to espouse the ultimate goal of the country's independence. The gap here, however, is not impassable for on the one hand the moderate Communists would like to expand Poland's autonomy, and on the other hand the moderate oppositionists recognize that at present complete independence is unattainable, and, consequently, at least for the time being, that gradual expansion of internal freedom is the only practical course to follow.

More important is the fact that the Communists and the non-Communists also differ over the tactics which they should pursue to attain their overlapping goals. Many of the non-Marxist moderate realists are convinced — coming close here to the political idealists — that a continuous resistance against Communism is useful in expanding Poland's autonomy from the Soviet Union. They believe that popular pressure keeps the Jaruzelski regime on its toes and compels it to probe the outer limits of the country's freedom from Moscow.

The tactic of applying popular pressure upon the Communist government, however, is restricted in its usefulness and could even be
counter-productive. The Soviets clearly will not agree to any conces-
sion to the Jaruzelski regime which they would consider detrimental
to their essential interests in Poland. They were certainly pleased not
to have to intervene there in 1981, but should the Polish army have
failed to suppress Solidarity, they would have done so; and, no doubt,
should a similar situation develop in the future they will not refrain
from taking this step. The Soviets must also be well aware that while
an intervention in Poland would be militarily and politically costly
to them, the losses which the Poles would suffer would be greater;
they do not see, thus, the threat by the Polish political idealists to
resort to arms as credible.

The Soviets probably also perceive that the Polish moderate realists'
tactic of winning small concessions is ultimately aimed at restoring,
in a piecemeal fashion, the country's complete independence. They
may reason, then, that granting the Poles any greater freedom would
only encourage them to strive for more, and that the whole process
would never end until the country's sovereignty were fully restored.
The Soviet leaders, thus, may calculate that keeping the Jaruzelski
regime on a short leash is the best policy. And, the wide gap separating
the Communist government from the Polish society may be not detrimental, but advantageous to them in doing so.

Yet, efforts to restore strict Communist control over Poland may
prove to be counter-productive too. After the crisis in 1980-81 the
Communist ideology has been thoroughly discredited in the eyes of
most Poles and attempts to re-impose it would compromise all political
realism and make the Poles embrace the radical idealist programs.
The opposition might acquire its own momentum, and, despite all
odds, might resort to trying to overthrow the Communist government
by force. Such an outcome would amount to an act of despair similar
to that of 1863, and, likewise, would lead to a national catastrophe.

* * *

Most of the Communists and some of the non-Communist realists,
thus, advocate the opposite course. They argue that strong popular
pressure upon the Polish Communist government is counter-productive
for it weakens it internally and externally makes it even more dependent upon Moscow; and, conversely, the stronger the Polih Communist government is at home, the more concessions it can obtain

from the USSR.* They recommed, therefore, that instead of opposing it the Poles should throw their support behind the Jaruzelski regime. This is precisely the platform which has been advocated by the Patriotic Movement of National Revival.

Yet, there are various risks involved for the Poles in abandoning all pressure upon the Communist government. For while the Polish Communists may find the support at home useful in expanding their own autonomy from Moscow, they may not necessarily use it to expand the freedom of the Polish society, and, instead, may continue to rule the country in an autocratic style. Indeed, without any popular pressure pushing them in that direction, they may not even strive for any concessions from Moscow. And, freed from the pressure of the democratic opposition, the Jaruzelski regime would still be exposed to counter-pressure from the party conservatives to fall closer into line with the USSR.

Needless to add, such a development in Poland would be an ideal solution for the Soviet Union. It would free Moscow from any pressure from the Polish Communists for an expansion of the country's autonomy, and, in turn, would enable it to press the Jaruzelski régime — both directly and through the Polish party conservatives — to proceed apace with the Communization of Poland along the Soviet lines. Abandoning all opposition by the Poles, thus, could amount to the voluntary acceptance on their part of a foreign rule — in effect, to national suicide.

After the Solidarity period which has re-awakened their patriotic feelings, and instilled them firmly among the younger generation, the prospect that the Polish people *en masse* would willingly succumb to the Communist rule is remote. But there is another way that a similar situation could arise. After the suppression of Solidarity large segments of the Polish society have sunk into helplessness and resignation. Seeing no chance of success they have simply forsaken all political activity.

The people who have adopted this posture do not support the Jaruzelski regime, but they do not oppose it either. The boycott of the local government elections in 1984, recommended by the underground Solidarity, according to its own estimates was a blatant failure — some 15 million people participated in them. They voted, as the underground spokesman admitted, "for the sake of peace and quiet".[20] And next year the boycott of parliamentary elections also did not materialize. Paradoxically, thus, side by side with the growing agitation

---

*For fuller discussion of this view see: Andrzej Walicki, Appendix 11.

by the radical underground groups, there is also a progressive depolitization of the Polish society. And the two trends are not incompatible; in fact, they tend to reinforce each other. The more utopian the programs advocated by the radical groups become, the less use the Poles have for them.

From the Soviets' point of view such a development if Poland falls short of their ideological expectations, but politically may not be unacceptable. If they cannot have Poland as a reliable Communist ally — and they probably realize that at present this is not attainable — the next best thing is to keep the country as a weak satellite. The Poles' turning away from all politics — leaving the country's urgent problem unresolved — may be helpful to the Soviets' desire to at least neutralize the Polish nation.

If the trend toward depolitization of the Polish society were to continue uninterrupted over time, even without another popular explosion it might produce an atmosphere similar to that following the uprising of 1863. In a piecemeal fashion it may lead the Poles to embrace extreme political realism, amounting to yet another form of a national surrender.

* * *

There is no easy way out of their predicament for the Poles. The principle of *Primat der Aussenpolitik* still ruthlessly applies in their present position and the cherished Polish goal of national independence remains as elusive as ever. The extreme idealist and realist programs do not offer the Poles much hope; indeed, the adoption of either one of them would carry the threat of a national catastrophe. And the moderate idealists and realists also offer no clear solutions to the country's present dilemmas. And, rather than coming closer together, they are drifting even further apart on the political spectrum.

Turning away from all politics, of course, offers no escape.* Precisely because the country's situation is so grave, and pregnant with even greater dangers, the Poles must cope with it the best way they can. They must not abandon all political pressure, but they also must learn how much pressure should be applied at any given moment. What the Poles, then, urgently need are new and imaginative political programs. And when, searching for such programs, the Poles look back for inspiration in the past, the experiences called up must reflect

---

*For a discussion of the negative impact of the Poles' following such a course see Gella, Appendix 12.

accurately the historical facts. Fortunately, there are signs that at least some Poles are beginning to respond to this challenge.

One example of how historical analogies can be used in an illuminating political fashion is an essay published in 1985 by a young, though already quite well known historian, Aleksander Hall, entitled "The Two Realisms".[21] The author, after examining the period from the uprising of 1863 until the early stages of the 20th century (a period similar to that studied by Blejwas and Fountain), not only differentiates between idealism and realism, but also between the two types of realism. These were epitomized on the one hand by the program of the conservatives and Aleksander Wielopolski, and on the other hand by that of the national democrats and Roman Dmowski.

Hall notes three common features of all the realist programs. First, there was disbelief in any effective assistance to Poland by the western powers. Second, there was the repudiation of an armed struggle as the only way to regain independence. Instead, there was the stress on organic work aimed to strengthen the nation economically and culturally. And third, there was persistent striving to expand the Polish autonomy under foreign rule. In these three respects there was little difference between Wielopolski and Dmowski.

Yet, the two Polish leaders also differed in some major ways. Wielopolski followed what can be labelled "governmental realism". He thought that the situation in Poland was primarily determined by the external forces and, consequently, he gave his first attention to ingratiating himself to the Russian authorities. At the same time he tended to ignore, or even to distrust — having no faith in their political maturity — the Poles' aspirations and sought no support from them. Wielopolski's attitude was well expressed in his famous dictum that: "One can do something for the Poles, but never with the Poles".

In contrast, Dmowski espoused what may be termed a "dynamic realism". He was well aware of the significance of the external forces, but he did not neglect the internal ones. On the contrary, he strove to arouse political consciousness among all the Poles and to forge them into a mass political movement pressing to expand Poland's autonomy, and — when the international situation was ripe for it — to reach for independence. It was precisely by following the program of "dynamic realism" that the national democrats contributed to the rise of modern Polish nationalism and the revival of the Polish state in 1918.

After the sobering experience of martial law, observed Hall, there has been a revived interest in realist political thought, and perhaps a new realist movement is now in the making.* Yet, he added: "It is not enough to declare oneself a realist. It is also necessary to define what realism means and what concrete political program derives from it." As to the young historian himself he made his position quite clear — he declared himself an ardent supporter of Dmowski's "dynamic realism".

In his essay (as well as in his other writings) Hall indeed follows closely in Dmowski's footsteps. The young writer rejects both extreme idealism and extreme realism — the thesis and antithesis — and instead tries to combine their moderate versions into a coherent political program. In doing so he consciously strives — as Dmowski did early in this century — to arrive at the synthesis between the two traditional approaches in Polish politics which would best fit the contemporary circumstances.

---

*For Hall's extensive discussion of the reasons why he has embraced the national democratic tradition see Appendix 14.

## NOTES

1. "Stan swiadomosci spolecznej w Polsce". *Niezalezne Pismo Katolikow - Spotkania,* reprinted in *Zwiazkowiec* (Toronto), June 10, 1986.

2. "Panorama politycznej opozycji polskiej", *Niepodleglosc,* No. 25, January 1984, reprinted in *Trybuna* (London), No. 47/103.

3. "Dead Victims of Martial Law in Poland", RAD Background Report/168, (Poland), Radio Free Europe Research, September 5, 1984.

4. For this author's assessment of the importance of Father Popieluszko's murder see: "Poland at a Turning Point?", *Newsday,* December 4, 1984.

5. "A Register of Political Prisoners in Poland", RAD Background Report/70, (Poland), Radio Free Europe Research, July 22, 1985.

6. Jacek Kuron, "Macie zloty rog", *Tygodnik Mazowsze,* reprinted in *Informacja* (Montreal), No. 5, July 21, 1982.

7. Wladyslaw Hradek, *Tygonik Mazowsze* in "Informacja", *Ibid.*

8. "Niepodleglosc", *op. cit.*

9. *Ibid.*

10. "Coming out of the Fog, One Man's View of the Political Geography of the Polish Opposition", *Biuletyn Miedzywydawniczy,* No. 5-6, reprinted in Committee in Support of Solidarity REPORTS (New York), No. 28, October 28, 1984.

11. "Fighting Solidarity - Our Calling Card for Russians and Ukrainians", *Ibid.*

12. "An Interview with Kornel Morawiecki", *Czas,* No. 1, October 1984, reprinted in RAD Polish Underground Extracts/11, Radio Free Europe Research, July 31, 1985.

13. Henryk Wereszycki, "Znaczenie powstania styczniowego w dziejach narodu polskiego", *Tygodnik Powszechny,* May 30, 1982.

14. For this author's personal impressions of John Paul II's visit to Poland in 1983 see: "The Delicate Dance of Pope and General", *Newsday,* July 1, 1983.

15. A.V. Kuznetzov, "O teoretichieskikch knotseptsiiach odnogo polskovo politologa", *Voprosy Filosofii,* No. 12, December 1983.

16. Witold Olszewski, "Polskie myslenie", *Lad,* June 27, 1982.

17. Kierunki dalszej pracy Zwiazku — fragmenty refereatu prezesa Zablockiego", *Lad,* June 20, 1982.

18. Stanislaw Stomma, "Komentarz do sytuacji" (Mimeographed, Warsaw). For complete text of Professor Stomma's statement see Appendix 10.

19. John Darnton, "Primate Demands Poles Free Walesa", *The New York Times,* August 27, 1982.

20. "An Interview with Kornel Morawiecki", *Ibid.*

21. Aleksander Hall, "Dwa realizmy", *Tygodnik Powszechny,* July 14, 1985.

# IV

# THE LEGACY OF ROMAN DMOWSKI

There are similarities between the situation which existed in Poland before the uprising of 1863 and that in Poland in the late 1970s and early 1980s — stemming from the fact that in both cases idealism was on the rise. However, while the defeat of the insurrection in 1863 marked a decisive shift from idealism to realism, the suppression of Solidarity has not produced the same reaction, and idealism continues to be ascendant in Poland. In my polemic with Henryk Wereszycki in 1982 I suggested that, in fact, the latest (the third) rise of political romanticism has more in common with the last (the second) phase at the turn of the century, than with the more distant (the first) phase which preceded 1863. I also pointed out the similarities between the popular upheaval in 1980-81 and the revolutionary ferment in 1905-06 — in the sense that neither of these events (in contrast to the uprising in 1963) marked a decisive shift from idealism to realism.[1]

It is not only that the contemporary Polish adherents of idealism have embraced most of the tenets of its traditional political program; but they have also done so for reasons similar to those which influenced their predecessors at the turn of the century. First of all there has been a generational change — the leaders of the democratic opposition, of Solidarity and now of the various underground organizations being predominantly young people in their twenties and thirties, free from the defeatist memories of their fathers. The difference in outlook between the two generations was well summed up in 1985 by Andrzej Micewski. The young idealists, he wrote:

commit an error exactly the opposite to that which we made when we were young. After the loss of six million people during the war we were preoccupied with the program of the biological survival of the nation and the principles of geopolitics. [In contrast, the young people today] tend to believe that "wanting" is the same as "achieving" without taking into account the circumstances of place and time... [They seem to forget] that politics consists of an interplay of various actual forces, and the capability to conclude compromises is an integral part of it...[2]

The young Poles' decision to follow in the footsteps of the idealists from the late 19th and the early 20th century, moreover, was deliberate. Many of them were well aware of the similarities between the two situations. A prominent leader of the democratic opposition, Marek Tarniewski, compared the situation in the late 1970s to "the point of departure at the turn of the century".[3] Indeed, the young Poles were explicitly encouraged to fashion themselves after the revolutionaries among their grandfathers and great-grandfathers. A historical book published in 1971 by a young Catholic writer, Bogdan Cywinski — which depicted the fortunes of the "irrepresibles", who against great odds resumed the struggle for independence at the end of the 19th century — apparently made quite an impact among the young generation.[4] *The Solidarity Lexicon* issued in 1981 described it in the following terms:

... by presenting the story of two magnificent generations of the intelligentsia whose heroic efforts were crowned with independence [the book] served as a true inspiration to the generation presently in their thirties. It could be said without any exaggeration that it shaped the views of many activists of August 1980.[5]

The parallel between the revival of the Poles' aspirations at the turn of the century and today could, in fact, be carried a step further for there exists a widespread belief among them that now, as prior to 1918, their efforts are ultimately to be crowned with independence. This sentiment was well articulated in 1984 by Lech Walesa, who, while defending his renunciation of violence, resorted to a characteristic historical metaphor:

A policy which rejects solutions by force has the best chance and is the most responsible at present... We must realize that the proper historical moment has not yet arrived and this is not a propitious time for a Pilsudski to step in,* bringing his idea of independence with him.[6]

\* \* \*

If my parallel between the present situation in Poland and that existing after the revolution in 1905-06 is correct, then, it follows that the national democratic program which was dominant in Poland at that time is particularly relevant today. Indeed, at least two aspects of Dmowski's political thought from that period already seem to have been adopted by the contemporary Poles. First, it was the national democrats who in 1905-06 prevented the socialists from turning the revolutionary ferment in the country into a fully-fledged armed uprising and channelled the energies of the Poles into non-violent political activities. In this respect the course of the present moderate realists (including Lech Walesa, although he still seems to be more impressed with Pilsudski than with Dmowski), follows closely the example of the national democrats early in the century. Second, Dmowski's emphasis upon the need to synchronize the internal changes in Poland with those in the international sphere remains valid today. After their painful recent experiences many Poles have taken his advice to heart and since 1981 they are paying closer attention to the realities of their country's geopolitical position.

It is, however, precisely in comparing the geopolitical position of Poland early in the 20th century and today that the parallel between the two periods breaks down. Dmowski early anticipated an outbreak of the conflict in Europe which would open up opportunities for Poland to improve its position in the international sphere. Indeed, after

---

*Walesa's reference to Pilsudski illustrates another characteristic trait of Polish political thinking: the belief in the rise of some charismatic leader who will overcome Poland's geopolitical predicament — a myth which, incidentally, was deliberately cultivated in the inter-war period by the Pilsudskiites to enhance their political standing.

Paradoxically, it was Pilsudski's close friend, General Kazimerz Sosnkowski, who first alerted me to this Polish predilection. When, during a visit to his retirement place in Arundel, Quebec in 1953 I pleaded with him to go to London to take charge of the Polish Government-in-Exile, he impatiently retorted: "The Poles expect their leader to resolve all of their problems for them". Apparently, he did not believe that his assuming the leadership of the Polish emigrés in the West — given the international situation at that time — could change the situation of Poland; and, consequently, he chose to remain in his retreat in Arundel until his death in 1969.

publishing his masterly study of the country's geopolitical position, *Germany, Russia and the Polish Question,* in 1908, he turned his primary attention to international activities. In particular he cultivated contacts in the West which paid off handsomely when he headed the Polish National Committee in France during World War I, which paved the way toward Poland's regaining its independence in 1918*. At present, of course, such calculations on the part of the Poles would be futile. A war in Europe is unlikely, and should one happen it could result in a nuclear holocaust in which Poland would be one of the first victims. The prospect of an East-West conflict, thus, offers no relief for the Poles; on the contrary it threatens them with national extinction.

The similarities between the situation in Poland at the turn of the century and nowadays, then, demonstrate merely the existence of the cycle between realism and idealism, and they do not re-affirm the traditional linear view of Polish history. The ardent hopes of the political idealists that their efforts will inevitably culminate in another 1918 do not appear to be warranted. On the contrary, it appears that Poland's position in the international sphere can be improved only in a peaceful fashion and over a long period of time. In those circumstances the most promising course for the Poles is to follow the precepts of political realism.

Yet, as Hall rightly observes, in going back to realism the Poles should not opt for its extreme brand, but rather a moderate one (coming as close as possible to a synthesis with idealism), such as was espoused by Dmowski. And here we come to still another aspect of the national democratic leader's political thought that is highly relevant today, namely, his advice to his compatriots that while waiting for a more favorable turn of events in the international sphere they should concentrate upon developing the nation's internal strength.

* * *

Was Dmowski a revolutionary? — asks Fountain. It is a very pertinent question and the answer should be in the affirmative. In the sense

---

*Pilsudski also anticipated early the conflict in Europe, although during World War I he followed a different political path than Dmowski. He first threw in his lot with the Central Powers, and only after the defeat of Russia in 1917 did he switch over to the side of the Western Coalition. Nevertheless the activities of both Polish political leaders — by winning concessions from both sides — supplemented each other and paved the way for the restoration of the Polish state at the end of the war.

of departing from the 19th century Polish political thinking the national democratic program was no less revolutionary than that of the socialists. It was also aimed at a radical transformation of the Polish society in the direction of its modernization. These aspirations of the national democrats were best articulated in Dmowski's work *The Thoughts of a Modern Pole*, first published in 1903.

Dmowski was highly critical of the romantic tradition. It was not only that he regarded the incessant armed struggle as futile, but he saw the Poles' addiction to it as a major flaw in their national character. In his book he ruthlessly castigated as immature the Poles' emotional approach to politics.* He attributed this to their intellectual laziness. He was particularly critical of the dilettante and mystical nature of 19th century Polish political thought — heavily influenced by literature — which he sharply contrasted with practical and precise western political ideas. The Poles, he observed sarcastically, "transformed patriotism into a religion. But even the most religious people know how to light their churches with electricity, while in our national temples we are still using candles."

The national democratic leader, thus, strove to change the Polish national character by eliminating from it the obsolete traits, and so to bring it closer to the most advanced nations. For him politics was a serious exercise requiring strenuous and persistent endeavors, and, above all, profound intellectual exertions. In his writings Dmowski lived up to those expectations: his arguments were clear and well developed from premise to conclusion, and he used a crisp, yet powerful prose. He still ranks as one of the greatest Polish political authors of this century.

Dmowski's writings had an evident didactic character. His goal was to transform the Poles into a nation which would be energetic and skillful, inspired by deep patriotism, and yet guided in pursuing its interests not by emotions but by reason. He urged his compatriots to depart from their past traditions and to adopt new concepts fitting modernity. In this context he attached great importance to the national awakening of the masses. If it is true, he argued, that Poland is on the move once again, it is due to "... the masses of people — young, vibrant, ambitious, striving for action with their newly awakened instincts; it is not really a revival of the old Poland, but rather the emergence of a new one composed of the social strata which had been passive for centuries."

---

*For excerpts from Dmowski's writings relevant to this section see Appendix 1.

Dmowski was well aware that he was coming out against the dominant current in the Polish political thought, and he had no illusions that, in trying to transform traditional Polish character, he faced a long uphill battle. National policy, he wrote, "is a system which is developed over generations — a system to which each generation makes its own contribution and which is subject only to a gradual change". Given the odds with which he was faced Dmowski was remarkably successful. He created the political movement which remained dominant on the Polish political scene from the beginning of the 20th century until 1918; he also effectively countered Pilsudski's two attempts at staging an anti-Russian insurrection, in 1905 and in 1914.*

Yet, in the inter-war period, although the national democracy remained the single strongest political movement in the country, political power eluded it and most of the time belonged to the Pilsudskiites; at the same time the romantic tradition was revived and was continued during World War II, culminating in the tragic Warsaw uprising in 1944. Furthermore, after its eclipse in the 1950s and the 1960s, political idealism was once again resurrected in the 1970s.

* * *

The continued strength of the romantic tradition was demonstrated not only in the many *samizdat* publications, but by the debate over Tomasz Lubienski's book: *To Fight or Not to Fight?* which took place in the late 1970s in the official press. It reviewed the Polish uprisings against Russia in 1794, 1830 and 1863. The book was not really an historical work, but rather a popular pamphlet, and because it did not give an explicit answer to the question posed in its title, it offered

---

*The importance of the latter episode is generally not appreciated in Western historiography; yet, it contributed to the final outcome of World War I in a major way. Had Pilsudski succeeded in his efforts to stage in August 1914 an uprising in the "Polish tongue" of the Russian Empire, Samsonov's offensive into East Prussia would have not been possible. And since the stopping of Samsonov by Hindenburg at Tannenberg required recalling German troops from the western front, this, in turn, may have well determined the outcome of the battle of the Marne, where the German advance upon Paris was checked. If this interpretation of the opening gambits in World War I is correct, then, the Poles made a major contribution to the final victory of the Western Coalition over the Central Power and, thus, Dmowski had every right to participate in the Paris Conference representing Poland as one of the victors.

even greater scope for different interpretations. It provoked a lively and prolonged debate in the various major Polish papers, with some of the discussants even going beyond the historical events which it covered, and reaching into more recent episodes, and especially the Warsaw uprising.

In the debate the romantic interpretations of history clearly predominated. Several authors strongly defended the positive effects of the uprisings which, in their opinion, re-awakened the Poles' national consciousness and stimulated their will to independence. Jerzy Lojek even argued that the autonomy of the Congress Kingdom in the Russian Empire (which was abolished after the insurrection of 1830) was not worth preserving for it could have led to "the disappearance of the small Polish stream in the mighty Russian river.[8] If nothing else, he argued, this uprising served to encourage the next armed struggle for freedom in 1863. And Ernest Skalski offered even still more sweeping generalizations upholding the insurrectionist tradition:

> If in the period of over a hundred years of foreign rule the national consciousness remained alive, it was because of the uprisings... To put it simply, after each uprising there grew a new generation for which the burdens and the costs of the struggle were abstract, and who were fascinated by the struggle in itself. [Thus] a lost uprising was useful even if it just led to another uprising, by the next generation. For in history it is survival of the nation, and not of the individuals, which really counts.[9]

Skalski, significantly, attributed the same positive effects to the Warsaw uprising of 1944. With the demise of the last participants in it, he claimed, there will disappear "the sense of its uselessness, the bitterness of suffering, the stigma of defeat and the pain of its consequences".[10] What will remain will be the memory of an adventure which will dominate among the younger generation.*

Some participants in the debate went beyond attributing the armed uprising just to the striving of the young people for adventure, but — since it had served the national cause — raised it to the status of

---

*Skalski was right, for when at the Solidarity Congress in 1981 one of its advisors, a prominent economist, Witold Trzeciakowski, warned the young hotheads against going too far, and illustrated his point by showing his hand scarred by a bullet during the Warsaw uprising, he encountered an entirely unexpected reaction: "How exciting! We wish we could go through an adventure like this too."

an ethical issue. The insurgents, they claimed, were always right and their opponents were wrong. In addressing himself to the uprising of 1794, Marek Hryniewicz unfavorably contrasted the rational policy of the last King of Poland, Stanislaw August, with the moralistic posture of the leader of the insurrection (which led to the last partition of Poland a year later), Tadeusz Kosciuszko. What was most important, Hryniewicz argued:

> was the lasting memory of the insurrection... Transmuted into a legend, it played a great role in preserving the national consciousness.... And coming from the weaker party, Kosciuszko's appeal to ethical values deprived the partitioning powers of effective propaganda arguments.[12]

\* \* \*

There were some other voices — closer to Dmowski's position — in the debate over Lubienski's book too. Skalski himself raised some questions in the realist vein, such as: whether maintaining the autonomy of the Congress Kingdom after 1830 would not have helped the Poles in the international sphere during the Crimean War of 1855, or whether the Polish uprising (rather than having been staged in 1863) should not have been synchronized with that conflict of Russia with France and England? Yet, he quickly dismissed these questions as irrelevant and once again emphasized the insurrections' role in preserving the Polish national consciousness. One can conclude from this, Skalski added pointedly, that had the uprisings not taken place, at the beginning of the 20th century Dmowski, who was so critical of them — would have had no one to discuss the Polish question with.[13]

Another writer, Franciszek Ryszka, like Skalski, addressed himself to the question of the Warsaw uprising of 1944, but he reached different conclusions. By comparing Lubienski's review of the uprisings in the 18th and 19th century with the study of the activities of the Polish underground during World War II, he offered quite a sober assessment of the latter. In 1939-45 the question whether to fight or not to fight, he argued, did not really exist, for the war was imposed upon the Poles by the Germans. The question, then, rather was how the struggle should be conducted. In Ryszka's opinion it was, unfortunately, not conducted well. At the root of the Warsaw uprising was the political assumption that after a victory over Germany "a future Poland would find itself in a position basically the same as that in the inter-war period". And that assumption was wrong. Thus, Ryszka concluded, it is not a question of fighting or not fighting, but rather one of adopting the strategy best fitting the existing conditions and "corresponding to the requirements of realism".[14]

The most sober answer to the question raised in Lubienski's book came from Jan Demborog. He took strong exception to raising it to the level of an ethical issue and criticized Lubienski's statement that "the basic weapon of the weak is that they are right and that the law is on their side". In contrast, Dembrog adopted a thoroughly Dmowskian realist position. Law and moral rightousness, he wrote:

> are important only among the people who are bound by basic solidarity. In international conflicts law and morality — an, to be precise, legalistic and moralistic arguments — can be used also by the strong, and, indeed, they can put these arguments to better use. The weapons of the weak are knowledge, truth, realism and imagination, and if in these respects they are not superior to their adversaries there is no room for them in this world.[15]

The outcome of the debate over Lubienski's book — even though it was overshadowed by the historical debates conducted at the same time in the *samizdat* publications — was nevertheless highly significant. Perhaps, precisely because it took place on the pages of the official press, it demonstrated how deeply, even if unconsciously, the Poles are still committed to the idea that only through an armed struggle can they regain their independence.

Indeed, the debate revealed even some deeper layers in the Polish national psyche. It not only confirmed the Poles' profound predilection toward legalism and moralism, it also demonstrated a lack of confidence on the part of the political idealists in the strength of Polish nationalism. They clearly believe that compromising with the enemy would inevitably lead to a national surrender: the disappearance of the separate Polish national identity. In their opinion the Polish national consciousness can be maintained only in the emotional pitch of battle; otherwise it would cease to exist. The political idealists then feel that it is necessary to continue the struggle regardless of its costs.

The legalistic and moralistic traits of the Polish national character came to the surface once again in the late 1970s and the early 1980s. They were aggravated by the strong influence which was exerted at that time by the people who, once again, were dilettantes at politics: the writers, poets, producers, and actors. The novels of Tadeusz

Konwicki and the poems of Stanislaw Baranczak as well as many contemporary plays and films — all conveyed a strong idealist message. And the emotional song by Jan Pietrzak, "Let Poland be Poland", during the Solidarity period virtually became another national anthem.[17] The romantic atmosphere of those days, however, was best epitomized by the popular slogan: "It is better to die free than to live on one's knees". Yet, when the moment of truth came in 1981 the Poles abstained from violent struggle. Apparently, Dmowski's lessons were not altogether lost on them.

It is, then, in challenging the romantic traits of the Polish national psyche that Dmowski's political thought is particularly relevant today. His distrust of the literary treatment of politics, and his suspicion of moralistic slogans, go against the practices so widely spread in contemporary Poland. In fact, Dmowski was convinced that this realist position was morally superior to that of the political idealists, because what count in politics are not the intentions but the results.* The true policy for regaining independence", he wrote, "is not the one that just wants it, but that which brings it nearer and has some chances of success." The modern Poles would do well to take this advice of the national democratic leader to heart.

Yet, above all, Dmowski repudiated an incessant armed struggle for independence because he had greater confidence than the political idealists in the Polish nation. He did not believe that a compromise with foreign powers would be fatal to the Polish national consciousness; in fact, in so far as this would advance, even if only partially, their national goals, it could be conducive to it. And here we touch upon another aspect of Dmowski's political thought which remains profoundly relevant today, namely, his concept of nationalism.

\* \* \*

Dmowski watched with admiration the rise in the 19th century of modern nationalism in Western Europe, which permeated all social classes and provided those nations with a sense of cohesion and common purpose. He unfavorably contrasted this with the Polish nationalism, which well into the 19th century remained basically confined to the landowning class: the *szlachta*. He was also opposed to the concept of the Polish state to which this class — especially in the eastern provinces — was committed, namely, the recreation of the

---

*This aspect of Dmowski's political thought was well developed half a century later by Stanislaw Stomma. See: Appendices 4 and 5.

old, multi-national, Polish Commonwealth. Once again in this respect Dmowski strove to transform Poland into a modern nation.

As in Western Europe at that time, Dmowski's concept of Polish nationalism was influenced by the Darwinian idea of "the survival of the fittest". "Struggle is the foundation of life", the national democratic leader wrote, "nations morally degenerate and decay whenever they cease struggling." Roman Dmowski regarded Bismarck as the arch-enemy of Poland, yet he subscribed to the principles of *Realpolitik*. He believed, particularly since vis-á-vis the Germans the Poles represented the weaker side, that they had no choice but to follow a similar course.

Yet, it was not Charles Darwin, but rather Ernest Renan who seems to have impressed the young Dmowski the most. In Dmowski's writings there is a direct echo of Renan's celebrated lecture given at the Sorbonne in 1881 in which he perceived modern nations not just as linguistic or ethnic groups, but as communities linked by conscious desire to stay together, "having accomplished great things in common in the past and with the will to accomplish them in the future." In the most rousing lines of *The Thoughts of a Modern Pole*, the national democratic leader exclaimed:

> I am a Pole ... not only because I speak Polish, because the others who use the same tongue are spiritually closer to me and I understand them better, and because my personal affairs are more closely linked with them than with the foreigners, but because I am conscious of a collective national life of which I am part.
>
> I am a Pole: which means that I belong to the Polish nation across its entire territory and throughout its entire existence, today, as well as in the future.

In Dmowski's concept of nationalism there was no room for cultural or racial arrogance.* He wanted to assert the rights of the Polish nation — and whenever necessary he was prepared to do so in a forceful fashion — but he respected the same rights of other nations. "True patriotism", he argued, "need not be based on the notion of superiority of one's own nation over other nations." Indeed, he admitted that Poland profited a great deal from the civilizational progress of other

---

*For excerpts from Dmowski's writings relevant to this section see Appendices 2 and 3.

nations and urged his compatriots to intensify their efforts in this domain. Should not our pride, he asked:

> guide us toward civilizational and creative achievements from which in the future other nations can benefit as much as we have benefitted from them in the past and are still benefitting today? And should this not be the most noble obligation to humanity?

Their modern nationalism led the national democrats (and here great influence over Dmowski was exerted by Ludwik Poplawski) to embrace the idea of a Polish state based on ethnicity. They were the first important political movement to concede that the eastern provinces of the old Commonwealth — populated predominantly by the Ukrainians, Byelorussians and the Lithuanians — were irrevocably lost to Poland. Applying the same principls, however, to the western provinces — where the Germans represented the upper social strata, but were in the minority — the national democrats insisted that they should be a part of the restored Polish state. With the ethnic groups, however, hopelessly mingled together the delimitation of Poland's territory along those lines after World War I proved to be difficult, leaving large minority groups on both sides of the border.

\* \* \*

The concept of a unified Polish state, in turn, led the national democrats to emphasize the role of Catholicism. At first their relations with the Catholic church were lukewarm — with the Polish hierarchy leaning toward the conservatives and the Vatican being indifferent to the issue of Poland's independence — but gradually they become closer. In the inter-war period, and especially in the 1930s, the national democracy identified itself as a manifestly Catholic movement and many leading churchmen openly supported its program.

Once again of a crucial significance in this evolution of national democracy was the position taken by its leader. A rationalist as a young man and well into his middle age, Dmowski remained rather indifferent toward religion, but then he underwent a conversion. In his pamphlet *The Church, the Nation and the State,* published in 1926, he underlined the historical role which the Catholic church played in the development of the Polish national consciousness. Indeed, Dmowski argued that the Catholic religion and the Polish nationality are inseparably linked together. Catholicism, he wrote, "is not an adjunct to Polishdom, merely coloring it in some special way, but is inherent in its very core and to a large extent constitutes its very essence". And, he added, any attempt to divide the two "strikes at the very essence of our Nation".

In many respects Dmowski's concept of modern nationalism has been remarkably successful. In the inter-war period the national democratic ideology exerted powerful influence in the Polish society, expecially among the younger generation. By the late 1930s even the Pilsudskiites, particularly when they formed the Camp of National Unity in 1937, had adopted some of its tenets as their own. Meanwhile, the process of the Polish national consciousness permeating all social classes made important strides, and by World War II it was completed.*

The Polish state which emerged after the war, paradoxically under Communist rule, fitted well the vision of the national democrats. It lost its eastern — ethnically mixed — territories, but it stretched far into the west, including the lands which had been Polish in its early history under the Piast dynasty. Poland also emerged from World War II as one of the most homogenous nations in the world. Ethnically its population was over 98 per cent Polish and overwhelmingly Catholic.[18]

The legacy of its close association with the national democracy in the inter-war period (although for obvious political reasons the ecclesiastical leaders carefully avoided stressing it directly), can easily be detected in the line which has been followed by the Catholic church in the post-war years. An echo of Dmowski's views about the close links between Catholicism and Polishdom can be found in various statements by Cardinal Wyszynski and John Paul II. In the case of Wyszynski, who before the war had been close to national democracy, it was probably conscious. "For us", he declared in 1974, "next to God, our first love is Poland". In the case of Wojtyla, who as a young priest in Cracow was close to the "Znak" group, it has been

---

*The pride in this phenomenon was displayed to me in a conversation which I had in 1968 with one of Dmowski's close collaborators, Jerzy Zdziechowski, who was then 88, but still remarkably lucid. When I expressed concern about the political crisis unfolding in Poland at that time, he dismissed this: "Don't worry", he said, "those are the inevitable consequences of the participation in the national life of all the social classes." Zdziechowski's statement applies even more to the events in 1980-81.

less pronounced (he probably inherited it indirectly from Wyszynski), but nevertheless it is still there.*

The influence of Dmowski's political thought upon the Catholic church in Poland in the post-war period has been most clearly manifested by the tactics which it adopted vis-à-vis the Communist government. Primate Wyszynski pressed the Communist regime hard for concessions to the church as well as to the Polish people. Yet, whenever there was danger of an outright insurrection — as in 1956, 1970 and in 1980 — he held the Poles back. And in this respect Primate Glemp has steadfastly followed in the footsteps of his predecessor.

* * *

Yet, Dmowski's concept of modern nationalism has by no means been universally accepted by the Poles. In 1920, ignoring bitter opposition from the national democrats, Pilsudski undertook the military expedition to Kiev in an effort to recreate the ancient union between the Poles and the Ukrainians. It ended in near disaster for the young Polish state with the Bolshevik counter-offensive stopped only at the gates of Warsaw. Yet, in the inter-war period the dominant wing of the Pilsudskiites subscribed to the so-called Promethean program aimed at subverting the USSR and restoring the Jagiellonian Commonwealth, composed, in addition to the Poles, of the Ukrainians, the Byelorussians and the Lithuanians.

These plans persisted during World War II when the various underground groups influenced by the Pilsudskiite ideology ceaselessly advocated restoration of the Polish state stretching from the Baltic to the Black Sea. And in London the Polish exiles advanced the less boisterous, but equally unacceptable to the USSR, program of a Polish-Czechoslovak federation which was to serve as the nuclous of a broader union of all the Central and Southern East European countries, as a barrier separating Germany and Russia.

In the post-war period the Jagiellonian tradition was continued by the Polish emigrés. It was subscribed to by the old Pilsudskiites, the

---

*For illustrations of Cardinal Wyszynski's and John Paul II statements along those lines see Appendices 7 and 13; and for interpretations by Zablocki and Hall see Appendices 8 and 14.

neo-Pilsudkiites* and the socialists, who exerted the dominant influence among the Polish exiles in the West. It was also consistently
advocated by the Paris *Kultura*. Following the rise of the dissident
movement in the USSR in the late 1960s and the early 1970s, its chief
political commentator, Juliusz Mieroszewski, wrote a series of articles restating the Pilsudskiites' hopes for a collapse of the Soviet
Union, paving the way for a renewal of Poland's role in the east.[20]
And these emigré delusions, in turn, spread among the various opposition groups in Poland.

The revival of Dmowski's political thought, thus, was bitterly
resented in most of the democratic opposition circles inspired by the
socialists' or the Pilsudskiites' ideas. They repeatedly denounced the
national democracy — often in terms not much different from those
applied by the Communists — as a reactionary political movement.
In 1977 the clandestine Polish Coalition for Independence came out
with a strong denounciation of the national democratic tradition,[21]
and a member of the Committee for Defence of the Workers, Barbara
Torunczyk, undertook writing a book highly critical of Dmowski's
activities in 1895-1905**, which, however, was published only in
1983 after she left for the West.[22]

In mid-1981, during the climax of the Solidarity period, there
appeared an essay — at first issued by an independent publishing house
and then reprinted by the Paris *Kultura* — on the nature of Polish
nationalism written by a prominent literary critic and leader of the
Committee for Defence of the Workers, Jan Jozef Lipski.[23] It was

---

*The neo-Pilsudskiites, composed mostly of young officers, diplomats and
journalists, formed in exile a political group called Independence and
Democracy. It repudiated the Pilsudskiites' dictatorship of 1926-39 and supported parliamentary democracy, but it continued to subscribe to their main
tenets in foreign policy. Its leader was a nephew of the old Marshal, Rowmund
Pilsudski, and among the group's young followers was Piotr Wandycz (who,
in fact, started his academic career with a monograph about the plans for
Polish-Czechoslovak federation during World War II). Susbequently, dissillu-
sioned by the lack of interest in the fate of Eastern Europe in the West, many
of the leading figures in Independence and Democracy (including Pilsudski
and Wandycz) have moved closer to the realist positions. Some others, however, have stubbornly clung to the idealist program.

**Torunczyk's book covers the same period of Dmowski's life as does
that of Fountain, although she does not seem to be familiar with it. The contrast
between an objective treatment of Dmowski's political activities at that time
by a detached American historian, and that of a Polish author — properly
trained in history, yet so deeply involved in politics — is striking.

written in an idealist fashion *par excellence,* criticizing the national democracy for its alleged xenophobia, and it openly reverted to the Jagiellonian tradition. The essay expressed regrets for the Poles' past errors toward their eastern neighbors (although it pointed out their mistakes too), and advocated forgetting the old prejudices and a closing of ranks among the Poles, Ukrainians, Byelorussians and Lithuanians, as well as the Russian dissidents, in their common struggle against Soviet Communism. It also called — in a fashion not atypical of the political idealists — for a reconciliation between the Poles and the Germans, which it presented as an indispensable prerequisite for Poland's return to the West.

Lipski's essay, however, is interesting not only for its political ideas, but also for the style in which it is written — it exhibits all of the features which Dmowski found so repugnant in the Polish approach to politics. It is written in a highly emotional manner and to support its arguments it relies upon literary masterpieces rather than historical and social works. It also displays the narcissism of the Polish intellectuals: the belief in their special role in Poland and beyond.* As such it falls into a xenophobic trap of its own: a strongly accentuated Polonocentrism — the belief that Poland has to play a special role among the neighboring countries and, indeed, in Europe as a whole.

Last but not least Lipski, evidently unaware that it was from there that Dmowski derived his doctrine, reveals a remarkable naiveté about the nature of nationalism in the West. He ignores the fact that the policies of the western powers (starting with West Germany) are shaped, above all, by their hard-nosed national interests.

An indirect, but nevertheless pointed, lesson to the Poles like Lipski was given right after the suppression of Solidarity by American historian Ronald Steel. In an article significantly entitled "Realpolitik", Steel assessed the present position of Poland in the international sphere in the following fashion:

> The division of Europe is, for the foreseeable future, a fact of life, a fact that reflects the complementary interests of the superpowers. It

---

*The narcissism of the Polish intellectuals particularly struck me in a conversation which I had in 1974 (shortly before he died in a car accident) with a prominent poet, Antoni Slonimski. He was clearly irritated by the attention given at that time in the western media to the activities of the Soviet dissidents, while the opposition in Poland — which was then in eclipse — was scarcely mentioned. Slonimski enjoyed considerable prestige in the Polish intellectual circles; among others he was a political mentor of Adam Michnik.

cannot be repaired by force. Indeed, any dramatic change could unhinge both alliance systems. If Poland wrenches itself free from the Soviet bloc, East Germany would be isolated. Bonn might then look East, tempted by visions of reunification, and question its links to NATO and the Common Market. The threatening specter of the unified Reich would loom on the horizon, bringing a new element of danger into European politics. At the very least, West European nationalism would increase and the United States' hold over its allies would sharply diminish.

While the division of Europe is regrettable, almost any conceivable alternative, under present conditions, poses great risks... This is why every European Government has been restrained in its reaction to the crackdown in Poland. And it is why the Reagan Administration, even while enjoying Moscow's embarassment, must recognize that if the Russians lose control over Poland, all of Europe becomes unstable.

Americans and West Europeans have shown their sympathy for the Polish people. But sentiments are personal. People have sentiments, nations have interests. And it is an unfortunate fact of political life that the interests of the Western alliance, as well as those of the Soviet Union, demand that the Polish boat not be turned upside down.[24]

Steel's sober evaluation of Poland's present position in the broad context of East-West relations illustrates eloquently the limits of its action. The Polish Promethean program is rather Sysyphean, i.e. no matter how tenaciously it is followed, it stands no chance of success. The modern Poles would do better by adhering strictly to Dmowski's precepts of *Realpolitik*.

## NOTES

1. See my: *Poland, The Protracted Crisis* (Oakville, 1983), p. 242.
2. Andrzej Micewski, "Zmiana pokoleniowa", *Tygodnik Powszechny*, January 13, 1985.
3. Marek Tarniewski, *Ewolucja czy rewolucja?* (Paris, 1975), p. 181.
4. Bogdan Cywinski, *Rodowody niepokornych* (Warszawa, 1971).
5. *Solidarnosc, leksykon zwiazkowy* (Gdansk, 1981), pp. 22-23.
6. "Now I Shall Be Myself: An interview with Lech Walesa", *Tygodnik Wojenny*, August 30, 1984. Reprinted in RAD, Polish Samizdat Extracts/10 AG, Radio Free Europe Research, October 25, 1984.
7. Tomasz Lubienski, *Bic sie czy nie bic?* (Krakow, 1978).
8. Jerzy Lojek, "Moze jednak sie bic", *Zycie Literackie*, September 17, 1978.
9. Earnest Skalski "Raczej sie bic", *Kultura*, October 22, 1978.
10. *Ibid.*
11. As related to this author by Professor Trzeciakowski.
12. Marek Hryniewicz, "Historia po polsku", *Nowe ksiazki*, April 1978, p. 73.
13. Skalski, *op. cit.*
14. Jerzy, Janusz Terej, *Rozstajne drogi. Ze studiow nad obliczem i modelem Armii Krajowej* (Warsaw, 1978).
15. Franciszek Ryszka, "Rozstajne drogi", *Kultura*, January 7, 1979.
16. Jan Demborog, "Dalszy ciag debaty", *Tygodnik Powszechny*, September 3, 1978.
17. For a more detailed discussion of this subject see my: *Poland, The Protracted Crisis* (Oakville, 1983), pp. 240-1.
18. In 1956, all the minority groups in Poland amounted to a half a million people, representing 1.8 per cent of the total population (*Zycie Warszwy*, July 11, 1957). For a more detailed discussion of the contrast between the pre-war and the post-war Poland and its political consequences see my: *Poland's Politics, Idealism vs. Realism* (Cambridge, Mass. 1967). Ch. 13.
19. For an excellent presentation of Cardinal Wyszynski's political tactics see: Aleksander Hall, "Poland's Future" in my *Eastern Europe in the Aftermath of Solidarity* (Boulder, Co., 1985), pp. 188-9.
20. Juliusz Mieroszewski, *Materialy do refleksji i zadumy* (Paris, 1976). Especially pp. 110-135, 175-186.
21. Polskie Porozumienie Niepodleglosciowe, "Tradycja niepodleglosciowa i jej wrogowie", *Tydzien Polski* (London), April 23, 1977.
22. Barbara Torunczyk, *Narodowa Demokracja, Antologia mysli poltiycznej Przegladu Wszechpolskiego (1895-1905)*, London, 1983).
23. Jan Jozef Lipski, "Dwie ojczyzny, dwa patriotyzmy", *Kultura* (Paris). October 1981. Originally issued by the *samizdat* publishing house NOW-a in Poland in June 1981.
24. Ronald Steel, "Realpolitik", *The New York Times*, January 3, 1982.

# V

# TOWARD A SYNTHESIS

Dmowski's nationalism has been directly opposed to Marx's inter-nationalism, and, as a result, on several occasions in the past the national democrats have clashed head-on with the social democrats and later with the Communists. In 1905-06 the national democrats helped to extinguish the revolutionary ferment in the country, and during the Polish-Russian war in 1918-20, of course, the national democrats and the Communists found themselves on opposite sides. Still, in 1926 the Communists supported the Pilsudskiites' military coup to prevent the national democrats from coming to power.

In the late 1920s and the 1930s the national democrats embraced — as was happening all over Europe at that time — a more militant version of nationalism. The older, more liberally minded leaders of the party were pushed aside, and even the aging and ill Dmowski, although he was revered until his death in 1939 as the movement's founder, gradually lost his grip on it. Under the new leadership the movement's name was changed to the "Nationalist Party" and it moved distinctly to the right although it never went — if only because of its traditional aversion to Germany — as far as fascism.* The

---

*Strictly speaking the name of the party was the "National Party" (Stronnictwo Narodowe). The pre-war national democrats, including Bielecki, argued that this was a deliberate move to accentuate their difference from the Nazis, who were "nationalists", while they only were the supporters of the "national idea". Yet, in English the party's proper denomination seems to be "nationalist", although, of course, in Dmowski's and not in Hitler's mold.

splinter group which moved furthest in that direction — and for a while collaborated with the Pilsudskiites' Camp of National Unity — were the Falangists, led by a young Boleslaw Piasecki, yet even they aped the Italian or Spanish, and not the German, brand of fascism.*

The widening gap between the national democrats and the left led to another bitter confrontation between them and the Communists. During World War II the national democrats in exile in London, led by Tadeusz Bielecki, drifted toward the idealist position. They opposed the efforts of the Premier of the Polish Government-in-Exile, General Wladyslaw Sikorski, and his successor, the Peasant Party leader, Stanislaw Mikolajczyk, to arrive at an accommodation with the Soviet Union. Toward the end of 1944 in London they joined the socialists and the Pilsudskiites in the new government opposed to any change of the Polish eastern boundary. As a result they closed the door for themselves on any participation in the government prescribed by the Yalta Conference and established in June 1945 in Warsw, which was dominated by the Communists, but included several genuine non-Communist political leaders. At the same time the partisan units, formed by the national democrats during the war to fight the Germans, turned against the Soviet and the Polish Communist forces. Some of them, called the National Armed Forces, carried on their struggle into the late 1940s. And the national democratic underground, directed from London, continued to operate in Poland into the early 1950s.

The national democrats paid dearly for their idealist course during World War II and its aftermath. Under the Communist rule they became the most persecuted political movement in the country. Thousands of them were thrown into prison and many perished there.[1] Those who survived were released after 1956, but many of them were broken men. And for many years afterwards the national democracy was branded by the Communists as a "fascist" movement, and the only references to it permitted in the official publications were derogatory. It was only in the late 1960s and in the 1970s that the history of the movement was allowed a somewhat fairer — although still far from objective — treatment.

---

*Paradoxically, the former Falangists re-emerged on the Polish political scene in the post-war period as the "Pax" group, which Piasecki led until his death in 1980. In a conversation which I had with him in 1978 Piasecki explained this political evolution on his part in two terms: i) political realism, which he attributed to Dmowski; and ii) the commitment to radical social changes, which, even though on the extreme right, the "Falangists" shared with the Communists.

The first political groups openly reverting to the national democratic program appeared in Poland in the late 1970s. They ranged from the Polish Committee for the Defence of Life and Family, which advocated reapealing the lenient abortion laws, to the Movement of Young Poland, composed of young intellectuals (one of whom was Aleksander Hall). The latter group, centerd in Gdansk, subsequently played an important role as moderate advisors to Solidarity. They were joined there by a few older national democrats and the Christian democrats, notably a prominent lawyer Wieslaw Chrzanowski.*

Meanwhile, the national democrats abroad underwent a political evolution, returning to Dmowski's original thought. They broke with the Pilsudskiites and the socialists and assumed a more realist stance toward the political development in Poland.** They centered around the monthly *Mysl Polska,* published in London and edited by Antoni Dargas, who, after the death of Bielecki, also assumed the group's leadership. Gradually contacts were established between the young followers of Dmowski in Poland and the older national democrats abroad. The writings of the national democratic authors living in the West, notably those of Jedrzej Giertych and Wojciech Wasiutynski, penetrated into Poland.

In 1981-84 the official organ of the Polish Catholic Social Union, *Lad,* a weekly, was edited by Witold Olszewski, who in the 1950s and the 1960s published in Paris a national democratic monthly, *Horyzonty.* After returning to Poland Olszewski grouped around him some young admirers of Dmowski, some of whom joined him on the

---

*The ties between the national democrats and the Christian democrats who came into being in the inter-war period, have been traditionally close. The political fortunes of Chrzanowski illustrate this well. During the war, as a young man, he participated in the national democratic underground. After the war he led the youth wing of the Christian democratic party — for which he served several years in prison. Acting as one of the chief legal advisors to Solidarity, Chrzanowski was joined by a former Christian democrat, and another prominent lawyer, Wladyslaw Sila-Nowicki.[2]

**The course followed by Jerzy Zdziechowski was symptomatic in this regard. In the early 1950s he still headed the executive of the then main emigré political body in the West: the Political Council. After 1956, however, he parted with the political emigrés and visited Poland, where he established high level political contacts with the Gomulka regime. In the late 1950s and the early 1960s he edited in Paris a quarterly, *Cahiers Pologne-Allemagne,* which was devoted to the defence of the Polish western boundary against the German revisionist claims. Subsequently, when he was in his mid-eighties, he returned to Poland to retire.

editorial board of *Lad,* and gave that paper a distinctly national democratic flavor.

At the same time several unofficial groups adhering to the national democratic tradition, composed mostly of young people, came into being in Poland. The best known among them is the successor to the Movement of Young Poland, centered around the journal *Polityka Polska* (the name of which is significantly derived from Dmowski's work: *Polish Politics*). Its chief publicist has been Aleksander Hall, (whose writings have appeared also in the official Catholic papers and were reprinted in *Mysl Polska* in London). The various groups are only loosely connected and they tend to emphasize somewhat different aspects of the national democratic program. Yet, they are all inspired by Dmowski's thought and strive to modernize it to fit the needs of contemporary Poland.

* * *

After the upheaval in 1980-81 the historical role of Dmowski has eventually gained recognition even among some writers from the ranks of the democratic opposition. Piotr Wierzbicki, who in his previous writings castigated the Polish intelligentsia for submitting to the Communist regime, after the martial law period (when he was temporarily interned), completely shifted gears, and has now accused them of engaging in a futile opposition. In 1985 he came out with a book entitled *The Thoughts of an Old-Fashioned Pole* — to signify that the "modern" Pole of Dmowski's period has now "matured". It is an uneven volume, but lively and containing several provocative themes. It proclaims the bankruptcy of the Polish Left and advocates a return to the traditions of the Right, and particularly to those of national democracy.

Wierzbicki fully endorsed Dmowski's middle course, rejecting both extreme idealism and extreme realism. The Poles, he writes, tend to subscribe to two opposite programs, each of which restricts their aspirations. On the one hand there is blind servility, and on the other hand there is blind protest. Dmowski aptly analyzed these two tendencies and attributed them to the long subjugation of the Poles to foreign rule. After all, "shifting from blind servility to blind protest is a typical behavior of a slave".[4]

Dmowski's third course is superficially just a combination of the two, but in fact it is superior to either because it represents a reaction not of slaves, but, on the contrary, of a free people. It is a "sophisticated program followed by the advanced, strong and cultured nations. It is a program of systematic political activities aimed to attain specific political goals."[5]

Wierzbicki clearly admires Dmowski as a master of such conscious and persistent political activity. It culminated in the national democratic leader's role at the Paris Peace Conference in 1919 where he managed to successfully uphold both Poland's independence and its borders. But, adds the author, these attainments did not come easy to Dmowski. For to conduct such a "refined, calculated, policy, inspired more by logic than emotions" required years of intense preparations on his part.[6] He not only had to think through his own program, but also to create a powerful political movement supporting it.

The behavior of the present Polish intelligentsia, according to Wierzbicki, follows the traditional patterns of slaves: either submission or protest. Yet, they must overcome this and follow the example of the national democrats from early in the century. A prerequisite for this is the adoption of a thorough realism, which the author defines as: "seeing the Polish problems as they are, distinguishing between our wishes and the realities surrounding us, including the unpleasant ones ... and accepting the entire truth without any exceptions and embellishments."[7]

Even a prominent leader of the Committee for Defense of the Workers, Adam Michnik, has undertaken at least a partial rehabilitation of Dmowski. In an essay written in internment in 1982 he addressed himself to an extensive, and in some respects profound, historical analysis of national democracy.[8] He admitted that one of the reasons for doing this was because he found his previous writings on the subject "tainted with an anti-national democratic stereotype,"[9] Michnik recognized that Dmowski was a great political thinker. Not all the predictions of the national democratic leader came true, the author argued, but Dmowski's diagnosis probably was "the best type of analysis of the Poles' political position".[10]

Michnik, like Wierzbicki, has upheld Dmowski's middle course between extreme idealism and extreme realism.* In fact, the former leader of the Committee for Defense of the Workers came close to conscious searching for a synthesis between these two strands of Polish political thought like the national democrats of the early century. "In

---

*It is interesting to observe, however, that Michnik's fellow-interns who read the draft of his essay — and represented the cream of the former Committee for Defence of the Workers — strongly disapproved of his evaluation of the national democratic tradition as too apologetic.

Polish political thought'', he wrote, ''there was a dualism between romanticism and positivism and in Polish political activity, a dichotomy between armed insurrection and organic work. Overcoming these was an indispensable precondition for a new style of political thinking''.[11] But, he stressed, the repudiation of insurrectionist tactics should not lead to just conciliation with foreign rulers. Rather it ought ''to be aimed at searching for new means of attaining independence''.[12]

Yet, Michnik's rehabilitation of Dmowski (although much more sophisticated than that of Torunczyk), also remained partial and in some respects even tendentious. In his analysis of the national democratic thought he deliberately denigrated the realist, and stressed the idealist elements, and particularly Dmowski's qualified endorsement of conspiratorial activities. In short, Michnik focused on those aspects of Dmowski's tradition which fitted into the program of the democratic opposition in contemporary Poland.

In doing so, of course, Michnik distorted the national democratic program. For the fact is that Dmowski regarded conspiracies only as a last resort, and when opportunities for open political activities existed he distinctly preferred them. The national democratic leader adopted them after the revolution in 1905-06, and he probably would have done the same today. This mistake of Michnik's was pointed out in an essay written in 1985 by a prominent Polish historian, Andrzej Walicki: ''There is no doubt that in the situation of People's Poland — the existence of a non-sovereign, but nevertheless Polish, state — the true followers of Dmowski are the people who try to expand its independence by using to that end the existing political institutions, rather than by opposing the state wholesale.''[13]

The strength of the national democratic tradition in today's Poland, however, does not lie in its political influence.* Nor does it lie in the numbers of its avowed followers. The remnants of the pre-war national democrats, both at home and abroad, are a fading force — they can at best serve as a conduit for their ideas to the younger generation. And the conscious adherents to Dmowski's political thought

---

*Although at least two former national democrats, both of whom advanced through the ranks of ''Pax'', made it to the top levels of the Jaruzelski regime. Zenon Komender — who at the end of the war was imprisoned for his participation in the national democratic underground — in 1983-85 was a Deputy Premier, and at present is a member of the State Council. And Jan Dobraczynski — who during the war served as an officer in the national democratic military underground — since 1983 has been the Chairman of the Polish Movement of National Revival.

among the younger people are still very few — they are certainly overshadowed by the supporters of the Pilsudskiite and even the Marxist
traditions.

Dmowski's program, moreover, must not be accepted uncritically.
As with most prolific writers, there are better and worse aspects in
his political thought. Dmowski himself was aware of this, and warned
his followers not to be dogmatists. And, of course, with the changes
in Poland and in the world during the 20th century some aspects of
the national democratic program have simply become obsolete. They
have to be verified against the passage of time and, whenever
necessary, brought up to date.

Yet, the revival of Dmowski's political thought in contemporary
Poland is not as strange as it may appear. It is not only that most
of his ideas uniquely fit the country's present conditions; it is also
that, even among those people who have never read Dmowski's works,
they have permeated broad segments of the Polish society. Above
all, the influence of national democracy is quite visible among the
Catholics — both layment and clergymen. But it can also be discerned
among the Polish Communists.

* * *

Despite the very different historical roads which the national democrats and the Communists have traveled, there have also been some
aspects of their programs which they have had in common. In their
formative stages they were both influenced by the positivists' repudiat-
ing, after 1863, the tradition of a futile struggle for independence;
and, both turned to searching for inspiration to improve Poland's fate
in the contemporary western thought — except, of course, the national
democrats were impressed with the liberal ideas while the early social
democrats looked up to revolutionary Marxism.[14] Still, they were both
highly critical of the 19th century Polish national character — and
especially the dominant influence over it of the *szlachta* tradition —
and strove to modernize it.[15] Furthermore, the national democrats,
like the social democrats, early appreciated the significance for Poland
of the internal changes in Russia; although the former placed their
hopes in its evolution toward constitutionalism and democracy, and
the latter in a revolutionary upheaval against Tsarism.

Despite the Bolshevik revolution in Russia in 1917, toward the end
of his life Dmowski remained convinced that Poland should maintain
proper, if not friendly, relations with its eastern neighbor. In 1920

he bitterly opposed Pilsudski's military venture into the Ukraine. Ten years later he wrote a series of articles rejecting Poland's participation in any plans of intervention in the USSR.[16] And in 1981 he, once again, emphasized the importance of proper relations between Poland and the Soviet Union: "Russia", he argued, "represents our most important neighbor ... here is the crux of Poland's future".[17]

Paradoxically, it was their attention to the developments in Russia which pushed the social democrats back to the romantic tradition. Their common struggle with the Russian revolutionaries against Tsarism, dating back to the 1880s, led them to embrace the insurrectionist tactics. The drift on the left toward romanticism was accelerated a decade later by the Polish Socialist Party, which combined in its program the goal of social revolution with that of Poland's independence; and it was carried to its logical conclusion early in the 20th century by the Pilsudskiites' abandoning their socialist pretences and giving their first attention to freeing Poland from Russia through military struggle.

After the Bolshevik revolution in Russia it was the Communist Party of Poland, formed in 1918, which inherited the mantle of being the chief advocate of close relations between the two countries. Yet, the Polish Communists viewed Poland's intimate bonds with the USSR — indeed, Poland's becoming a Soviet republic — exclusively in ideological, and not geopolitical terms. Their romantic élan pushed the Communists toward seeking cooperation with the strongly anti-Russian socialists, and even with the Pilsudskiites, rather than the pro-Russian national democrats. As a result the Communist Party fell between the two stools and had a negligible popular following in the country. Furthermore, almost totally dependent upon Moscow, it was caught up in the internal rivalaries among the different factions in Soviet party, and in the late 1930s it was formally disbanded by the Comintern and its leadership was decimated by Stalin in the great purges. The romantic course, thus, was highly destructive to the Polish Communists (somewhat resembling the fate of the national democrats a decade later). On the eve of World War II an organized communist movement was non-existent in Poland and its surviving leaders were shattered and demoralized.

It was only during World War II, and actually only after the outbreak of the Russo-German war in 1941, that the Polish Communists reorganized and moved closer to political realism. The Polish Workers' Party advocated a close alliance between Poland and the USSR — yet, significantly, no longer Poland's becoming a Soviet republic — not only in ideological, but also in geopolitical terms. It still underlined its close affinity to the Communist Party of the Soviet Union, but at the same time it emphasized strongly the unity between the two nations in their struggle against Germany.* This new course was continued in the immediate post war years until 1948, as long as Gomulka remained at the helm. Afterwards the party, now led by Boleslaw Bierut, and especially after it was merged with the left wing socialists into the Polish United Workers' Party, reverted to the strict ideological justification of Poland's close bonds with the USSR, amounting to its strict subordination to Moscow.

The geopolitical arguments in favor of the Polish-Soviet alliance were revived after Gomulka's return to power in 1956. Side by side with his emphasis on the close ideological bond between the two ruling parties, Gomulka often defended the alignment between the two countries in a realist vein *par excellance* — presenting the USSR as the most effective guarantor of Poland's western territories against the West German revisionist claims, and stressing the ambiguous position taken in this regard by the western powers. Implicit in his statements, although naturally never articulated in this fashion, was also his disbelief that Poland could count on the support of the West in any attempt to leave the Soviet bloc.[18]

Gomulka's political reasoning has become an integral part of the Polish United Workers' Party political program, and has been repeated — particularly at the moment of political crises — by his successors: Gierek, Kania and Jaruzelski. At one time or another they have all underlined that the Polish-Soviet alliance is not only rooted in proletarian internationalism, but is an integral, and unchangeable part of the post-war settlement between the great powers in Europe. In fact, Jaruzelski explicitly defended the introduction of martial law and the suppression of Solidarity in 1981, as the necessary move to protect the European system from being de-stabilized; and, implicitly, to prevent a Soviet invasion of Poland, which would have not been challenged by the Western powers.[19]

\* \* \*

*At the end of the war and in the immediate post-war years the Polish Communist leaders were apparently aware that their geopolitical arguments followed closely the national democratic line. One of them, Edward Ochab, in a conversation with me in 1983, after admitting how weak the Communists were when they came to power in 1944, added that the national democrats could have been their natural allies. "Except", he observed, "that we were at that time divided by an impassable ideological gap".

The realism of the Polish Communists, however, has always been closer to the tradition of Wielopolski than to that of Dmowski. The differences among the various factions in the Polish United Workers' Party over how much autonomy Poland should obtain from the USSR have been restricted in scope — and the people who have moved beyond them have either been excluded from the top positions in the party or even expelled from its ranks. The Polish Communists have never really gone beyond the program of the 19th century conciliationists. And with the growing concern on their part over their privileged social position — especially blatant during Gierek's years — it is no wonder that in the eyes of the Poles they have come to resemble the old-fashioned conservatives.

If the Jaruzelski regime really wishes to overcome the barrier separating it from the Polish society it has to go beyond its predecessors. It not only has to proceed with the modernization of the country (where it has not been particularly successful so far), but it also has convincingly to demonstrate that it is striving to expand Poland's autonomy from the USSR.* This is the only way it can win over to their side the moderate Polish realists. In other words the Polish Communist government must abandon its Wielopolski-like stance and adopt a program more similar to that of Dmowski.

The limits of Poland's autonomy, of course, are determined not only by the strivings on the part of the Polish Communists to expand them, but also by the willingness on the part of the Soviet leaders to accept these as legitimate, and try to arrive at some mutually acceptable accommodation. As of now — as has been pointed out — the USSR has envisaged two solutions to the Polish problem: to continue the sovietizing of Poland, hoping against hope that at some future date it is going to bear fruit; or to keep Poland as an unreliable and weak satellite, and to muddle through its repeated internal crises.

---

*So far, the faction in the ranks of the Polish United Workers' Party which has taken the most visible nationalist stance, has been the partisans, led by General Mieczyslaw Moczar, which was prominent in the latter part of the 1960s. The Moczarites' program, however, was a curious amalgam of the realist and idealist strands in Polish history. While they stood for an expanded Polish autonomy from the USSR, like the Pilsudskiites in 1926-39 they would allow for no democracy at home. In fact, they aped the Pilsudskiites in trying to use the wartime exploits of the Communist partisans as a legitimization for their governing Poland. And yet, since their achievements during World War II had not been comparable to those of the non-Communist underground, they only added to the Home Army legend, and this way contributed to the revival of the classical romantic insurrectionist tradition.

The first solution, as the Soviet leaders should have realized after the events in 1980-81, is not going to work in the foreseeable future. The chances of sovietizing Poland are at present even more remote than they were in the immediate post-war years. And the second solution may work for some time, but in the long run it threatens with new — and potentially even more dramatic than ever in the past — popular explosion in Poland. Indeed, the persistent efforts to pursue the first solution may only increase the risk of such confrontations.

There are valid reasons, then, for the Soviet leaders to adopt a more imaginative and viable policy toward Poland. The country is the most important western neighbor of the USSR, and continued unrest there would weaken the Soviet position in Eastern Europe and have detrimental effects upon East-West relations. Thus, an internally stable Poland, friendly toward Russia — along the lines envisaged by the Polish moderate realists — is a third solution, and the optimum one, available at present. This, however, would predicate de-emphasizing the ideological bonds between the two countries, and instead a stressing of their common geopolitical interests, as was advocated in the inter-war period by Dmowski, and at present by Hall.*

The geopolitical arguments are not alien to the Soviet leaders, all of their commitment to Marxism-Leninism notwithstanding. They have always defended their dominant position in Eastern Europe not only in ideological, but also in geopolitical terms.[20] It was precisely the latter reasoning which has made them show a good deal of restraint, above all by avoiding direct intervention in the Polish crises in 1956, 1970 and in 1980-81; as well as their relative tolerance in the post-Stalinist period of various Polish internal changes deviating from the Soviet model of Communism, such as non-collectivized agriculture and the existence of a powerful Catholic church. At present, at least in principle, the Soviet leaders accept the need for continued domestic reforms in Poland as espoused by the Jaruzelski regime**; and at one time or another they may conclude that even bolder

---

*For Hall's views about the future of Polish-Russian relations see Appendix 14.

**Gorbachev's address at the Polish Communist Party Congress in June 1986 seems to have fitted into this pattern. His was quite antagonistic toward Solidarity and made it clear that had the Polish Communists not crushed the free trade unions, the USSR would have. At the same time, however, he admitted that the Polish workers' grievances were not unfounded, indicating that he would be tolerant of limited reforms in Poland.

measures by the Polish Communist government to win the Polish society to its side, are needed.

The long term evolution in the USSR seems to be conducive to such a development in Polish-Soviet relations. Shedding off by the Soviets their rigid Marxist-Leninist outlook and fitting it into modern world has been a slow process, but it is there. The recent ascendancy to power in Moscow of younger and more progmatic leaders under Mikhail Gorbachev may well prove to be another step on this road. In turn it may lead toward adopting by the Soviets more imaginative and flexible policies in Eastern Europe than in the past. And the marked revival of Russian nationalism may encourage them to seek more compromises along the traditional geopolitical lines. In order to terminate the centuries-long Polish-Russian animosity *Realpolitik* must be followed not only by the Poles, but also by the Russians.

*NOTES*

1. For a first-hand account of the persecution of the national democrats in the post-war years see: Leon Mirecki, "Porownania", *Lad*, August 23, 1981.
2. For Sila-Nowicki's role in Solidarity see my: *Poland, The Protracted Crisis* (Oakville, Ont., 1983), pp. 234-5.
3. Piotr Wierzbicki, *Mysli staroswieckiego Polaka*, (Glos, Warszawa, 1985).
4. *Ibid.* p. 12.
5. *Ibid.*
6. *Ibid.* p. 20.
7. *Ibid.* p. 57.
8. Adam Michnik, *Szanse polskiej demokracji, Artykuly i eseje*, (Aneks, London, 1984).
9. *Ibid.* p. 215.
10. *Ibid.* p. 220.
11. *Ibid.* p. 213.
12. *Ibid.* p. 214.
13. Andrzej Walicki, "Tradycje polskiego patriotyzmu", *Aneks* (London), No. 40, p. 74, 1985.
14. For the evolution of early Marxism in Poland see my: *Poland's Politics, Idealism vs. Realism* (Cambridge, Mass. 1967), pp. 19-25.
15. For a discussion of the affinities between Dmowski's early political thought and the Marxist, see: Leszek Kaminski, *Romantyzm a ideologia, Glowne ugrupowania polityczne Drugiej Rzeczpospolitej wobec tradycji romantycznej* (Warsaw, 1980). Especially pp. 62-64.
16. "Przeciw wojnie". Subsequently included in Dmowski's book *Swiat powojenny i Polska* (Warsaw, 1931). The articles, although with a foreword highly critical of the author, were also published in pamphlet form in the Soviet Union. See: Roman Dmowski, *Kommivoyazher v zatrudnenii* (Moscow, 1930).
17. *Swiat powojenny i Polska,* 2nd ed. (Warsaw, 1931).
18. For the relevant aspects of Gomulka's program see my: *Poland's Politics, Idealism vs. Realism* (Cambridge, Mass., 1967), pp. 108-112.
19. For a penetrating analysis of Jaruzelski's policies seen in this light see: Jerzy Wiatr, "Professional Soldiers and Politics in Poland: The Experience of 1980s". Inter-University Seminar on Armed Forces, Chicago, October 18-20, 1985. (Mimeographed).
20. For a discussion of the role of geopolitical factors in Soviet post-war policies toward Eastern Europe see my: *Eastern Europe in the Aftermath of Solidarity* (Boulder, Co., 1985). Ch. II.

# VI

## MAGISTRA VITAE

History remains very much alive in today's Poland. The dramatic upheaval in 1980-81 has only stimulated new interest in it. And history, as ever, is being used for political purposes. Analogies with the past events are widely, even if often inaccurately, used in the current political arguments. No end of this peculiar Polish habit is in sight.

Many western observers of the contemporary Polish scene have been impressed with this fact. Elisabeth Kridl Valkenier wrote in 1985: "The predillection of the Poles to manipulate their collective memory in order to rationalize the present according to some particular vision of history is a living legacy of their historical experience". And she rightly added: "the past will continue to be a highly charged issue as long as society remains to be dissatisfied with the present."[1] Also in 1985, Rudolf Jaworski came to the same opinion. In Poland, he argued, the "feeling for history and tradition are matter-of-fact, even instinctive in the people of this country and are very much alive even to this day."[2] And in the same year, Andrzej Walicki reached a similar conclusion:

> One of the most peculiar features of the intellectual climate in contemporary Poland is an obsessive fascination with national history... The language of historical analogy has always been used in Poland but never so widely as today... Both the opposition and the ruling party dress themselves in historical costumes and try to play the roles already played in Polish history, though of course, with their own different interpretations of these roles.[3]

103

Indeed, the programs of the opposing movements at the two extremes of a political continuum: the conservatives in the Communist party and the radicals in the underground, are directly derived from their own specific visions of Polish history. The former still cling to the Marxist notion of history conceived as a class struggle, while the latter cherish the concept of history viewed as incessant struggle for independence. At the center of the continuum this division is less apparent, but it is there and serves as an ultimate dividing line between the supporters of the government and of the opposition.

By now the Marxist historiography has considerably evolved from its crude version of the early 1950s. In the succeeding three decades it has shed much of its rigid ideological character and has moved closer to scholarly objectivity. Since 1981 this trend has slowed, but has not reversed. In fact, one of the main achievements of the Solidarity period, "the right to pursue factual inquiry into Poland's recent past [has been] preserved in a modified form"[4] This is evident not only in purely scholarly writings, but also, and perhaps even more, in the popular historical articles, and the polemics over them, which appear in the official press.

Nevertheless, the party historians still find themselves constrained by the binding Communist ideology. Paradoxically, they are freer to write about the history of other political movements than that of their own; and any unorthodox interpretation of Polish-Soviet relations remains taboo. Occasionally they may sneak through the censorship a somewhat more truthful presentation of the past; and since only they have access to the party archives their findings may even be revealing. Yet, until such time as they may be freed from their ideological bondage most of their work will remain stilted and fragmentary.*

Among the non-Communist historians since 1981 there has been some shift toward greater objectivity, too. After intoxication with freedom during the Solidarity period, its defeat apparently has had a sobering effect upon them. They have looked more closely at the traditional Poland's constraints in the international sphere. Some of them have even taken into heart Samsonowicz's advice and examined critically the activities of Solidarity itself.

---

*The fate of the report prepared by the Kubiak Commission in 1981-83 which investigated the sources of the repeated crises in the post-war Poland illustrates this well. In its original version it was more forthcoming than in the final one which was released for publication. Apparently the report was revised, and circumscribed, by the party authorities several times.[5]

Yet, in the highly charged political atmosphere in the country, which five years after introduction of martial law still has not completely calmed down, the non-Communist historians find themselves under strong popular pressure not to carry their impartiality too far. And the deeply-embedded narcissism of the Polish intellectuals does not help them to withstand it. Paradoxically, they are most restricted in writing objectively about the very subjects which are most abused by the Marxists. It is considered strictly *de rigeur* among them not to say anything positive, (for this could be considered as approval of the existing political system) about any aspects of the history of the Communist movement in Poland or of Polish-Russian relations. And any open criticism of the view of Polish history as a continuous, and noble struggle for independence is still largely inadmissible.

So, the two linear, and erroneous, views of history — even if in somewhat modified forms — persist in today's Poland side by side.

\* \* \*

The Marxist version of Poland's past is unlikely to achieve its political objectives. It has never captured, and after the Solidarity period is even less likely to do so, the imagination of the Poles. It is adhered to ritually, but not really taken seriously, even by the great majority of Communist party members. Indeed, the Marxist historical writings will probably keep producing effects opposite from those intended. By affronting the Poles' national pride, especially over the sensitive issue of Polish-Soviet relations, the Marxist version will only reaffirm them in their commitment to the concept of Polish history as incessant struggle for independence.

The political significance of the traditional interpretation of Polish history, with its firm belief in the ultimate triumph of Poland's independence, is undeniable. As a nationalist ideology it played a crucial role in the survival of the Polish nation during the era of the partitions. Subsequently, during World War II it helped the Poles to withstand the onslaught of Nazism, and in the following decade to resist, and ultimately to overcome Stalinism. And in the last thirty years it has repeatedly induced them to challenge the Communist government in efforts to expand their freedom.

It is precisely because of the political role of the traditionalist concept of Poland's history that many historians are reluctant to come out against it. Even if privately they do not subscribe to it, they still refrain from questioning it openly. They are apparently afraid that to do so might weaken the Poles' resolve to strive for independence and this way contribute to an acceptance by the Polish nation of its satellite status vis-à-vis the Soviet Union.

Thus, however, the non-Communist historians indirectly reaffirm the traditionalist view of Polish history. They leave criticism of the romantic legacy primarily to the Marxists, which weakens the credibility of the analysis. And they also convey the impression of sharing, even if unconsciously, the major fallacy of the traditionalist approach, namely its lack of confidence in the ability of the Poles to promote their interests in any way other than by repeated uprisings.

Yet, the fact is that the romantic view of Polish history, like the Marxist, is largely a political myth. During the last two hundred years Poland was truly independent for only twenty years. And the goal of restoring a Polish state such as existed in 1918-39 is as elusive as ever. That the Polish nation has survived since the 18th century is not just because of its repeated uprisings, but also because of its ability to hold its own under foreign rule through one form or another of compromise with the dominant powers.

At least one Polish historian had the courage to acknowledge it openly. Tadeusz Lepkowski admitted that in the past two centuries Poland has mostly not been an independent nation. It was dependent, he wrote: "in different ways — as a subordinate state only formally independent, as an autonomous territory, as a state belonging into an alliance dominated by a foreign power, or, finally, as a nation totally deprived of its state." The Poles tried to change this situation and to regain their independence, Lepkowski went on, but when it was not possible, they tried at least "to reduce and ease" their dependence.[6]

As a nationalist ideology, thus, the realist interpretation of Polish history may be less exciting than the idealist one, but it offers a more practical program of action. And if it does not represent the whole truth, it is certainly closer to the truth. Yet political myths, even if not supported by facts, are also a part of reality; so the romantic view of Polish history must not be entirely discounted. It will continue to inspire the Poles in trying to expand their freedom from foreign rule, and, indeed, at one time or another it may push them into another open, even if futile, rebellion. For myths that are widely adhered to, even if they are wrong (as all myths are) are still politically significant.

Some of the Polish scholars are well aware of the tendency to abuse history for political purposes. A political scientist, Remigiusz Bierzanek, has explicitly warned against "selecting historical facts... to justify and popularise the current political programs" — a practice he labelled "politics projected backward."[7] And a historian, Karol Gorski, has asserted that such efforts are "not history at all... but rather articicial constructs reflecting one's own outlook which is then affirmed by selecting appropriate facts."[8]*

Yet, if only for political reasons the Marxist and the romantic presentations of Poland's history will go on. And, paradoxically, they will continue reinforcing each other. The Polish historians striving to offer a more objective view of their country's past will still face an uphill battle.

* * *

In view of the awkward situation of Polish historiography at home, the work on recent Polish history in the West will continue to be of a major significance. The foremost task of the western scholars is to bare the truth. Stating the facts is also the greatest service they can render to the Poles. For as Janusz K. Zawodny beautifully put it: "facts should matter, especially when they are written on the tomb-stones of millions... At least we should not rob the dead of the dignity of the cause which they served."[10]

The western historians' stating the facts is the best way to counter the Marxist writers' distortions. In these endeavors incidentally, it is not necessary to adopt anti-Communist positions; it is quite enough to be a non-Communist, or simply objective. Indeed, in this fashion the western scholars should fill the gaps in the mainstream Polish historiography, i.e. the history of the Marxist movement itself. Since they have no access to the primary sources this is not an easy task. Yet, as the works by Kamil M. Dziewanowski or Zbigniew A. Pelczynski have demonstrated, it can be done.

Yet, the same obligation applies to other aspects of Polish history. Regardless of their personal sympathies for the Poles' legitimate striv-ings for freedom from foreign rule, the western writers must not be uncritical of the interpretation of Polish history as an incessant struggle for independence. First of all because it is not true. And, moreover, because it does not necessarily help the Poles. For cultivating among them delusions, no matter how noble, — especially when the impetus come from the West and, therefore, is more likely to be accepted —

---

*As an example of a pseudo-historical study Gorski pointed Antoni Choloniewski's *The Spirit of Polish History* which presented a *par excellance* romantic view of Poland's past and in the inter-war period was widely used by the Pilsudskiites to vindicate their own political program.[9]

is of no use for them.* The Poles are better served by being presented with the facts — and these should be treated in a comprehensive fashion, including the unpleasant ones. Even Piotr Wandycz agrees with this. While criticizing Jan Karski's book: *The Great Powers of Poland, 1919-1945* as perhaps unduly pessimistic, Wandycz observed with melancholy: "One also needs books which are not only written for enhartement."[11]

Indeed, studies conforming with the above requirements, written in western languages, should be made more broadly accessible to the Poles by translating them into Polish. This way the major gaps in Polish historiography could be filled and the influence of the two fallacious concepts of Polish history, i.e. the Marxist and the romantic one, should be mitigated. Studies of Poland's position in the international sphere — dealing with its relations both with Russia and with the West — as well as histories of the programs of various political movements, are a special significance here. By concentrating their efforts in these fields the western scholars could make a major contribution to Polish historiography. And since the study of history plays such an important political role in Poland they could also help the Poles to formulate superior contemporary programs. Armed with true knowledge about their past, the Poles would be in a better position to defend their present interests.**

Yet, to consistently follow this approach is not always easy for the western scholars. Some of them may be genuinely concerned that by criticizing the romantic concept of Polish history they would undermine its role as a political ideology, and, therefore, would weaken the Poles' resolve in their struggle for independence. And others may simply be influenced by the views predominant among the Poles themselves and not to have enough intellectual courage to challenge them.

---

*Dmowski was well aware of this fact. In *Thoughts of a Modern Pole* he underlined the role which the western opinions of them played in formulating the Poles' self-image. See Appendix I.

**One thing that the western scholars of Polish background could usefully do, would be to write basic textbooks in political science, economics, sociology, etc. based on the latest achievements of western social sciences, in Polish. Such books, of course, would not be used as official textbooks in Poland, but nevertheless they would be placed on the shelves in the university libraries and might even be recommended by some professors as "alternative" readings. Yet, I know of no such volumes published in the West. And I also am guilty here. For I have toyed for years with the idea of writing an introductory textbook on international relations in Polish, but have never found the time to do it.

It must be remembered, of course, that the western students of Poland, by the very nature of their profession, maintain close links with the Poles — and not only with scholars like themselves, but with ordinary people who are generally critical of the existing political system there. Even those western scholars who are not of Polish background, at one time or another, have usually lived and studied in that country and formed many close ties with Poles. And many of them are actually of Polish origin and even in the second generation, still have relatives in Poland. Then there are the emigrés of different vintages — ranging from those who left the country during World War II to those who did so after 1981 — who have since assumed academic posts at various western universities. And among the Polish emigrés from the post-Solidarity period especially, political emotions still run high. These people tend to see the events in 1980-81 as a continuation of the traditional struggle for Poland's independence and hope that, against all odds, it will go on. Any western scholar, thus, who does not subscribe to this view is likely to be accused by them of tolerating, if not sympathizing with the Polish Communist regime.

Even among many thoughtful Poles, moreover, there is a deeply ingrained cliché about the alleged division of roles between the people who live in Poland and those who live in the West. The former, so the argument goes, by necessity have to conform to the existing situation and to make the best of it by following a realist course, reconciling themselves to the Communist dominance and Poland's dependence from the USSR. The later, however, since they are free to articulate their sentiments in western democracies, should resolutely support, and indeed wage by whatever means are available to them, the struggle for Poland's independence. And anything short of that on their part amounts to a betrayal of the national cause.*

---

*This conception of the role of the Polish communities in the West has, in fact, impeded the growth of independent academic studies on Poland there. Nowhere this is more amply demonstrated than in the United States. The Polish American Congress, which prides itself on representing over 10 million Americans of Polish descent, has shown singularly little interest in promoting Polish studies in that country. Instead, under the influence of the post-war emigrés, it has focused on political activities as a lobby in Washington supporting the oposition in Poland. It has made no effort to assist in developing the Polish studies programs or to found chairs at prominent universities (as the Ukrainians did at Harvard).

As a result the academics who have risen to prominence in the United States (like Zbigniew Brzezinski) have achieved this entirely on their own; and those who have expressed opinions different from the dominant line (like Andrzej Korbonski) have even been publically taken to task. And the small Polish Studies Center at Indiana University in Bloomington (the only one in existence in the entire country) is shunned by the Polish-American organizations because it maintains links with the academic institutions in Poland!

* * *

Fortunately, not all the emigrés subscribed to such oversimplified views. At least some of them share my view that the scholars' first duty is to bare the truth. And they also believe that the Poles are best served by being faced with the facts, no matter how unpleasant. Indeed, they deem it their duty to explicitly warn the Poles not to indulge in delusions and to follow, at least in their present situation, a realist political course.

Two recent examples of such writings stand out. Jan Karski a war-time hero (who was a courier between the Polish Government-in-Exile in London and the underground at home, and who subsequently has for many years taught international politics at Georgetown University), came out in 1985 with a thoroughly sober evaluation of Poland's position in the international sphere. From a standpoint of American foreign policy, he argued:

> the most important issue is to secure some degree of stability with the Soviet Union... Whether such a cooperation, uneasy by nature, will emerge is a matter of speculation. As I see it, it will emerge because it must. Once this happens the support of Polish and other Soviet dominated countries will probably weaken. Naturally no one can expect the USSR will permit those countries to ge out of their control voluntarily.[12]

This is not, Karski explained, because the United States is unfriendly to Poland, but simply because America is preoccupied with other problems in the world that are greater than that one. In its "tremendous tasks Poland *per se* cannot represent much more than a marginal issue. Any Pole who thinks otherwise lives in a make-believe world".[13] In such a situation, Karski continued, "it would be a mistake on the part of the Poles to challenge the Soviet Union." The Polish people are in a stronger position than the Jaruzelski regime and they could overthrow it. And Jaruzelski knows this, so:

> they are right when they press the regime for concessions, and to some extent they have been successful. But any demands, pressures, challenges or confrontations which might threaten the very existence of that regime would be ill-timed. The regime has Soviet power behind it. One telephone to Moscow would be enough and the Red Army would enter Poland. What then would happen in the West? Nothing... Expectation that the West would

be willing to confront the USSR just because there was some national upheaval in Poland is simply unrealistic.[14]

The Poles, concluded Karski, must not abandon hope for independence. "History is not inert, nor is it predictable." Yet, hope alone is not enough. It "must be accompanied by a sense of realism, patience and hard work".[15]

Another wartime hero, Stefan Korbonski, (who was the last chief of the Polish underground and since the late 1940s has lived in Washington), has offered the Poles similar entirely realistic advice. Pointing to his own experiences when the Soviet army entered Poland at the end of World War II, he argued that the "Solidarity underground as well as any future mass underground organizations have no chance of conducting effective struggles under existing conditions." Resistance against the Communist regime, thus, must follow a different concept. It must be based, Korbonski asserted,

> upon the principle that the attainment of the major Polish political objective i.e., gaining freedom, independence, and a democracy is not presently possible. In any case, without deviating from this main goal, it is essential that more limited temporary Polish political objectives be substituted in those areas where Soviet controls offer relief and will not precipitate an invasion or direct Soviet occupation of the country. The main purpose of this limited program would be to preserve the substance, the national identity and the culture through limited actions with the use of peaceful means in the specific areas in which these issues are endangered.[16]

Karski and Korbonski are right. History, of course, is not inert. At one time or another it may also have some pleasant surprises for the Poles. There may be changes, as there have been over the years, although slow and hesitant, in the USSR. Detente between the United States and the Soviet Union, which Karski so clearly anticipates, would not eliminate Moscow's dominant position over Eastern Europe, but it might contribute to the relaxation of its controls there. And in the more peaceful and interdependent world the very traditional notion of independence may lose its former significance.[17]

Any major improvement of Poland's position, however, would presuppose a basic shift in the international sphere. Until such time the principle of *Primat der Aussenpolitik* will remain binding in Polish politics, and the Poles will continue to oscilate between idealism and realism.

The characteristic political cycle in Polish history, asserted Norman Davies in his latest work,

> was put into motion not merely by the loss of statehood but rather by inter-vention of foreign powers ... and must be expected to continue as long as foreign oppression exists. In this light, the Romantic and Positivist generations of the mid-nineteenth century must not be seen as merely the successors of Stanislaw Leszczynski and Stanislaw August, but also as predecessors of Wladyslaw Gomulka and Lech Walesa.[18]

Yet, if it is true that there is a cycle in Polish history, for the time being the Poles would be better off, as Karski and Korbonski remind us, by following the realist rather than idealist course. They need not go all the way back to Wielopolski; a modernized version of Dmowski's program, as Hall observed, should serve their present needs just fine.

* * *

In order to fulfill their potential role Polish studies in the West, however, should not be conducted at random. Selecting the topics for new doctoral theses should not be left just to the fancy of graduate students or their professors. It should rather reflect a purposeful effort to fill up the existing gaps in our knowledge. Only when Polish studies fit together into a coherent intellectual pattern will they live up to their academic (and, incidentally, also political) expectations.

To transform Polish studies in the West into a systematic sub-discipline in history and social sciences, several steps should be taken. First of all, of course, the work of the western scholars ought to be carefully coordinated with that done in Poland. There is no sense in duplicating what is being done effectively in that country. In fact, valuable new Polish works should be published in translation in the West.

In this regard various existing gaps from the past should be filled. Feldman's history of Polish political thought prior to World War I, as well as Micewski's works on the programs of the Polish political movements in the inter-war period, should be made available (perhaps in an abbreviated form) in English. More attention should be given to preparation of anthologies of Polish political thought. Selected writings of Roman Dmowski, Jozef Pilsudski, Wincenty Witos and other prominent past figures in Polish politics should be made accessible to the western readers. Instead of just writing commentaries about Poland's history and politics, more western scholars should address themselves to this task.

The western students of Poland should certainly increase cooperation among themselves. Especially those living in those countries where major work on Poland is being conducted: the United States, Britain, West Germany, France and Canada, should stay closely in touch. They should regularly exchange information about their activities. Systematic issuance of bibliographical information on what works have lately appeared in the field of Polish studies, and what doctoral dissertations are under way, would be particularly helpful. And some regular forum of personal exchange of ideas — beyond the sporadic contacts at some international conferences and congresses — would also be important.*

Above all, the western scholars — because of their freedom of research and access to modern methodologies — are uniquely equipped to search for overall patterns in the past and present Poland's history. Such models, like all paradigms, would be just approximations of reality. Yet, they can serve a useful intellectual function in transforming Polish studies into a true sub-discipline — not just a random, but a purposeful activity. For progress along this road close cooperation between the historians and the political scientists is a prerequisite, but contributions from other social scientists could be enlightening too.

It was exactly in an effort to sort out the complexities of Poland's politics in the preceding hundred years that I came out in 1967 with the model conceived as a dichotomy between idealism and realism. I should like to believe that at least to some extent my model has served its purpose. More and more western scholars, some with achnowledgement and others unconsciously, have used it as a framework for their analyses. And, especially after 1981, it has had some impact in Poland too.

If nothing else, I think that my model does offer some insights into directions for research into the past as well as into contemporary

---

*The idea of establishing a standing Polish studies group affiliated with the International Committee for Soviet and East European Studies was floated at its Congress in Garmisch Partenkirchen in 1980. Yet, so far nothing has come of it. Perhaps the plan should be revived and brought to fruition at the next ICSEES Congress in Harrowgate, England in 1990.

political events in Poland. By pointing out the principle of *Primat der Aussenpolitik* as a source of the perennial split between the idealists and the realists, it underlines the significance of a continuous re-examination of Poland's position in the international sphere, and its linkages (which work both ways) to domestic political developments.

The model could also be helpful as a guide to more systematic study of history of the Polish political thought. It points out the need of less uncritical acceptance of the view of Polish history as an incessant struggle for independence. The role of that view as a political ideology inducing the Poles toward repeated struggles for freedom must not be ignored; yet its political shortcomings, which have resulted in repeated defeats, should not be lost from sight. And a great variety of the romantic programs — those from the 19th century, the inter-war period and during World War II, and the last decade — should be systematically examined, pointing out their continuity as well as their differences.

At the same time more attention should be paid to the realist political thought in Poland. Indeed, since so far it has been ignored in most of the western writings on Poland, it should be given definite priority. And, as with the idealist thought, the various metamorphoses of the realist political programs — from Wielopolski to Dmowski and from Stomma to Hall — should be examined.

I should like to believe that in this context valuable insights into the history of the Marxist movement in Poland could also be gained. For the study of this subject must not be conducted on terms imposed by the Communist writers *à rebours* — amounting merely to refutations of the notion of Polish history as a class struggle. Instead, the subtle, but unmistakable relationship between the Marxist thought at its different stages of development with the concurrent romantic or realist political programs, should be investigated.

And, above all, my central hypothesis that the dominant feature in Poland's politics over the last two hundred years has been the perennial split into the idealist and the realists resulting in the sort of self-repeating historical cycle, should be inquired into, and, if necessary, challenged. Yet, the writers who repudiate my model should not just confine themselves to statements that history is full of surprises and that trying to make some sense out of it is futile. Surely, history is full of unexpected twists. But there are also some long-term trends in it, and there are the situations which, not exactly, but largely, repeat themselves. And it is the task of the historian to try to discern these. If my model is unsatisfactory its opponents should present a better model of their own.

\* \* \*

The fact remains that the western students of Poland, even if their first obligation is to sound scholarship, cannot completely avoid political implications of their work. Political scientists' accounts of the developments in that country, and especially their normative studies recommending responses to the Polish events by the Western government may influence (depending on how much weight they carry), Poland's position in the international sphere. And the same is true of the works by well-established economists or sociologists. The historians play a different, but no less significant, role. Because their discipline is so important in shaping contemporary Polish political programs, they may have an indirect, but still profound influence upon the conduct of the Poles themselves.

These are grave responsibilities. To meet them individual scholars must fulfill some basic obligations. Above all they must be intellectually honest. In that endeavor they should not be swayed by any other motives than the urge to present the facts as they truly see them. And they should remember that silence can be a form of deception too; and that they should report all the facts, including the unpleasant ones.

To live up to true scholar's vocation, thus, one also needs courage. In the last instance one must use one's judgment in accordance with one's own individual conscience. And to do this one must be prepared, if necessary, to go against the dominate trends among the public and even in one's own profession. As Antoni Maczak put it, true scholars should claim autonomy from any pressure. Their duty is "to introduce into social thought those problems which they themselves consider as important.:"[19]

Yet, these burdens on the western students of Poland should be eased by the conviction that, by remaining faithful to the principle of intellectual honesty, they also render the best service to the Polish nation. For by presenting the truth they help the Poles to use history as a real *magistra vitae.*

## NOTES

1. Elisabeth Kridl Valkenier, "The Rise and Decline of Official Marxist Historiography in Poland, 1945-1983". *Slavic Review*, Vol. 44, No. 4. Winter 1985. p. 680.

2. Rudolf Jaworski, "History and Tradition in Contemporary Poland", *East European Quarterly* Vol. XIX, No. 3. September 1985.

3. Andrzej Walicki, "The Paradoxes of Jaruzelski's Poland" *Archivum Europae*, Vol. XXVI, 1985. pp. 174-5.

4. Kridl Valkenier, *op. cit.*, p. 676.

5. For extensive exerpts of the Kubiak Report in English see my: *Eastern Europe in the Aftermath of Solidarity* (Boulder, Colo. 1985), Appendix I.

6. Tadeusz Lepkowski, "O formach zaleznosci". As reprinted from *Tygodnik Powszechny* in *Zwiazkowiec* (Toronto), July 8, 1986.

7. Remigiusz Bierzanek, "Doswiadczenie historyczne w badaniach nad stosunkami miedzynarodowymi", *Studia Nauk Politycznych*, No. 1 (43), 1980, p. 36.

8. Karol Gorski, "Ethos profesora", *Tydonik Powszechny*, January 30, 1983.

9. For discussion of Choloniewski's book in English see my *Poland's Politics, Idealism vs. Realism* (Cambridge, Mass. 1967), pp. 36-7.

10. Janusz K. Zawodny, "The Great Powers and Poland 1919-1945: A Pawn Under the Table", *The Polish Review*, Vol. XXX, No. 4, 1985, p. 414.

11. Piotr Wandycz - Janusz K. Zawodny, "Dwuglos o ksiazce Jana Karskiego "Wielkie mocarstwa a Polska 1919-1945", *Zeszyty Historyczne*, Vol. 74, 1985. p. 167.

12. Peter Mroczyk "An Interview with Jan Karski", *Studium Papers* (Ann Arbor, Mich.) Vol. 9, No. 2. April 1985. p. 72.

13. *Ibid.* p. 73.

14. *Ibid.* p. 74.

15. *Ibid.* p. 76.

16. Stefan Korbonski, "The Polish Underground - Past and Present", *Studium Papers*, Vol. 9, No. 3, July 1985. p. 85.

17. For an argument along these lines see my: *Polska Weltpolitik* (London, 1975).

18. Norman Davies, *Heart of Europe, A Short History of Poland* (Oxford, 1984). pp. 213-4.

19. Antoni Maczak, "Prawda i otucha", *Tygodnik Powszechny*, January 23, 1983.

*APPENDICES*

# I

## THE DEAD END OF OUR THOUGHT*

### Roman Dmowski

For a long time I have felt that the fundamental paradigm of our political thought, to the extent, indeed, that there is one, is based on falsehood. On the most important matters concerning the very substance of our national existence — our attitudes toward other nations and our prospects of surviving as a separate political and civilizational entity — we accept, and even cherish, opinions which when confronted with reality, prove to be groundless.

I have always felt an instinctive aversion toward these falsehoods, but, in my youth, not being able to grasp their origin, I could not perceive their true nature either. They have occupied such a prominent place in our political thought that it was difficult to believe that there was no substance to them. So my young mind, eager for independent thought, but still uncertain of itself, did not dare to challenge them outright and, instead, respectfully avoided facing them. As I grew older, as I came to know life — my experiences enriched by work among my own kind and by travel among others — my mind matured and I gradually came to grips with these falsehoods. Then I felt an even greater urge to overcome them.

By comparing our own nation with others I became convinced that many of the lies which poison our thought — absurdities divorced from all reality which in other societies are espoused only by

---

*Roman Dmowski, *Mysli nowoczesnego Polaka*. Originally published in 1903. From the seventh edition (London 1953). Pp. 31-7.

119

hidebound bigots — are adhered to among us by serious men: by the leading opinion makers and social activists, who use them to arrive at their judgments of history and their political expectations.

Those lies, which often are honest and noble, and at times even claim descent from the great minds of past eras, and which are supposed to embody the advancement toward moral perfection of all humanity, are constantly demonstrated in life to be worthless. Yet, we fail to accept them as such and keep repeating them like one who, in mortal danger, loses his mind and, distracted, mumbles the same phrases over and over again.[...]

Despite the fact that in the history of mankind we see that the territories occupied by given peoples change — either expanding or shrinking, or, simply, shifting — and that they have no eternal boundaries determined by Providence, but are exclusively shaped by the nations' internal strength and drive to expand — and that in accordance with these capabilities some nations grow, while others decay or even perish — we insist upon the existence of some specious boundaries among nations which cannot be crossed either with sword or with civilization. What is more, we trust that in the future these frontiers will continue to be generally recognized and respected.

Everyday experience teaches us that in the real world there is less and less respect for the weak and defenseless, and that less and less attention is being paid to those who passively suffer injuries: yet, we keep displaying our physical weakness and elevate it to the rank of a virtue, as something which supposedly even entitles us to judge the conduct of others.

In the inventory of our thought there are plenty of such lies, obvious to anyone who knows life and the severe, ruthless facts of our existence. Everywhere they blur our horizons. And even those who are unafraid of the truth, and who would never think of avoiding it, and who are trying to see life as it is, still fall under the spell of this curse of our thought. They tend to adopt one or another falsehood, as if to satisfy some deeply rooted psychic need.

These falsehoods which lie at the foundation of our thought also have immense influence over our conduct. Had we not deceived ourselves — had we not retreated from the naked truth, trying to clothe it in faded rags — we would have understood that our patriotism and our commitment to the national cause are lies; and that our concepts of civic duty are lies; and that our deeds, so scarce in the public domain, are often suicidal rather than worthy of a nation competing with others in the civilizational endeavors.[...] These sanctimonious lies satisfy and appease our conscience and lead people to persist in conduct which is, to put it bluntly, treasonable.

Searching for the roots of those falsehoods, I found them inherent both in our character and in our minds. In order to face the truth one needs a strong character, and this is a rarity in our society. We like peace and passivity, and we dislike fighting - we prefer to stay quiescent and to let ourselves to be rocked by the waves. Whenever the public good, or even our own private good, requires more daring action, we retreat. And, unable to face our own laziness and ineptitude, we prefer to appease our conscience by lying to ourselves and to others, claiming that any action would be useless or possibly even harmful.

Our contemporary thought has some strange characteristics. The virtues of the Polish mind which were stressed by the past writers: clarity, sobriety and realism, are missing today when we approach the most urgent problems of our national life. When faced with the national questions the educated Pole ceases to be realistic and modern.

In our country people who in the fields of technology, economics and even foreign affairs are acutely aware of the latest achievements of human thought, when it comes to the Polish national problems reason as if the second half of the 19th century had never happened. They can think clearly about Russia, Germany, England or France, taking into account the experiences of those countries in the last half century, but when it comes to Poland they reason as if they have been asleep for the last fifty years. Poland is treated as an exception: the other nations can have even the most brutal kind of self interests and strive for expansion — this is regarded as natural; yet, for Poland these would be improper — incompatible with its spirit. How often do we hear the opinions such as these: "It is better that we have not gained independence, for this would have involved establishing state institutions and adopting policies which could have had detrimental effects upon others" or, "Slavery is better than ruling over others"? And how often, even when we accept it as quite natural that the other nations fight, do we try to moralize our position to our adversaries by preaching to them about the Christian values?

The inability to think about Polish problems in the same fashion as we do those of other nations stems, in my opinion, above all from the fact that, for us, the problems of other nations are alive and constantly changing; while the Polish question is something abstract, as if it were a literary matter or a carefully cultivated idea, or even a religious dogma to be protected from any new influences.

Where does it all come from?

I think there are two sources. First, there is the incompatibility between our life and our ideals. After the last uprising there emerged such a gap between what the nation strove for and its actual fate, that intellectual power did not suffice to bridge it. It was simply too painful to compare what was actually happening in life and what reason had wanted to bring about. Outside forces created a reality so far divorced from our national ideals that they became irrelevant. Life went on, but the national thought remained stagnant, attached to the old ideals, and, when even these eventually became lost, to the old concepts.

This affected particularly the older generation, the people who participated directly or indirectly in the great national upheavals and who were still in their prime when they suffered the defeat which marked the fatal change in the conditions of the national existence; and those who, upon entering life, had been faced with the still-fresh tradition of defeat and who found themselves in the atmosphere of pain and disillusionment.

Among the younger generation there appears to be the same reaction, but for different reasons. Due to the absurd Germanic system of education followed in all three parts of the country as well as the conscious distortions of thought in the Russian schools in Poland, the people of the younger generation are capable of learning only from books. And from life they can only comprehend (and often they cannot even do this) those facts which illustrate what they have learned from books. They are incapable of observing facts and drawing conclusions from them on their own.

Probably there is no other country where the intelligentsia includes so many individuals who have a broad, although often superficial, knowledge drawn from a wide range of books and newspapers, but who at the same time are quite naive about even the most elementary facts of life, and especially social life.[...] The new generation is acquainted with the latest philosophic, literary and social trends in the West and it has its own opinions in those matters. Even when it comes to current affairs or to social changes abroad they think as modern men. They know the facts because they have learned of them from the books and articles. Yet in the most important domain, namely, their own national existence and how it is influenced by life, they have no books to rely on. So they remain blind to it.

The national question either does not exist for them at all or it exists merely as an obsolete practical formula adopted from the West prior to 1848, or else as a literary matter as defined in our great patriotic poetry. There are many people, who while discussing foreign problems, quote statesmen and historians and use facts and figures, but when it comes to the crucial issue of their own national existence are incapable of going beyond Mickiewicz, Slowacki and Krasinski! [...] It is probably true that their genius did probe deeper into national-political questions than any other poetry in the world; yet, it is also true that our political culture is so backward that in order to be "good Poles" we must transform patriotism into a religion, and every religion must have its holy books. But even the most religious people know enough to light their churches with electricity, while in our national temples we are still using wax candles.

The inability to think of our own nation in the same fashion as about other peoples inevitably leads us to regard ourselves as exceptional and exempt from all social laws — in other words, as a chosen nation. And from there stem our tendencies toward messianism as manifested by some segments of the modern generation. Their minds are so weak and so lazy that they are incapable of perceiving the universal laws which govern the lives of nations and of drawing from them the conclusions which would apply to a nation living in such exceptional circumstances as ours; so they prefer to claim that we are a "chosen nation".[...]

I do not want to be accused of trying to oversimplify matters and of dealing in just a few lines with such a complicated phenomenon as the spirit of Polish messianism. All I want to do is to point out the messianistic element which influences the approach to the national problems among many people, in whom intellectual passivity superficially seems to resemble the tragic trials of great spirits seeking an exit from the confused labyrinth of their country's existence.

From the establishment of the [Napoleonic] legions until 1863, Poland was such a strange, such an unprecedented social entity, that it was difficult for the human mind to perceive it, or to classify it among other peoples. Whichever formula was adopted, could be easily discounted. It was impossible to evaluate its physical strength, its social organization, its degree of civilizational achievement, its moral conditions and its material life — everywhere there were only questions, but no answers. Our own views of our country wavered from firm belief in its great future to the utter despair and hopelessness; while others' views about us ranged from the greatest admiration to the utmost contempt. It was necessary then to seek answers to those questions, which reality evaded, in poetry and the prophetic revelations of the great geniuses.

Today the times have changed. Life swiftly marches on, destroying the old and creating the new elements of national life. The institutions upon which the old social structures and relationships were based have collapsed; the revolution in the means of communication has intensified our contacts with other nations, bringing our society closer within the economic framework of Europe, and necessitating its adjustment to the needs of modernity. The social tissues which in the old Poland were in decay have begun to grow once again, and those which were in excess have been reduced. The nation has become more like the other European peoples — it has ceased to be an unknown quantity.

For many people this is a matter for concern: we are losing our originality — we are becoming like the Western European nations. Yet, what we are losing is just our monstrosity, while we are becoming a viable, healthy and modern society — at least in so far as our abnormal political conditions permit this. Step by step we are moving toward a higher and more modern type of society. The internal relationships linking us more closely together into a coherent whole are strengthened, and they are, furthermore, involuntary, inherent in the new social structures by which an individual is constrained, and, as such, more solid, more permanent and less subject to transitory whims.

Those internal changes, advancing today with great swiftness, have also brought changes in the attitudes toward us abroad. Except perhaps in the oldest generation of the Europeans, today no one praises or admires us excessively, but there is also less contempt and disdain toward us. Among the younger generation which, after a time when we were altogether forgotten, only now learns of our existence, there are new opinions — still not completely free from the past prejudices, but generally striving at a more objective and concrete evaluation of our position. This changing outside view, in turn, should accelerate the changes in our self-perception. We have to start thinking in the same categories accepted by civilized men everywhere. And by using the same yardstick toward ourselves as toward the others we can better assess our own position, strength, ability to live and to progress, and to become aware of what exactly is our originality and our national individuality — in other words we can come closer to an evaluation of what position we occupy among the civilized peoples and what road of future development we should take.

The character of our national life is obviously changing so quickly that the human mind cannot keep up with it, and this affects, above all, the most intelligent part of our society, precisely because that part was most strongly affected by the past traditions. Among the young people, not so exposed to the past, the new concepts follow the new elements of life more closely; but among the older ex-*szlachta* intelligentsia there are still many Don Quixotes desperately clinging to the old ideals, the old concepts and the old, faded slogans. From the new manifestations of intellectual life they tend to adopt only those elements which affirm their old illusions. They prefer to adhere to the superficial products of sickly minds, either the quite esoteric or the popular humbugs, and they turn away from the substance of modern life, especially as it applies to their own country.

The people who are eager to learn about all the modern inventions and all the modern intellectual trends — indeed, about everything that is fashionable and modernistic — do not know how and do not try, to perceive what is the core of modern nations' existence and what are the foundations of contemporary life and thought. In this regard they remain half a century behind without realizing that their concerns amount to just the preservation of our poetry or of the revolutionary European thought of a time when the political situation in Europe was altogether different and the social structure in Poland was unlike that of today.

The very concepts which embodies the impressive ideals of the great spirits in the past era of national life, or of the powerful popular movements in the by- gone period of European history, today are just ridiculous rags worn by the weak spirits, who are unable to cope with the existing reality, its problems and challenges. To tear away these rags: to face the truth and to uncover the problems of our modern national existence — these are the greatest tasks of today's Polish minds.

# II

## A MODERN POLE*

I am a Pole: and this, in its deeper sense, means a great deal.

I am so, not only because I speak Polish, because those others who use the same tongue are spiritually closer to me and I understand them better, and because my own affairs are more closely linked with them than with the foreigners, but also because, my personal life apart, I am conscious of a collective national life of which I am a part - because, simultaneously with my own affairs and interest, I am aware of the national problems, the interests of Poland as a whole: the supreme interests for which one ought to be prepared to sacrifice what for personal interests must not be sacrificed.

I am a Pole: which means that I belong to the Polish nation across its entire territory and throughout its entire existence, today, as well as in the past, and in the future; that I feel close affinity with Poland in its entirety - that Poland of today which suffers from persecution and enjoys only limited autonomy, which either works and fights, or remains slovenly passive and uneducated and is not even conscious of its national identity; and that of the past which rose a millennium ago, collecting together primitive tribes devoid of separate political individuality, and that which midway through its history expanded, repulsed its neighbors with its power and advanced swiftly along the road of civilizational progress, and that which later declined and civilizationally stagnated, paving the way for the disintegration of its national power and the collapse of its state; that which subsequently struggled for freedom and independence; and, finally, that of the

*"Mysli...". Pp. 26-30.

future, regardless whether it wastes the work of the past generations, or wins back its independent state and secures for it a place among the leading nations. Everything that is Polish is mine. I cannot renounce any of the legacy. I am entitled to be proud of what is great in Poland, but at the same time I must accept the blame for what is pitiful in my nation.

I am a Pole: so with all my spiritual life I participate in its existence, its emotions, thoughts, needs, strivings and aspirations. The more I am a Pole the less in the national life is alien to me, and the more do I aspire to what is worthy in that life and should be shared by the entire nation.

I am a Pole: so I have Polish duties - the better man I am the higher they are and the more I subscribe to them.

For the more I spiritually participate in the collective life of the nation the dearer it is to me, and the more I feel obliged to contribute to its entirety and progress. At the same time the higher is my moral development the more I am driven in this direction on my own. At the lower level of personal morality one's attitude toward other men is determined either by sympathy toward them or by a fear of retribution and punishment either in this life or beyond. With civilizational progress, however, our propensities are determined more by our own morality. A civilized man avoids disgrace above all because he respects himself. This self-respect also fashions an appropriate attitude toward the nation on his part. The feeling of dignity which prevents a man from begging or stealing also prevents him from benefitting from the national good without contributing to it and upholding and expanding it. A sufficient degree of intelligence enables a man to comprehend how the national good is essential to his individual development and how he benefits from it; and an appropriate moral maturity compels a man to accept the fact that by benefitting from the national good without contributing anything to it, he is indebted to the society like a beggar living on welfare: and his very sense of self-respect, regardless even of his actual attachment to the country, makes him accept his national duties: to work for the country, to fight for it, and to give it as much as he gets in exchange from it.

On entering life we discover its form and organization ready-made through the work of many generations which created, built, expanded upon and improved it. Are we not ashamed at the thought that we can depart without a trace — without adding anything to this structure built over centuries and without improving it in any way? The duties we owe our country are obligations not only to today's Poles, but also to the past and the future generations.

From the same source we derive our duties to other nations and to humanity as a whole. As a man accepts his obligations toward today's Poland in his own name and in that of his generation, in the same fashion he accepts obligations toward all of humanity in the name of his own nation. Our nation has benefitted over centuries from the experiences, the accomplishments and the spiritual resources of other nations which have attained higher civilizational levels. In proportion to what we have derived from them we have contributed very little to the humanity. Should not, then, our pride guide us toward civilizational and creative achievements from which in the future other nations can benefit, as much as we have benefitted from them in the past and are still benefitting today? And is this not the most noble obligation owed to humanity?

There are people for whom such sentiments, notions and duties do not exist. But patriotism is not a philosophic concept to be either accepted or rejected by the individuals at a given level of intellectual development, it is rather the moral attitude of an individual toward the society — its acceptance at a certain moral level is a moral imperative, and, conversely, its repudiation testifies to a moral inferiority and decline. In normal circumstances the nation is placed within the coercive structure of the state which compels all the individuals to perform their civic duties; we do not have such a structure and for this reason we so often encounter open evasion of service to the country. It is precisely for this reason that we have to emphasize even more the moral obligations, so they will serve as an effective substitute for the state's coercion.[...]

The deep feeling of communion with the nation, its interests and aspirations, does not depend on whether we approve or disapprove of the country at any given stage of its historical development. It should be manifested in all the historical stages regardless of whether the country is free or enslaved, and when it is necessary to defend it as well as to attack in its name. Only upon such a kind of patriotism can the future of the country be founded. And if we feel too little love for our country to fight for its freedom, it is likely that we should suffer even more from the same deficiency were we living in our own self-governing state. An independent Poland, perhaps more than that of today, will need true patriots — people whose attitudes toward the nation and its needs will be both serious and profound; and should these be lacking she may be even more threatened then than at present.

True patriotism need not be based on the notion of superiority of one's own nations over other nations; and, conversely, the feeling of inferiority in no way should detract from the nation's moral strength. His attachment to the nation should not affect an individual's judgment and blur his critical faculty; it must not blind him in objectively evaluating what is dear to him, for clinging to gratifying delusions about one's own worth is the more harmful the more these delusions are divorced from the truth. For if the strong and advanced nations convinced of their superiority tend to cultivate those features which contribute to their strength, then the weak and backward ones idealize those characteristics which perpetuate their weakness. And we have been weak for a long time, though there are in us the elements of great strength.

In terms of national power, in its number and wealth our nation remains far behind those peoples who today determine the fate of the world, and raising our material resources is one of the most important tasks ahead of us. The history of mankind, however, has demonstrated that even more decisive in the fortunes of a nation is its moral strength. But it is necessary to remember that the moral strength of a nation is not demonstrated by its defenselessness or its innocence - as we often tend to believe — but in its striving for real life, in its determination to intensify its wealth and influence, and its readiness to make sacrifices in accomplishing these national goals. Poor and small nations through their moral strength have often won struggles and have greatly influenced the events in the world.

I believe, and I am even confident, that precisely such a strength is beginning to emerge now among the masses of our people. And I believe that side by side with that, the level of national morality among the educated segments of our society is also rising.

The difficult conditions under which our society exists cannot stop this progress. There is no situation from which a vibrant nation, which has reserves for the future, cannot derive some advantages.

One of the advantages of our present plight — the unheard of oppression under which we find ourselves and the political partitioning, although this is still accompanied by a strong sense of national unity — is that the urgency to reconsider the essence of our national existence and the nature of our tasks and duties is for us greater than it is among other nations. No nation has a stronger motivation to turn its thoughts in this direction. It was precisely in response to such a challenge that we once produced a patriotic poetry such as no other nations possesses; poetry which in the strength and depth of its love of country is unparalleled in any other literature. Who knows whether in response to the same challenge we shall not at one time or another pave the way for new trends in ethics and politics? Should the Polish spirit, while taking into account the broad experiences of other nations, be able to learn from the extraordinary conditions of the Polish life which are unknown to the others, then perhaps we shall be able to create at some point in the future such a strong national morality, and so intensive — purely national and free from any outside influences — a type of politics, that it will become our lasting source of an extraordinary strength.

So far, however, the situation is exactly the opposite. Today our national morality is tarnished by empty sentimentalism — it is characterized by a complete absence of positive affection for the country, and the political views of our enlightened public differ from those of other nations in that they are devoid of the very foundation of healthy politics, namely, the instinct for survival. We are a nation with a distorted way of political thinking.

The roots of this situation can be found in our distant past. For several centuries our society, having once lost its historic destiny, departed further and further from the course which could have assured it a great future. Promising in history to be one of the leading nations of Europe and owning a large and steadily expanding territory, our nation fell into the rear of civilizational progress, lost its independence and found itself in a worse position than the peoples who never possessed their own states. While they, as minors, never enjoyed independence, our nation was submitted to a humiliating foreign curatorship like a habitual loser, who after a string of bankruptcies is deprived the right to run his own affairs. Unable to return to the road of its former greatness through a national revival, in despair it sporadically tried to shake off its chains, while in the meantime passively accepting its slavery.

With the growing tendencies to accept its miserable fate, our nation gradually developed the mentality which facilitated the ultimate abdication of its historical role. Ineptness became known as generosity, cowardness as prudence, servility toward enemies as civic duty, and treason as patriotism. Almost all the political concepts were turned upside down. The nation began to live in a realm of political delusions, and, adjusting to such an existence, it began to suppress all of the healthy tendencies, and all manifestations of the instinct for survival.

Yet, with this sickly trend in Polish thought, under the influence of new legal and economic conditions, there also began a healthy social development. From the lower strata of the nation — which for centuries had been ignored and had been regarded as immature, and which had never participated in the running of the commonwealth, but also had never squandered any part of it — there began to emerge new social forces and new social aspirations. This is the reality which will re-shape the entire nation's soul. And the sooner this happens the better for us.

At present, when at the foundations, among the broad masses, there begin to appear the new elements of a national policy, it is there that our nation gains the broad basis for its moral and political rebirth. Should Polish political thought take advantage of this, we shall soon enter into the road of basic and healthy political creativity. And, then, there will come the new period of development for the Polish spirit which will open for it new horizons of action and which will provide the basis for an extraordinary moral strength.

# III

# THE CHURCH, THE NATION AND THE STATE*

## Roman Dmowski

The essential social unit in our civilization, the result of the process of historical evolution, is the modern nation. The moral unity of the people constituting the nation is today the major driving force of history.

We speak and write extensively about the nature of this or that nation and the spiritual bonds which hold it together, but we often do not appreciate what a great role in forging both has been played by Religion and the Church.

Without the historic contribution of Christianity and the Roman Catholic Church modern nations would not have come into existence. It was the Church's accomplishment to cultivate the individual human soul as reflected in its moral conscience, and in this way to develop the person's sense of duty and responsibility. It was the Church which brought all the tribes together, with their different cults, into a single great religion, and, at the inception of the modern European nations, early in the Middle Ages, assisted in creating their states — for the Church's members were the only educated people, without whom the development of neither the states nor international relations would have been possible. It was also the Catholic Church which has passed over to the people the great legacy of Rome: its civilization and law, which rest at the very foundation of the entire western world and which

---

*Roman Dmowski, *Kosciol, narod i panstwo* Originally published in 1926. Second edition, (Dilligen 1946). (Pp. 9-11, 17-18, 20-21. Italics by the author.).

shaped the social instincts of the modern nations. To appreciate this
role of religion and the Church we need look no further than the history
of our own country.[...]

In the pre-Christian era our predecessors did not consider themselves
an entity. They were, rather, divided into tribes which fought each
other. There was really no unity among them until the end of the Piast
dynasty. In their spiritual consciousness those values which distinguish
us today as individuals and as a nation, and unite us into a single entity,
were still missing. The people were kept together by the coercive
power of the state, to the extent that one existed. It was the Church
— either as a supporter or opponent of the state — which over the
centuries guided the human soul toward its maturity, improved the
mores (which at that time were not as noble as many of us would
like to believe), and strengthened the family (which in the tribal system
was weak). The rulers either helped the Church in those endeavors,
or opposed them, so these tasks could have been finally accomplished
only by a powerful, universal Church, independent of the state and
able, if necessary, to stand up to it.

During the feudal division which threatened to completely dis-
rupt the work of the early Piasts, the Polish church was the main
force upholding the state's unity, paving the way for its reconstruction by Przemyslaw, Wladyslaw I the Short, and Casimir the
Great, and without these efforts we would have never become a Great
Nation. [...]

When we examine the elements in our souls which make us
today a modern European nation, we can find their roots in both
our ancient ethnic origin and the existence over centuries of the
Polish state, as well as in our millenium-old attachment to Catholicism.

Catholicism is not an adjunct to Polishdom, merely coloring
it in some special way, but is inherent in its very core and to
a large extent constitutes its very essence. Any attempt to divide
Catholicism and Polishdom, to separate the Nation from the religion and the Church, then, strikes at the very essence of our
Nation.[...]

In accordance with Christ's teaching human existence in this world
should lead to eternal life. The task of the Church is to guide the
individual through faith and conduct in accordance with God's
Commandments, to eternal life.

This does not mean, however, that the Church should not concern
itself with temporal matters and should confine itself merely to
spreading the faith.

Only quite exceptional characters can consistently be governed in their conduct by reliance on their own principles, as only the saintly can constantly keep their every step in conformity with God's Commandments.

The conduct of an average person is, rather, determined by the historical experiences which have been accumulated over generations in the customs and institutions and which shape his social instincts, and by the education he receives both in the family and at school. The Church's role is of great significance in influencing the society's customs and the state's institutions as well as the education offered by both the family and the school.

A truly Catholic nation, then, must be concerned that its laws and state institutions conform with the Catholic principles and that the young people should be brought up in the Catholic spirit.[...]

*The Polish state is a Catholic state.*

*This is so not just because the great majority of its population is Catholic, not even because the size of that majority is so overwhelming. It is fully Catholic because our state is a national one, and our nation is a Catholic one.*

This has profound consequences. It means that the state should guarantee freedom for all denominations, but the principles of the ruling religion should be observed by the state and the Catholic Church should represent religion in the state activities. We have among our nation non-Catholics who are often among the most conscious and conscientious members of our nation. They understand, however, that Poland is a Catholic country and they act accordingly. The Polish Nation [...] does not deny any of its members the right of beliefs different from those of the Catholics, but it does not allow them the right to conduct policies incompatible with, much less, contradictory to, the nature and the needs of a Catholic nation.

*The Great Nation must hold high the banner of its faith.* The people must hold it even higher when the state authorities fail to do so, and to cling to it even more firmly when an attempt is made to take it away.

# IV

## IDEA AND POWER*

### Stanislaw Stomma

There is a painting by Grottger titled the "Reading of the Golden Manifesto". It depicts a minor historical episode from the uprising of 1863 which is not widely known. A group of young noblemen, Polish, naturally, went into the countryside to arouse the Ukranian peasants against the oppressive Russian Tsarist government. The young men's patriotic-revolutionary pilgrimage did not last long and it ended in disaster. They were attacked in a village by a band of armed peasants and cruelly murdered.

What was the program offered by this handful of young idealists who, with their "Golden Manifesto", went to the people? The answer is simple: they had no program. A noble idea flared in their minds and their hearts: to go to the people, to fraternize with them and then to undertake a joint struggle — just that. In the name of this idea — which for them was obviously right and inspiring — they left their palaces and mansions in the Ukraine and undertook an activity fraught with mortal danger of which possibly they were not even fully aware.

We respect the memory of these young hotheads, although we are shocked and almost appalled, by their extreme idealism and the complete impracticality of their commitment. Considering the specific social and national conditions which at that time prevailed in the Ukraine, what other results could they expect? They were noblemen who came from the mansions so the Ukrainian peasants regarded them

*Stanislaw Stomma, *Mysli o polityce i kulturze* (Krakow, 1960), Pp. 28-34.

as class enemies. They were also Poles and Catholics appealing for an insurrection against the Orthodox and Russian authorities in the name of some new, but nevertheless Polish and Catholic republic.

We single out this episode because it is very characteristic. The young men with "The Golden Manifesto" were inspired by idealism, but they took action without a proper evaluation of the existing social reality. They marched out with their idea — which they obviously believed in and loved while completely ignoring its socio-political context. They blindly ran into reality. As such it was a typical behavior. It represents a kind of activity which is governed by what we might call a "pure" idea, yet without a program based on social reality and accounting for objective necessity. This type of action and the attitude it embodies we regard as manifestations of political idealism. Thus, political idealism could be defined as the following in politics of some comprehensive idea, but without any concrete program as to how it could be implemented in a way that is appropriate to the existing conditions.

It is difficult to find arguments with which such political idealism could be defended either in theory or in practice. Following a pure idea in politics is like deciding to cross the Atlantic in a sailboat without taking into account the directions or velocity of the winds.

In the contemporary Polish, non-Marxist writings about public affairs there is emerging a new trend called — although just in the political sense — "positivism", or "neo-positivism". I am regarded as one of the exponents of this trend. I do not know whether this terminology is accurate, but, in any case, before accepting it I have to put forward some pre-conditions.

One must reject that type of positivist thinking which denies the existence of all ideas in politics. Realism must not imply the absence of ideas.

Opportunism in politics is expressed by excessive striving for material benefits while resigning all moral goals. But political realism is not necessarily associated with opportunism. If cases of such do exist they are accidental. There are also examples of realism assisting in the implementation of some ideas. For instance, in the policies of Lenin. Or in the role of Cavour in the unification of Italy. Thus, let us make it clear once and for all that realism — or, if one prefers, political positivism — does not negate ideas and can be even of assistance to them, but at the same time it accepts the limits within which they can be implemented in the concrete historical circumstances.

When in 1948 in Cracow Wyspianski's drama *La Varsovienne* was put on stage some people who adhered to positivist attitudes almost instinctively were repelled by it. One can understand their reaction. Yet, it was a misunderstanding, for the author's objective was to bring about exactly this effect. Wyspianski wrote his drama because he hated all pathos, destruction and martyrdom. He could not stand such heroic-martyrological posturings, widespread among the Polish people, and their condemnation is perhaps the central theme of his play.[...]

Yet, it is characteristic that members of the audience for *La Varsovienne* often fail to perceive the author's real intention. This is because the poetical genius of Wyspianski was also sensitive to what was truly great and monumental in the actions of his characters. This genius spontaneously detected these values and underlined them in the drama. Thus, in a play which condemns the falsehood of suicidal heroism, Wyspianski also presents a captivating vision of everything which in the tragic moment was beautiful and worthy. And it would be wrong not to see it.

Near the white mansion in Grochow a battle is waged: the national uprising is under way which sooner or later is doomed to defeat. The fate of Poland is sealed, yet the people who are gathered at the white mansion live in an idealistic ecstasy for they hear the wings of Nike flying over the battlefield. And this reaction is also correct. Such intense sentiments are also a part of the national history, and in its "treasury" (an ugly material word) represent concrete and lasting values. For the nation is something alive and changeable, it has its ups and downs, and is educated by its history.

The glory of dedicated struggles for great and pure causes, even when they are lost, is also a part of the national education. Such hopeless upheavals as those in 1794, 1830, 1863 and 1944 influenced the national character too. It was not in this school that the Poles learned about political realism, prudence, patience and persistence; but from there they derive their readiness to sacrifice, their commitment to a cause and the great truth that the moral values are supreme over individual material benefits. Those experiences and trials have made a lasting contribution to the national ethos.

I stress that this not to justify the uprising. It was a typical product of political idealism — an attempt to cross the ocean by sailboat without taking into account the direction of the winds. I underline this point to emphasize that positivism must not be narrow and ignore the idealist and moral values.

Heroism is valuable *per se* and as such remains in the treasury of national history and the national education. And furthermore the wrong political decisions and the events that turn against the wheel of history do not detract from the greatness of the ideals that inspired the nation and led it into action. Yet, this does not change the basic dramatic point inherent in *La Varsovienne* and does not diminish the frightful *j'accuse* which it expresses. The tragedy lies in the fact that from the outset the circle is a closed one. The participants in *La Varsovienne* live through a great idealistic catharsis, but they are doomed to defeat. And there is no way out of that circle.

The curse of the Polish fate in the last few centuries is that heroism has been always confined within the closed circle of inevitable defeat. It has been a defeatist heroism and the great national struggles could only be closed with the tragic saying: *gloria victis*. Positivism does not deprecate the glorious chapters of the Polish past and recognizes that heroism is a dynamic of history, but it double-checks the accounting between the decision and the chances of its realization.

There are times when a nation has to wage a hopeless struggle. Battle should be accepted when there is either a real prospect of victory, or it is inevitable; yet, an unnecessary battle without the chance of victory should not be accepted. It is for this reason that we all accepted the Polish-German war in 1939 and we are not unduly concerned about the tragic losses which we suffered during the seige of Warsaw at that time. We know that this could not have been avoided. In the same fashion we do not despair over the Polish graves in Narvik or Tobruk. Yet, we are more apprehensive about the bloodshed at Monte Cassino as until this day we cannot come to terms with what happened in Warsaw in 1944.

The case of the Warsaw uprising has already been discussed many times and it is not yet closed. I should not like to treat it superficially [...]so I shall make just one observation. The emigré authors who try to justify the uprising claim that it originated from a mistaken assessment of the situation. This is not a valid excuse. In such a grave matter an intellectual error brings a heavy moral guilt. The guilt is even greater for in this case it was not difficult to assess the situation correctly. I accept that there was no conscious intention to lead the nation to a defeat. But the crime of thoughtlessness is enough to burden the guilty ones with a frightful moral responsibility.

The title of this article is: idea and power. It is about the power of the idea, the indispensable quantum of power with which the idea can be realized, or — to put it in Thomistic terms — can be transformed from the potential into actuality. An idea can be implemented partially and gradually. And this is precisely what was not recognized by the 19th century Polish idealism. It adhered to the principle: all or nothing.

In 1860-63 Wielopolski advanced a concrete program for restoring independence, starting with regaining the autonomy of the Polish
Kingdom in the Russian Empire. This would have been a Polish
Piedmont — precisely what Cavour attained in Italy. The response
to this proposal was an uprising. The insurgents demanded Poland's
complete and immediate independence, and with its 1772 boundaries
including Minsk, Vitebsk and Kiev.

The program of gradual restoration of independence was proclaimed
treasonable and Wielopolski was branded a traitor. In this dilemma:
everything or nothing, of course, only the latter was attainable. And
for many years we clung to the thus defined idea, even though power
was still against us. This led to the antagonistic posing of idea versus
power and even a pejorative attitude toward power. It found its fullest
expression in the messianistic ideology of Krasinski.

In the realm of abstract ideas there is a perfect harmony. Everything
is simple and clear; only one thing is missing[...]contact with life.
The ideology of Krasinski's *The Dream* is, as Norwid put it, a
"nightmarish thinking about thinking". Krasinski's ideology belongs
to the past and there is no need to do combat with a shadow. But
the lure of political idealism — of a divorce from concrete life —
is still there.

"Reduction is a reduction", Norwid also said. To make an idea
concrete requires reducing it to its feasible limits. The Polish ethos
does not accept this. We prefer to run over all obstacles straight to
an idea. And, then, the fatal complex of *La Varsovienne* reappears:
the great idea reigns in a closed circle of a defeat.

In October 1956 we lived through great days in Polish history. And
a new thing happened which was a sensation for the world. This time,
contrary to the Polish traditions, the nation's idealistic upheaval did
not culminate in its martyrdom.[...] In October 1956 there was not
only the eruption of an idea in Poland, but also a concrete program
for its realization. And this is a novel situation.

December 1956

# V

## POSITIVISM IN THE LIGHT OF ETHICS*

### Stanislaw Stomma

Recently one of the readers of *Tygodnik Powszechny* [...] made it clear to me that he views positivism as political opportunism and ideological conformism. And Miss Pannenkowa in *Przeglad Kulturalny* (No. 12; 1957) went even further and depicted positivism as a sort of Machiavellism. I would like to protest strongly against such interpretations and to defend the moral value of positivism.

If such accusations against positivism are possible it only demonstrates that there are still basic misunderstandings about its nature. This is natural for the very notion of positivism is not clearly defined. So in order to clarify the discussion its very definition has to be made more precise. What exactly is political positivism, or neo-positivism, and what is it all about?

The term originated as a description of the ideological line of *Tygodnik Powszechny* without defining, however, which of its specific elements are concerned. In searching for its substance one can distinguish four different types of ideological-political views which have appeared in articles published in *Tygodnik Powszechny* which justify the use of this term and can be regarded as expressions of positivism. Positivism, thus, could be understood in the following fashions:

1. Positivism can be regarded as Poland's *raison d'etre*, especially in justifying its alliance with the USSR, which position is argued,

---

*"Mysli...", Pp. 16-27.

however, solely on the basis of national interest, regardless of — and even in contrast to — any ideological premises.

2. Positivism can be understood as a certain general political method. In this sense positivism is directly opposed to political romanticism. Its principles are modesty, prudence, a proclivity toward compromise and the repudiation of risky policies and the measuring of one's power by one's purposes.

3. Positivism also means the repudiation of the policy of prestige and a scepticism toward dramatic slogans as motivations for action.

4. Finally, positivism is known as a critical attitude toward the past and especially toward the so-called "heroic" episodes in our history.

It seems to me that the above four categories more or less exhaust the substance of the concept of positivism or neo-positivism.

Yet, strictly speaking, these are four different, although interconnected, topics which should be discussed separately; and, in any case in any discussion it is necessary to make it clear which one is being used. Most of the problems arise from use of the second and third and, as a consequence, the fourth.

Against the arbitrary opinions of my adversaries, and perhaps against the generally accepted tradition, I should like to assert — so far *a priori* — that despite all the appearances to the contrary, the positivist policy is more moral than the "heroic" one. Yet, this still has to be demonstrated.

Let us start from the ending, i.e. with the fourth usage. Miss Pannenkowa accuses me of subscribing to a single school of historiography, namely, the Cracow one. It is a mistake to overestimate the influence of the Cracow school on my political thought. It is not at the roots of political neo-positivism as it was formulated in the pages of *Tygodnik Powszechny*. A greater role was played by some — and I should like to emphasize, *some* — concepts of Roman Dmowski.

We decisively reject Dmowski's nationalism and we critically assess his social views as well as the totalitarian tendencies which he revealed toward the end of his life. Yet, we accept Dmowski's view of 19th century Polish politics and his general assessment of Poland's position between Russia and Germany. These views of Dmowski we adopt as our own.

Personally, I have to admit that in international politics I can say with Stanislaw Mackiewicz that "I love everything which I have burned, and I burn everything that I have loved". Emotionally I am closer to the people who fought against Russia and who sought assistance against the East from the West. Yet, the tragic events of 1939-1944 demonstrated that such emotional predispositions do not consort well with rational thinking. As a result, in international politics I have declared myself for Dmowski.[...]

I repeat that the views of the Cracow school are not at the roots of our political thinking, although I still regard them highly. But should this be a reason to condemn me? Anyone should be entitled to select the trend which appeals to him the most, and to accept some school as the foundation for his thought — which does not mean that he has to adhere to it entirely. Why should I prefer Choloniewski or Lelewel over Bobrzynski or Kalinka? I appreciate the Cracow school's courage to tell the truth. It seems to me that the novel views of the past which it advanced were correct and creative. This does not mean, of course, that it was right about every concrete problem. It appears to me, moreover, that many of its views are no longer all that novel or controversial, but, on the contrary, that they have been generally adopted by our society.

We are not dependent upon the Cracow school, but some analogy between them and us does in fact exist. New political trends appear in response to social needs. The Cracow school of political thought was a reaction to the fatal errors of the insurrectionist policy and the defeats which it brought upon Poland. The defeats and the tragic political errors which we have witnessed have also produced critical tendencies and have made us wonder whether the ideals of political "heroism" may not by any chance be a bad school of political thought? Such is the analogy between the Cracow School and our neo-positivism. Although this does not mean that we have abandoned our critical attitude toward its "loyalism".[...]

I remember, from a long time ago, our student debates in the seventh grade. We sneered at Mickiewicz's *Books of the Polish Nation and Pilgrimage* and we approved of Slowacki's *Tomb of Agamemnon*. I believe these reactions were proper. We did not search in those works for their artistic values, but rather we assessed them in a "programmatic" fashion. In the former we were appalled by the historical falsehoods and the latter appealed to us for its exposition of the ideological truth.

There are different types of lies. Some are conventional and others are pragmatic. Many are the pragmatic lies which serve good purposes. And quite often they are unconscious. In such cases the term "a lie" is improper, for subjectively it is not so. Nevertheless the truth is still distorted. Such a pragmatic lie very easily, and without notice, enters into the historiography and the political literature:

> God, give those people of yours
> Exhausted by the battle
> A quiet sleep, a sleep inspired
> By a wealth of shining hopes.

Slowacki rightly perceived the danger of this. Under foreign rule there was a temptation to offer the nation "a wealth of shining hopes" It can be seen in the Polish historiography.

Books written to enhearten the people can perform a positive role, but they make terrible reading for politicians. In politics there is no room for delusions. The more closely we become involved in political activity, the more strictly we should adhere to the truth. Here we touch upon the moral responsibility of politicians. I shall return to it.

This concludes the short defense of neo-positivism as seen in its fourth sense. Before closing, however, there is one thing I should like to reiterate. We approve of the Cracow school because of its searching for truth — which has a positive moral value. I may be wrong here, but I believe that Bobrzynski's enlightened revisionism in evaluating the past required courage to look the truth in the face, and courage to proclaim it. And I am attracted by such an approach to history, while, in contrast, I am repelled by all manifestations of national megalomania in historiography, and by all, even the most camouflaged, pragmatic lies.

Now let us turn to neo-positivism in its second and third senses.

In each profession there are special ethics, specific demands and responsibilities. Naturally the same is true of politics, although strictly speaking the politicians do not represent a separate professional group. The specificity of the rules of moral responsibility is particularly strongly marked when applied to public activity in all its ramifications.

The Decalogue is the same for all, but there are different rules of applying the same moral norms. When an individual fasts and mortifies himself, and he does so with good intent, this is generally accepted as good. But if a ruler were to decree that all his subjects had to observe ascetism and mortification, this would be bad. It would be improper for the simple reason that it is different when one mortifies himself voluntarily, than when one is ordered to do so. It is also noble when one distributes his riches among his brethren; yet, only in very special circumstances can the government require the citizens to give away their wealth. The same applies to the protection of life. Unless he commits deliberate suicide, one is free to risk his life; but the right to demand that others risk their lives is quite exceptional.

I repeat those obvious distinctions in order to emphasize the specifity of the rules binding in public life. In governing the country the tightening of the belt is done at the expense of someone else's stomach. The realization of this should suffice to condemn strongly the "heroic" decisions of the authorities that lead to dreadful bloodshed. Of course, the government is entitled to demand from the citizens the sacrifice of their lives. But this right should be exercised only in very special circumstances, when it is absolutely indispensable to uphold values even higher than life. Heroism means a willingness to sacrifice beyond the call of duty. In this sense the government has a right to expect sacrifice from its subjects. But any decisions to squander the citizens' blood beyond what is absolutely necessary is "heroism" and in its essence is immoral.

Now perhaps I can explain why I am attracted to positivism. I see in it the humanist values; the respect for man with his ordinary, earthly strivings which must not be lightly thrown away by an order from above. Such conduct would stand in contrast to Christian asceticism. For true asceticism must be voluntary, reflecting the inner motives and the moral maturity of a person.[...]

Miss Pannenkowa condemns casually and without any reservation Stanislaw August for his policy of cooperation with Russia and declares herself against it because of the disgusting personal conduct of Catherine II. This argument is grossly oversimplified. True, Catherine II was a whore ... so what? Was this a reason for Poland to adopt a suicidal policy? The personal morality of rulers, of course, is important. But it is necessary not to lose sight of the practical consequences of a maximalist moral stance.

First of all one should remember the maxim observed by the lawyers of the Renaissance era: *principes mortales sunt, respublica aeterna*. And what was at stake in Catherine's days were fundamental decisions concerning the general direction of Poland's policy that would extend beyond her rule. Next, one should ask whether there was any other solution? It is easy to adopt a maximalist stance and pass judgment when one bears no responsibility for it. But what was needed at that time was a practical solution. When one is faced with adverse political circumstances a moral gesture is not enough. One has to choose among concrete alternatives. Avoiding the decision and, even unconsciously, selecting passivity is also a form of choice. And such a choice is morally suspect too for in practice it amounts to accepting a certain alternative while pretending to make no decision.

One can in the name of moral maximalism abstain from deciding, but this means selecting the alternative which is *actually* induced by such a posture. So it is a false maximalism. In fact, one often has to select between greater and lesser evils. One can then, in the name of maximalism, opt out of deciding and wash one's hands, in order not to be tainted with acceptance of something which is less than good; but in this way, in effect, one accepts the greater evil. Such a false maximalism, thus, is hypocritical. It is nothing more than what I would term an easy "angelical" behavior. In every case one ought to make a conscious decision rather than try to avoid reality. Positivism compels one to face the pincers of life and does not tolerate an escape into the skies. When one is faced with a greater and a lesser evil, one must select with full responsibility the lesser evil. And is this stance not more moral than an "angelogy" which avoids moral responsibility?

This applies to our historical example too. In the Stanislaw August epoch Poland was undergoing a serious crisis: the choice was between Russia's "protection" (which, of course, brutally restricted the country's independence), or the partitioning of the Polish state. There was no third possibility. It seems, then, that the lesser evil was foreign "curatorship" over the entire state. One is entitled to a different opinion, but only when one consciously accepts all the consequences which flow from it. This means that one has to defend the view that the partitions would be preferable. Yet, one cannot defend such a view just by reference to moral maximalism. For this brings us back to the false "angelogy".

Using the above outlined criteria one can say that Stanislaus Augustus was a "positivist" and the Bar Confederation was "heroic". Which of them was morally superior? Who were their confederates and what their private morality may have been, is debatable. The fact is that in upholding their cause they resorted to the most noble Christian slogans. As Slowacki recreated it later, their song was:

> We shall never enter into an alliance with the king
> For we are subordinate only to God...
> We are Holy Mary's servants.

This verse sums up well the confederates' ideology. They proclaimed themselves the Knights of Holy Mary, but they carried out a concrete political activity aiming to achieve specific political goals. They defended the *szlachta's* golden freedoms and anarchy and their activities brought about civil war, foreign intervention and a partition of Poland. Which of the two sides, then, was more moral?

It is possible that in their private lives the confederates stood above the king who was a sceptic, a hedonist and a womanizer, but this does not detract from his public activities and their moral assessment.

I believe that in assessing morally a political action it is necessary to stress even more than in individual life the principle that one is responsible not only for the intentions, but also for the results. This is an indispensable ethical imperative inherent in the very nature of statesmanship. It includes also the responsibility — which may be a heavy one — for unintended wrong. A politician is guilty of bad, even though unintentional, consequences too; for he could, and in fact should, have anticipated them. The confederates, thus, were morally responsible for the misfortunes which they brought upon our nation.

I do not intend to elevate this example to the rank of a decisive argument. It is just an example and nothing more. Its objective is simply to illustrate how complex the problem is. It shows how unfounded are the claims of placing political "heroism" over positivism. I do not know whether the confederates were personally marked by heroism. But if this was so, what were the results of it for the nation? The waging of war, devastation and ruin, which the people did not accept voluntarily, but which were imposed upon them. And then a political defeat of the country: its partition.

If one does not like the example of the Bar Confederation, let him turn to any other historical analogies. Without drawing any superficial generalizations, I am thus inclined to believe that as a whole one should have more trust in positivist, than in "heroic" policies. The costs of political heroism are usually paid by others, so it is fine to have heroic soldiers, but not heroic politicians.

It is necessary to introduce here an important caveat. It is not true that positivism gives priority to material values. Even if at times this has been the case, this is not a general principle. In any case that is not the type of positivism which we espouse. The hierarchy of values should correspond to the Christian values. The material values are secondary to the main goals of man and the society. What is central here is the humanist respect for the man and the acceptance of his own judgment. This is the essential attribute of freedom which is denied by the Grand Inquisitor in Dostoyevsky's novel. Positivism does respect, as far as it is feasible, the human material needs, although it also recognized the limits there.

When in 1939 the war started everyone understood that there was no other way. probably there was not a single Pole who believed that the war could have been averted by some kind of surrender. And this was right. Yet, when one considers the misfortunes produced by the Warsaw uprising [of 1944], or those brought about by the 1830 or 1863 insurrections, the case is different. On those occasions "heroism" — both within quotation marks and without — was imposed by small groups, and the results were defeats, and only defeats.[...]

To see the truth without any distortions and without any pragmatic lies, and to observe the highest prudence in disposing other people's (even their very earthly) resources — these are the two axioms of neo-positivism. And both have positive moral connotation.

April 1957

# VI

# THINKING ABOUT THE FUTURE*

## Jan Szczepanski

To predict at the outset of the 1970s how far the Polish nation will advance in comparison with other nations in the march toward the year 2000, one must evaluate its capacity for progress and compare it with that of other peoples. We know what determines the progress, the ability to overcome small and great obstacles, of modern nations. We can list those factors. They are the demographic elements — the number and composition of the population; the natural resources — the soil, climate, etc.

We also know that those factors do not operate in isolation, but are influenced by other elements. Most importantly, there is the quality of the leadership — its ability to organize, utilize and multiply the existing resources, to channel the social energies, and to exploit the potential inherent in the large structures toward coordinated and effective activities. In Poland these large structures are the branches of the socialized economy, the armed forces, the judiciary and the educational and scientific institutions.[...]

In our society there are also structures which enjoy considerable autonomy from the government, such as the Church, which is able to conduct its own policies and influence the behavior of the believers. And, as in any society, there are large areas of communal life which develop on their own, such as local communities, the informal social

*Jan Szczepanski, *Rozwazania o Rzeczypospolitej* (Warszawa, 1971). Pp. 129-146.

and friendly circles, the generational layers, etc. And, finally, there are the manifestations of moods by the public, the spontaneous reactions of crowds which at times can seriously affect the fate of the entire nation.

I have listed those structures in a simplified fashion in order to demonstrate that in trying to anticipate the society's future one has to take into account all of the phenomena and all the processes, the entirety of all its structures and their significance in the nation's march toward the future. In a socialist society in which the nationalized economy is centrally planned and managed, the leadership plays a crucial role in developing the potential of the entire society. But the other structures are important too — including the spontaneous ones, which should be anticipated and integrated into an interdependent and coordinated process of development.[...]

I am interested here mainly in the mode of thinking about the future practiced by those individual citizens who in the last resort will influence what Poland is going to be like in the year 2000.[...] I am concerned with how one should behave in order to avoid such convulsions and crises as we witnessed in 1956 and 1970.[...]

How, since the beginning of the 19th century, have the successive generations of Poles viewed their future? It has always been a conditional thinking. There have been no uniform patterns of behavior with which every Pole could identify and embrace as his own — to see in them the reflection of his virtues and faults, his standards for educational and professional qualification, devotion to work, propensity for thrift, ambitions and aspirations — and on this basis to rationally calculate what his own prospects in life are. Hence, there emerged in our nation alternative models of personal life, career, ambitions and aspirations. The generations of the insurgents, or that of the Columbuses*, when looking ahead saw only suffering, struggles, hazards and defeats rather than success in work and accumulating wealth.[...]

The development of nations is conditioned by their historical experience. All who are concerned about the future of Poland, consciously or unconsciously accept as their point of departure the defeats of 1795 and 1939. The complex of these defeats is deeply rooted in the subconsciousness of each politically thinking Pole. Another historical

---

*The "Columbuses" refers to the generation born in the 1920s which carried the major burden of military struggle and was decimated during World War II. The term is derived from a popular novel by Roman Bratny, *Kolumbowie Rocznik 20* (Warszawa, 1961). (A.B.)

experience which has influenced us has been the spectacular progress of our neighbors.[...] And still another has been our tendency to search for the future in our past national models. In Poland this means reverting now to the 19th century positivism which strove to develop among us an attachment to reality, and the virtues of integrity, punctuality, thrift, discipline and effective organization. In other words, as a precondition for development we accept those virtues which are often seen as *petit bourgeois.*[...]

The Poles' thinking about the future has always been affected by concern that 1795 and 1939 should not be repeated. They have also striven to create the same material base which the developed nations achieved in the 19th century. In order to achieve these they have thought it necessary to cultivate characteristics which would make them needed and even indispensable in Europe.[...]

Looking back to our political literature at the end of the 18th century — when our neighbors, who modernized more rapidly, gained the upper hand over us and we became concerned for our very survival — one can see various trends of thought. The reformers at that time regarded as the most important task the improving of our political system and the government. And after the partitions our political thinkers concentrated upon developing those individual characteristics which were essential for regaining independence. For some this meant cultivating moral perfection and the readiness to sacrifice — this was the romantic tradition. The positivists, in contrast, emphasized energy and professional skills indispensable to economic progress through which the national goals were to be advanced.[...]

Today, in the early 1970s, none of these trends of thought, at least in their pure form, are adequate. For it is obvious that in a planned and centralized economy the way the country is run by the government is of a crucial significance. But the skills of the people — their abilities, training, and willingness to work — are essential for the government to promote its goals. In the second half of the 20th century the organization and the flow of information are of great importance too. When we look at the rapid economic progress of Japan, we can see how the old virtues of the positivists are especially conducive to achieving this end. For efficient organization requires from the people considerable skills, and above all, a high level of education: real competence, not just the possession of a university degree.[...]

Looking at the other nations which [...] have attained rapid economic growth we observe that their driving force has been their ability to channel the energies of the people. The American farmer or entrepreneur, for instance, always strove to exploit the opportunities before him to the utmost. Cultivated land had to produce an optimum crop, and the enterprise had to realize optimum profit. They did not stop half way at satisfying their own needs, but always strove to achieve the feasible optimum.

Is there room for adopting a similar attitude in the socialized economy and to exploit all the opportunities inherent in it? It seems that the current mechanisms for promoting such an attitude are quite unsatisfactory and while we are improving our economic model, we should be improving them, too.

The future can be shaped only by men who have something to contribute. So we are faced with two problems here. On the one hand we have to teach the Poles to rationally plan their own future; and on the other hand we have to channel their habits and aspirations to accelerate the development of the society as a whole.

Each individual has two prospects: either he can strive to promote his own welfare by any means, which could even place him outside the society; or he can try to improve his performance within the existing social system. The latter approach, however, in an economy where there are no appropriate mechanisms to reward individual initiative, may prove fruitless. Here we come to the central thesis of this essay, namely that in our country it is the activities of the political authorities which are of the crucial significance.[...]

But is there a chance of changing our psychological predilections — our national character?[...] In *The History Of Great Poland* Professor Lowomianski observes that tendencies towards waste were already characteristic of the Slavic leaders in the 7th century, and these, it seems, have remained with us in the next twelve ages. Is it possible then — assuming the continuity of our national character — to change the psychological profile of our people? Can we change the permanent attitudes with which we react to certain socio-economic and political circumstances, in just one generation? And, if it is possible, how can this be achieved?[...]

My answer is simple: we have to create an organized nation. This means we have to manage all of our resources — material means as well as our capabilities, energies, aspirations and strivings — in an organized fashion.[...]

If various elements coincide we should be able to do this. For when we are faced with a challenge we respond. And in December 1970 and the early months of 1971 we underwent such a serious crisis that it has brought the entire nation to an acute consciousness of the need for changes.

# VII

## WE ASK, WE INSIST, WE DEMAND*

### Stefan Cardinal Wyszynski

Looking at the life of Saint Stanislaw we see as the key element in his martyrdom a sense of pastoral duty which did not even stop at reprimanding the king for violation of God's law. For it is the duty of a bishop and a Catholic priest to obey God rather than people regardless of either their position or their power — whether entrusted to them by the populace or assumed by themselves. The Christian Church, through the Holy Father, the bishops and the priest has an obligation to teach all, and, whenever necessary, to point out their errors. Saint Stanislaw, Bishop of Cracow, fell a victim of this honorable task of admonishing God's People as well as those who lead them.

He did not do this arrogantly. For, reading The Holy Bible, we find there an excellent reminder given by Saint Paul to his beloved disciple Timothy. In the Second Letter to Bishop Timothy, in Chapter IV we read: "I charge you in the presence of God and of Jesus Christ who is to judge the living and the dead, and by his appearing and his kingdom: preach the word, be urgent in season and out of season, convince, rebuke, and exhort, be unfailing in patience and in teaching. For the time is coming when people will not endure sound teaching, but having itching ears they will accumulate for themselves teachers to suit their own likings, and will turn away from listening to the truth

---

*Stefan Cardinal Wyszynski, Prymas Polski, *Prymat czlowieka w ladzie spolecznym* (London, 1976). Pp. 149-161. Italics by the author.

and wander into myths. As for you, always be steady, endure suffering, do the work of an evangelist, fulfill your ministry."

Probably Saint Stanislaw the Bishop, read these words and derived from them inspiration for his pastoral mission. He did not hesitate when it was necessary to admonish the King — a ruler and a superior to whom for other reasons respect is due, as to all other authority.

Today the Church is doing just the same and is encouraging the bishops to admonish — in patience and love — remembering that the Holy Spirit has instituted them to rule over God's Church. Blessed is the nation who listens to God's Gospel. Blessed is the nation who knows how to accept the admonishment given in God's name, for such an admonishment, as we believe, always comes from God's wisdom. And today, dear Brothers and Sisters, in the Jubilee year of the Cracow Archdiocese, when this diocese is preparing itself to respect the memory of its Shepherd who devoted his life to the care of the sheep entrusted to him, look up to Saint Stanislaw. He was a shepherd, a faithful teacher and a guardian of morality. And the same duties rest with today's bishops as teachers of the faith and guardians of morality.[...]

It suffices to recall the words of Saint Paul to Bishop Timothy: "As for you, teach what befits sound doctrine." For God's people await light, the clear principles and sound teaching, and not the various erroneous and confused theories and opinions of which there are so many in the contemporary world. And today this is the most important duty of the bishops and priests in Poland, to offer — as the Apostle said — sound teaching to God's people. In our country the Church has done so for centuries, even for a millenium. We have embedded into the Polish soil the firm stones, the rocks over which the nation can safely walk toward its future. today we are responsible not only for our contemporary national and Catholic life, but we laboriously pave the way for the existence of the Catholic nation and the Church in the future.

And if today — as in the days of Saint Stanislaw — there are plentiful reasons which compel us to admonish, to explain, to ask, and when this is not enough, to demand, then a Catholic Bishop in Poland — like Saint Stanislaw — will not stop from performing his duty. He will teach and admonish, and when this does not suffice, he will demand, that God's rightful law be observed in our Homeland. Only then will Poland be able to proceed safely, in the spirit of the Gospel and following Christ's Cross, toward its far off and still unknown future.

And the Polish bishops today are aware of this responsibility for Christ's Poland, for God's people who are entrusted to them, and for their rights in the free Homeland, and especially the right to religion and sound morality. And for this reason the bishops in their many submissions directed to the appropriate authorities, have reminded them that the Catholics in Poland are entitled to religious freedom, to access to Catholic culture, to freedom of association in the realm of social, cultural, charitable and religious activities.

A matter which requires a special reminder — and when a reminder does not suffice an entreaty, and when an entreaty is not enough a demand — is *the defense of the Nation's life*. We address ourselves in this to everyone concerned: the parents at home, the citizens and all the state authorities, stressing that no one must be killed either in one's mother's womb, or in one's spiritual, moral or religious life. It is necessary to uphold the Nation's life and especially the unity of the family. Today the Catholic bishops have a duty to say, as John the Baptist said to Herod: thou shall not steal someone's else's wife; or as Saint Stanislaw said in Cracow: you must obey God's law, for authority and dignity do not free kings and rulers from respect for God's law, and, on the contrary, make them even more obliged to abide by it. It is the bishops duty, then, to defend the Nation's life and to demand that the laws, decrees and institutions aimed at the life of the unborn, be removed. Were Saint Stanislaw alive in Cracow today, he would certainly insist upon the same demands in defense of the Nation's life and the morality of the family.

It is necessary, moreover, to defend in our Homeland today *the working man and his right to relaxation.* [...]This morning I read in the Cracow papers an appeal — a very moving one and asking entirely on a voluntary basis — for work today [on Sunday]; and, unfortunately, not for tomorrow or for any of the other six days of the week, following the example of God who toiled for six days when he created the world and rested on the seventh.[...]

I read in the Cracow papers that some 300,000 citizens should report (they said, voluntarily) to work. And I have been told that those are party members, so you, the Primate, should not be concerned about them. A member of the party is also a man and deserves the right to relaxation. He may be (so they say) a believer too, and as such has a right to attend the Sunday mass. He toils and deserves a right to rest with his family, which is important to the family's unity and upbringing. I believe that I have a right to intervene on behalf of all the people whose rights are abridged and whose practicing of their freedom of conscience is restricted.

As Saint paul taught Timothy and Titus, as Bishop Stanislaw Szczepanowski inspired us, and as the Blessed Queen Jadwiga from

Cracow intervened on behalf of the exploited peasants, so we have a right to stand up for the working men, whose rights — at least on Sundays and holidays — must be respected. We do not seek new ways, but we walk over the stones and rocks which for a millenium — in accordance with the principles of Catholic morality — the Church has embedded into the Polish soil, so the Nation could walk over them in safely toward its future.[...]

It is, above all, the duty of a Catholic bishop to defend the faith and the place of God and Christ in educating the children and the youth. The Polish bishops have many times called upon the authorities in this matter, protesting against the compulsory atheistic, or the so-called secular, education. Should Saint Stanislaw be with us today, he would have also taught that the bishop's duty is, as Saint Paul put it, to "Preach the word, be urgent in season and out of season, show the error, and be unfailing in patience and teaching." Since we have already asked for this again and again, today *we demand* it. We have the same right as had Bishop Stanislaw who demanded from the king, as a man leading the Nation, that he set a good example for his subjects. And *today* we also demand that a good example of respect for the laws of God, Christ and the Church be given, at least to the children and the youth in our Homeland.

Similarly, dear Brothers and Sisters, our duty is *to defend our country's culture and history*. We can see what an enormous significance history has for us.[...] The national culture, and history — and especially the Christian one — gives us roots in the Polish soil as the growing oaks have roots in it. This way the nation is not swung back and forth by the winds and storms of war, and it cannot be pushed from boundary, to boundary, making us — as our neighbors to the west used to say, just a *Saisonstadt*. One might occasionally think that way, but we are a nation a millenium old, and we have grown into this soil which was given to our forefathers. We guard it and we work for it by maintaining our own tongue and our own culture.

For us, next to God, our first love is Poland. After God we must remain faithful to our Homeland and the Polish national culture. We will love all the peoples in the world, but only in such an order of priorities. Thus after God, after Jesus Christ and his Holiest Mother, after all God's order, our foremost love belongs to our Homeland, its tongue, history and culture from which we have grown on our Polish soil. And if we see everywhere slogans advocating love for all peoples and all the nations, we do not oppose this; but still, above all, we demand to live in accordance with the spirit, history, culture and language of our own Polish land where our predecessors have toiled for centuries.

Hence, the duty of defending our own culture. If this culture is deformed it is the duty of the bishops to uphold it. Christ said to the bishops: "Go, teach all the nations by baptizing them", so also: "Go, teach the Polish nation by Christianizing it". It is our duty to christen and to teach the Polish nation and to claim respect for our national culture, so we will not have to love first all nations and only at the last, and on special occasions, Poland.

Among the social rights which must be respected is also economic freedom. A man has a duty, while working for his Homeland, to support his children and family — no matter whether small or big. It is our position that the bigger the family the more rights it has. The families have a right to such material means as without difficulty, as a result of fair and honest work, can meet these obligations. Today we observe a painful situation: thirty years after the war, on the eve of a holiday, people idle away many hours lining up to buy a piece of cake.[...]

After thirty years of Poland's working so efficiently (read about it in the papers), it is still necessary to wait hours to buy a piece of cake! And where are our breads and cakes? Where are they all? And why is it so difficult to obtain a piece of meat before the holiday; why is meat rather available on Friday, and herring before Easter?

There is some disdain inherent there — a lack of respect for one's own nation. *The economy must belong to the nation* — this is the basic right of every working man. From what a man produces he should be paid. In the Old Testament there is written: "Thou shalt not muzzle the threshing ox". But among us on the eve of a holiday on Saturday, one must muzzle oneself, for, after a week of hard work, one has no opportunity to buy what is needed to put on the family table on Sunday.

There is a profound confusion in the hierarchy of values and in the hierarchy of the goods produced. This is not just an economic and political problem, but a moral one. God upholds the rights of every working man. In the Gospel Christ offers us the excellent example of vineyard workers who must be paid before sunset because it is their livelihood. It is difficult for a man who has worked the whole day to wait until his wife gets back after waiting in a line, bringing something which she has obtained by pure chance.

If the Polish Saints — Stanislaw walking about Cracow, Wladyslaw of Gielniow wandering the Warsaw district of Podwale, and Jadwiga exploring the poor parts of Cracow — were all sensitive to the needs of man, then it is necessary to be sensitive to them today. In the new system this sensitivity should be only intensified, for it is not a fertilizer, a factory, nor concrete and steel, but man who is the greatest asset. If his rights are respected, he will respond to all the demands made upon him, and willingly apply himself to a plow or a hammer, to honest work on weekdays. But if he has to work on a holiday and Sunday, then he will not work well on Monday.

When we say this, Dear God's Children, we adhere to the spiritual legacy of Cracow's shepherd, Saint Stanislaw, who devoted his soul and life to his sheep, to his brothers. What he did in the past is *our duty today*[...]

So *we embed into the Polish soil the rocks of moral and religious principles* which will lead us toward our longed-for better future. These rocks are: the Cross and the Gospel; service to the Church; love, sacrifice and respect for man; and, whenever needed, the defense of human rights. In history of mankind and our Homeland, the Holy Church has done just that.

We walk over these rocks, in God's light, searching for the millenium — from Dombrova and Mieszko, to, Saint Wojciech and Boleslaw the Brave; from Gniezno, Cracow and Wroclaw to Kolobrzeg; and from Stanislaw and Jadwiga to Zygmunt holding the cross in front of the Royal Castle in Warsaw — and we call upon all *to listen to God rather than to men.*[...]

Cracow, May 12, 1974

## VIII

## IDENTITY AND THE STRENGTH OF THE NATION*

### Janusz Zablocki

In order to understand Poland's present position in the world one must go back to when it was determined for the present historical epoch. What I have in mind, of course, is the end of World War II.

Two facts from that time deserve special attention, for they are the realities which have influenced all subsequent events and determined their outcome. First, despite Polish expectations, our country was freed from the German occupation, not by the Western allies, but by the Red Army. Second, the state of affairs which emerged at the end of the war, dividing Europe into the spheres of influence, and leaving Poland in that part where the Soviet interests were dominant, was accepted and confirmed by the accords among the great powers in the anti-Nazi coalition.

The major part of the Polish society was not prepared at the end of World War II for such an outcome nor for the type of state which was proclaimed by the Manifesto of July 1944. It created for the nation a completely new situation, breaking from its entire way of political thinking, its ideas and customs, its pattern of behavior and its capabilities of action. No wonder, then, that the first reaction — both in the emigration and at home — was a refusal to acknowledge the new situation, questioning its durability and nurturing hopes that it

---

*Janusz Zablocki, *Tozsamosc i sily narodu* (London, 1978). Pp. 30.

would collapse. Such expectations relied upon either transformations in the international sphere or changes inside the country.

Over the past thirty years there have been many hopes that transformations in the international sphere would bring about the changes in Poland. They have been linked to various developments and configurations in the world and to various forces operating there. We shall not try to analyze them here in detail, but we shall attempt to draw from these past experiences some generalizations.

At the root of the refusal to acknowledge the actual state of affairs in Poland and of the anticipation of change, were the traditional expectations, lingering from World War II, of assistance from the West. They were seriously undermined by the Yalta agreement, resulting in considerable disillusionment, and they were further weakened by the apparent weakness of Western Europe[...] Nevertheless they did not completely disappear. They merely shifted their basis from Western Europe to the United States, which in the post-war years emerged as the undisputed leader of the Western bloc and a world superpower.[...]

The only power which today can change the division of Europe sanctioned at Yalta is the United States. To do this, however, its leaders would have to accept the responsibility in respect of their own society and of mankind as a whole, for the inherent risks. And these include the danger of provoking a new world war, the outcome of which is incalculable and the costs unimaginable. When we look at the record of United States' policy we reach the following conclusion: the American people will approve of their leaders' risking a military confrontation to defend their sphere of influence, but not to expand it. A program of "liberation" of Eastern Europe may still evoke sympathy here and there, but for the average American it is not worth risking a war and nuclear annihilation.

This is the truth which cannot be concealed behind all the declarations about "human rights". I do not question the sincerity of these declarations nor their significance, I only note that they are not sufficient to influence the Poles' choice of their alignment. This is recognized by all reasonable and honest Americans, who understand that mutual trust and friendship cannot be based on half-truths and the nurturing of illusions. To convey the impression that one can count upon moral and political commitment, where there is none, and none is even intended, is a course which could be followed only by those who regard their Polish partners as mere pawns to be used in their own interests.[...]

What conclusions can we draw from all of this?

The essential difference between the position of the Polish nation early in the 20th century and today, as Adam Bromke correctly observed: "is the fact that war has ceased to be an effective means to improve its fate. A military confrontation between the two super-powers would mean a world catastrophe which inevitably would include Poland too.[...]So let us not pray for the 'peoples' war', but let us ask for a universal peace in the world."[1]

The long-term goal of Poland's policy should not be a change of sides in the present divided world. Such a change would undermine the fragile balance of power upon which peace in Europe rests and it would not be advantageous either to the East or to the West. Our goal should rather be such a restructuring of the world that its division would gradually disappear. The progress of détente and disarmament — which would create in Europe a system of collective security and, step by step, would overcome its division into antagonistic political, military and economic blocs, and in their place would advance manifold and diversified ties between the East and the West — this should be the optimum goal of Poland's evolution on our continent.[...]

\* \* \*

We noted two facts which at the end of the war were of decisive influence in determining the future of our country. There were that Poland was liberated by the Red Army, and that the division of Europe into the spheres of influence was confirmed by the great powers.

These facts, since the very inception of People's Poland, have determined also the political nature of the new state. Regardless of how we evaluate the correctness of these decisions and their impact upon our interests, the fact is that they were made without the Poles' participation. This was offensive to the dignity of the Polish society,[...] for the decisions in such vital matters, which should have been the result of the sovereign will of the nation, in effect were imposed through outside international pressure. This from the very outset adversely affected the attitudes of the Poles toward the new state, reduced the degree of popular identification with it, and prejudiced the relationship between the people and the authorities. Burdened by this original sin, throughout the entire post-war period the establishing of bonds between the society and the state has been the main problem in Poland. This has been particularly strongly manifested during the periodic political crises, but it has been present in everyday life too.

It still has not been overcome and it remains Poland's political problem "number one".

The impact of this problem on the Polish consciousness is so strong that it even prevents us from seeing what is constructive in our situation and what prospects we have ahead of us. In contrast to World War I, when the "Polish question", had to be strenuously promoted in the international sphere — both among the governments and in public opinion — during World War II the situation was altogether different. Regardless of its future boundaries the reconstruction of an independent and sovereign Polish state was not questioned by anyone in the anti-Nazi coalition. It was accepted not only by the Anglo-Saxon powers, but also by Stalin, who — in contrast to the method which he had adopted toward the Baltic countries — saw the future of socialist countries in Eastern Europe not as Soviet republics. but as sovereign and independent "people's democracies".[...]

This is for us of crucial significance. For without its own state no nation can fully develop and attain an appropriate place in the world; and in the long run even its separate identity may be threatened. In other words, the vital interests of a nation can only be effectively protected by a state acting as an organizational framework for its collective efforts. Thus, it is difficult to exaggerate the significance of the fact that from the turmoil of World War II the Polish nation managed to salvage its own statehood, as expressed not only in symbols but in the real attributes of legal sovereignty, even if the degree of popular influence over the beginnings of this state — as we have already observed — was unsatisfactory.

It must also be observed that it is not a truncated state, but it includes all the ethnically Polish territories. Within its boundaries is the entire nation. Thus, all analogies with the past situations: the partitions or the occupation, or such historical episodes as the existence of the Dutchy of Warsaw or the Congress Kingdom, are erroneous.

The achievement of territorial integrity, which brought together the entire nation, needs to be underlined, for such a state has its own dynamics promoting its fuller self-realization. In his book: *The Sources of Independence,* Wojciech Wasiutynski reminds us that at one time the minimalist program of Roman Dmowski was a unification of all Polish lands within the Russian state, but he also recalls the concern and anxiety which Sergei Witte expressed over such a prospect in his diary: "When Poland recovers its territorial integrity it will not be content with the autonomy which it was so stupidly promised. It will claim — and obtain — its absolute independence." The Tsarist minister, then, rightly perceived Dmowski's ultimate objective, which many Poles, who accused him of subscribing to a half-hearted and minimalist program, could not understand. "People who were excessively preoccupied with mere forms and symbols," adds Wasiutynski, "did not see that a political unit extending over a substantial territory, with a large population and a considerable industrial capacity, must in time attain effective political independence."[2]

* * *

At present, then, in contrast to the situation from before 1918, there is no problem of unifying all the territories inhabited by the Poles; nor is there any need to attain for Poland the status of a sovereign state. It is important, however, that our sovereignty — which the world universally accepts — should not just amount to a legal status, but should reflect more and more the actual state of affairs. The *de jure* sovereignty was granted to us, and all we have to do now is to retain it, but the *de facto* sovereignty must be striven for and constantly expanded. And this should proceed along with the strengthening of the nation; developing its consciousness of separate identity and of its need for independence. This will give an inexhaustible impetus for improving Poland's external position, in its relations with other states, and of internally increasing the citizens' participation in the determination of state affairs.

The actual power of a state vis-a-vis other states is undoubtedly influenced by its alliances, but it is determined primarily by what the nation itself accomplishes through its work, and what position it can attain in the international competition for a better place in the sun. If Poland is to count in this competition — if it is to come closer to the leading developed countries, and not to be pushed down — if it is to build strong foundations for its sovereignty and well being, then it must, in all the spheres: demographic, economic, scientific, technological and cultural, attain dynamic growth. For whoever does not advance falls behind. Furthermore, it must attain such growth not only to keep up with the others today, but also tomorrow, in the times and generations to come.

This, however, will not be possible without the development of a proper relationship between the state and the society, the government and the nation. Here we return to what we have called the Polish political problem "number one". [...]

Among the states where power belongs to Marxist parties, Poland is unique. It is a state which, despite all the integrationist pressures within the Council of Mutual Economic Assistance and the Warsaw Pact, has managed to preserve its own specific profile as a socialist country, which has avoided collectivization of agriculture, and where the entire society benefits from broader personal liberties and religious tolerance.

What elements have contributed to this Polish specificity? They, of course, are various. Our people, who ethnically and religiously are virtually homogeneous, have demonstrated a high degree of attachment to the traditional national and religious values. They have also displayed a considerable degree of political maturity. They have proven capable of effectively influencing the government, but at the same time have avoided open confrontations which could have led to a catastrophe for the nation, and even could have weakened its will to resistance. Last but not least the crucial role in the post-war life of the nation which has been played by the Catholic Church, must be underlined.

For if, in order to preserve the nation's identity, it is essential to maintain over successive generations some specific basic cultural elements, then we cannot omit Catholicism from among them. Catholicism, wrote Roman Dmowski in his work: *The Church, the Nation and the State,* "is not just an adjunct to Polishdom, merely coloring it in some special way, but is inherent in its very core, and to a large extent constitutes its very essence. Any attempt to divide Catholicism and Polishdom, to separate the Nation from religion and the church, then, strikes at the very essence of our Nation."[3]

Without entering here into a discussion of whether Catholicism represents the essence of Polishdom, let us at least agree that the Church, by introducing into our nation the Latin civilization, has for over a millenium played a major role in forming its consciousness — influencing its notions of what is good or bad, and establishing the hierarchy of values that are binding in a collective life. The preservation of these values in the national consciousness, both at present, and as ideals for future generations, will be decisive to our nation's maintaining its separate identity.

The fact that during the Stalinist period, in our country alone of all the socialist states the Church was neither undermined nor cowed into submission, but remained strong and independent — deriving its strength from close links with the people and, in turn, enjoying their trust — was of decisive importance. The very fact that there is, in Polish life under Marxist control, a powerful institution which has defied this control and has spoken with its own voice — not deformed by censorship — to the nation, in itself has made the Polish situation basically different. As a barrier to a complete conformity of Polish life, the Church has become an authentic spokesman for the aspirations of the nation, a guardian of its own cultural traditions, and a defender of pluralism and human rights.

\* \* \*

In the Poles' thinking about their future the question constantly recurs whether, in the existing circumstances, if Poland should embark upon a course which is not acceptable to the USSR, our country would be exposed to the danger of its intervention.[...]

In our opinion, after Czechoslovakia, the Soviet leaders are not interested in intervening in any socialist country and would do so only as a last resort. This does not mean that when all other methods fail, they would not do it. If the substantial political costs did not stop them from taking this step in Hungary and Czechoslovakia — which from the strategic point of view are more peripheral — then there is little basis for believing that they would hesitate to do the same in the case of Poland, which, after all, is of a greater significance to them. Let us remember that, except for Finland, Poland is the only country with a boundary separated by less then 1,000 kilometers from Moscow. Poland, moreover, lies between the USSR and East Germany, and the Soviet forces which are stationed both there and in Czechoslovakia, so Poland's withdrawal would undermine the entire western Soviet system of defence.[...]

So far, as a guarantee that the Soviet interests in Poland will not be undermined, it has been accepted that Poland must have a political system where — in accordance with the doctrine of the "dictatorship of the proletariat" — power is exercised by the Marxist party, which is trusted by the USSR.[...] This way of thinking in the Soviet leadership, however, is not necessarily unchangeable; like all historical phenomena it has been influenced by the specific circumstances of the time, and it may evolve. The indispensable guarantees expected by the Soviet Union from Finland differ from those expected from Poland. Next to tradition, rational political calculations also determine them. Generally speaking, the chances of evolution depend upon two developments: the progress of détente and cooperation with the West, which would diminish the significance of strategic elements in the Soviet political thinking; and the political program of an increasingly influential Polish society, to the degree to which it could be trusted in the same fashion as the Marxist party is, by the USSR.

We realize that hitherto the views of the Soviet leaders may have been influenced by their conviction that there is no other way to protect the USSR's vital interests in the region. As long as the Polish United Workers' Party and its political allies are regarded as the sole base for the Polish-Soviet alliance, then, any other political views must be perceived as potentially anti-Soviet and threatening to the relations between the two countries, and, indeed perhaps even representing dangers to the internal political system in the USSR itself. And if this situation persists, it is hardly surprising that the Russians look at internal changes in our country with suspicion and reserve.

Is this suspicion toward the Poles well-founded? Knowing the Polish society we are not sure. There are no rational bases for assuming that, had the Polish nation been really able to express its own wishes, and after the emotionalism had subsided, the overwhelming majority of the Poles would have not confirmed as their free choice an alliance and cooperation with the USSR, based on equality and partnership, as a realist policy fitting the true interests of Poland. And this would probably also have meant re-confirmation of some type of a socialist system, although in concrete matters different from this which has existed so far. Such socialism would correspond more closely to the specific Polish conditions and better reflect the Poles' peculiar national mentality by expanding the scope of freedom and pluralism.

The deepening of such views among those segments of the Polish society which demand greater freedom — and especially among those linked with the Church and guided by Christian social and national principles — is of a great significance for the future. It should be a matter of concern for all who would like to see the threshold of Soviet tolerance for democratic changes in Poland raised.

---

[1]Adam Bromke, *Polska 'Weltpolitik'*, (London, 1975), P. 25.

[2]Wojciech Wasiutynski, *Zrodla niepodleglosci* (London, 1977), P. 40.

[3]Roman Dmowski, *Kosciol, Narod i Panstwo* (2nd Ed. Dillingen, 1946). P. 11.

## IX

## THE NON-POLITICAL ELEMENTS OF THE NATION'S FUTURE*

### Jan Szczepanski

[...]The point of departure for all considerations of Poland's future, for understanding the attitudes of the Poles toward their own state, ought to be the historical changes which took place in the 18th century. At that time its ruling class, the *szlachta,* lost their sense of statehood, and the members of its leading segment, the aristocracy, rather than ruling their own state became courtiers of foreign powers. One of the largest states in Europe was not able to resist the small Prussian Kingdom, whose king invaded with impunity the Polish lands and carried conscription there, while the Polish *szlachta* kept sending complaints to him against their own king. Poland, thus, was partitioned without much resistance. Its ultimate calling upon the peasants to defend the country with only their scythes for armaments, eloquently testified to the disintegration of the state.

The fact that the leading classes lost the sense of the role which they should have been playing in the state — that they were unable to modernize it like its neighbors, which resulted in the Polish state's being powerless in conflicts with them; and, moreover, that they would not permit the rise of a middle class which, as in other countries, would have taken over from the *szlachta* and introduced the changes necessary to create a modern nation — "both of these developments

---

*Jan Szczepanski, *Pozapolityczne wyznaczniki przyszlosci narodu* (London, 1979). P. 31.

169

influenced our way of thinking about our state. This lasted for almost a hundred years until the peasants became aware that the Polish state could be their own.

Another fact which affected the Poles' political thinking was the emergence in the 19th century of the concept of the "nation's patriotism", as divorced from the "state's patriotism". Hence, when other nations were developing the strength of their states, the Poles, having no state of their own, focused upon cultural continuity and the national identity, while losing the sense of the state's significance as an element of power determining the nation's future.[...]The nation's patriotism can be helpful to the survival of the nation, but, conceived as an ideology which divorces the nation from the state, is suicidal. A nation without a state does not participate in the international power game, and, therefore, is discounted in it. The history of the "Polish question' in the 19th century serves here as a lesson which the Poles should not ignore.

A great deal of emphasis has been given to the impact which the partitions' period had upon the Polish attitudes toward the state as representing foreign occupiers, and to the transferring of these attitudes toward the Polish state after 1918. Yet, even in the 18th century the attitude that the state was a supreme common good, which prevailed among its neighbors, was missing in Poland. It is interesting to observe how many of these traditions and attitudes from the 18th century were revived after 1918. Hence, perhaps, the desperate, but unsuccessful, efforts of Pilsudski to implant among the Poles the notion of the role of the state as a coordinator of all political and non-political elements determining the nations' future.[...]

* * *

In order to understand the contemporary political thinking of the Poles it is also necessary to take into account the great influence exerted by their attitudes toward the occupying powers in the 19th century. In somewhat oversimplified terms, there prevailed at that time two types of attitudes. The first, above all dominant in Warsaw and the Congress Kingdom, was expressed in tendencies toward uprisings and stirrings in each next generation toward a new struggle. After the uprising of 1863 the Kingdom also went through a period of "organic work" and positivism, but in the 1890s it returned to romanticism.[...]

The other attitude was manifested in the Prussian part of Poland and was characterized by the efforts to attain, under foreign rule, through systematic work carried over generations, economic and cultural superiority over the foreign occupiers. It aimed at developing the Polish economic and cultural potential and seizing every opportunity to undermine the German influence. In these efforts hard work, persistence, determination and every day's toil were of decisive importance. The people espousing this course did not produce soldiers nor insurgents, neither did they attempt to organize armed forces, but rather they educated themselves as good craftsmen and skilled workers who contributed to the Polish strength through their purposeful and efficient work. They demonstrated, however, that they could also fight in an uprising; after all, it was their insurrection [in 1919] — carried out by those very craftsmen devoid of the romantic spark — which was the only victorious Polish upheaval.

It is necessary to remember that this second attitude is being tendentiously pushed out to the margins of the national memory, and Polish patriotism is systematically identified only with the insurrectionist tradition, while the romantic military struggle is presented as the only way to improve the nation's future. It is a vision of a nation deprived of its own state, consisting of martyrs and prisoners of war and taking pride in its emigrés, which takes precedence over that of a nation with a sound economy, prosperous cities and espousing the virtues of hard work. It is necessary to remember that the long struggles which the Poles conducted against Prussia and the German *Reich* were conducted by thrifty peasants, hard working and efficient craftsmen, the *szlachta* who carefully attended to their estates, and the aristocracy which guided the peasants toward economic independence and not insurrections. Why, then, was this type of activity, which has contributed so much to the real strength of the nation and the state, not repeated, at least to some degree, after 1918 or 1945?

In the revival of the Polish state in 1918 there prevailed first of all a reliance upon military power. Of course, it was necessary then to wage prolonged struggles to defend the new state's boundaries. I shall not try to assess their conduct nor objectives. What I am interested in is the question — which I shall also not be able to explore fully here — of what were the elements, and especially the internal ones, upon which the future of the Polish state could rest? Which were the factors which were to serve Poland's objectives, and, above all, could have secured for it a durable place in the post-war Europe beyond the existence of the Versailles system?

I have recently looked over what was written about this problem on the occasion of the sixtieth anniversary of independence[...]as well as my own notes from 1932-39. What struck me in all those materials was, above all, the Poles' passionate animosity, and even hatred, toward all the governments in that period, regardless whether they were led by Daszynski, Witos, Grabski or Pilsudski. At the same time there was an inability to develop a sound economy — free of low efficiency and poor productivity — the failure to overcome poverty and backwardness, resulting in contempt for the Polish economy abroad. Next came the propensity to evolve utopian political programs — such as the one by the Promethean Club which even in 1939 dreamed still of partitioning the Soviet Union — and the ideology of a great power, devoid of any real basis.

In the inter-war period there was a general lack of progress in developing non-political, economic and cultural elements to enhance the nation's work and organizational capabilities. It was as if the leaders from the Prussian provinces, who for decades had followed down-to-earth, but highly successful programs, suddenly disappeared; as if the rise of Polish independence deprived them of the opportunities to continue the good work they had conducted under the German rule.

One can, of course, make similar generalizations defending the opposite viewpoint. Yet, the fact remains that in 1939 Poland found itself isolated, with alliances which were of no help to it, and left alone between its two more powerful neighbors, who, acting in unison, disposed of it with no great effort. The campaign of 1939 was important in the overall context of an emerging anti-Nazi coalition; but it was not sufficient to protect Poland's national interests.[...]

\* \* \*

In 1945 the Polish nation found itself in a different state, under a different political system and within a new alliance structure. The Poles then could debate the wisdom of the decisions at Yalta and Potsdam, and that of the Warsaw uprising — arguing over the intelligence and talents of their political and military leaders; they could also keep shedding tears over the millions of victims and their burnt-down homes; they could try to console themselves with the military glories of Narvik and Monte Cassino and listen with disbelief to the stories of the battle of Lenino and the storming of Berlin. Yet, they also had to answer one basic question: what could they do to make sure that such events would not be repeated in the future? What elements of strength have to be developed to secure for Poland a better future: safety, economic development and cultural progress?

The answer given by the Polish Workers' Party, and then the Polish United Workers' Party, is well know. It espoused the alliance with the USSR, industrialization, educational strides, development of a numerous and skilled working class and strong technical cadres — in short the realization of a vision of socialist People's Poland. This program also stemmed from a conviction that the European order founded at Potsdam is basically a durable one.[...]

In contrast, the emigrés and the various opposition groups at home believed that the system established at Yalta and Potsdam will not survive and that the *Pax Sovietica* in Eastern Europe will collapse. So their program was first to tear Poland away from the Soviet bloc, and then to include it in the political and social system of western capitalism and NATO, reconstructing the Polish economy without central planning and nationalization of the means of production, along the model of a market economy and private property.[...]

After thirty five years of the Potsdam system these questions are still open. The hopes of the emigrés and the opposition at home that the system would collapse did not come true.[...]But the vision of a strong, industrialized, prosperous and efficient Poland also has not been realized. The political system underwent major convulsions in 1956, 1970 and again in 1976. There have been great accomplishments: hundreds of industrial plants have been constructed, cities and towns have been built, and millions of people have received secondary (and over 800,000 higher) education. Yet, the results still fall far short of those anticipated. The system of economic planning and management leaves a great deal to be desired. The quality of the products is low and the efficiency of labor is often not much higher than before the war. In their appearance today's cities and towns still resemble the neglected and dirty ones from the pre-war period. Alcoholism is a social plague. There is a lack of respect for both public and private property. The great efforts at modernization which were launched in the early 1970s have not brought about the desired results and at the same time foreign indebtedness has substantially increased.

* * *

In 1945 the Poles had several possible paths open to them. They could have followed the insurrectionist tradition, continuing the armed resistance and conspiratorial activities and this way tried to pave the way for the change of the Potsdam system.[...]Or they could have accepted the order established in Potsdam, striving to reconstruct their country and to advance their economy, industry, education and culture, thus developing the elements of strength in their state. They could, in fact, undertake such activities even without accepting the existing political reality and — as did the Poles under the Prussian rule — build the non-political elements of their economic, technical and cultural strength.

They could have, disregarding all politics, reconstructed their homes and their workshops and looked after their own well being. Such a road, similar to that in the Prussian provinces, was feasible, although it would have encountered two major obstacles. On the one hand it faced a government which in the planned economy was entrusted with all the macro-decisions; and on the other hand it ran into all the complexes of sorrow and despondency as well as the legacy of a lack of emotional discipline in economic activities expressed in solid work.[...]

[Thus, there spread in Poland the tendency] to justify poor work by patriotism, which often became a mere facade concealing laziness and sloppiness. The growth of alcoholism from year to year was blamed upon the government, the party and the sovietization of Poland — regardless that such arguments made the Poles out to be like children. Similarly poor performance and absenteeism at work were explained by reference to low wages, poor working conditions, poor planning and managerial incompetence.[...]But the poor planning and management was not the work of the devil, but that of Polish ministers, officials, planners and managers.

There developed a peculiar ideology: "the worse the better" — like the proverbial: "I shall punish my mother by freezing my ears"! — the conviction that poor work efficiency, drinking vodka on the job, corruption, etc., are activities beneficial to Poland and somehow detrimental to the "Soviets". In reality, however, they are harmful to Poland for they inhibit the economic progress of both the state and the nation living in it.[...]

Why did this happen? Why in developing their industry and gaining better professional qualifications did the Poles fail to perceive the obvious truth that this way they were also promoting a better place for themselves in the world, now and in the future? Various elements contributed: animosity toward the existing political system and the USSR, poor organization of the economy and its overcentralization restricting individual initiative and goodwill, the lack of confidence in the durability of the system, and the lack of confidence that it is possible to achieve good results under such a system. There is also the persistent propaganda that the system is soon going to collapse, and that it is a patriotic duty to contribute to this by poor work, as well as the systematic persuasion by the Cold War centres that whatever happens under Communism is useless and cannot be compared to the progress under democracy and capitalism.[...]

So, the cult of hard and persistent work from the Prussian provinces of Poland has not been carried into People's Poland. The opposition has become far more attracted to utopian political programs counting upon some good fortune preordained by Providence, rather than subscribing to a vision of good work carried through generations and developing the non-political elements of the nation's strength.

* * *

The elements of political as well as non-political strength are always developed by a nation organized in a state, and all its members regardless of their position participate in it. In the final analysis, if in a given state there is a bad government, even if it is unelected, it still reflects the nation. There are many examples of dictatorial regimes in different states which were not elected by the nation, yet led it along the road of progress. We even know of such examples in some socialist states, where the rulers were literally "brought in in the tanks", but who nonetheless have ruled wisely and have gained the respect of the people. Why then in Poland since the 18th century has the nation not selected a "good" government?[...]

Let's look at historical facts. In the 18th century the aristocratic government led the country into the partitions. Parliamentary democracy in 1918-26 ended in a military coup. The colonels' regime ended in a war defeat. The Stalinist rule culminated in the revolt of the Poznan workers in 1956, and the post-October ruling elite was overthrown by the workers' rebellion on the Coast in 1970. And the subsequent government by technocrats has produced the economic crisis and deep-seated political ferment. A coincidence? For 279 years, since the beginning of the Northern War, Poland has not been capable of selecting a competent government, and has not been able to create non-political elements of power which could effectively safeguard its national interests.

In the last instance the government is always a part of the nation; in the same fashion as the several tens of thousands of party members, administration and local government officials are a part of the Polish nation. They have been brought up in Poland and have been educated in Polish schools. They govern the best way they can, but their way of governing reflects the way they have been socialized in their families and at their schools. In other words they are the product of a specific Polish political culture. I am not saying this in order to accuse anyone, but merely to offer a sociological hypothesis to explain the amazing consistency in Polish politics ever since the beginning of the 18th century.

In the 18th century the Polish *szlachta* and aristocracy did not understand what the conditions are which a state must meet in order to remain strong and independent. They also did not perceive that after dropping out of the international political game as a viable partner, one can rejoin only by re-building the basic elements of strength. Whether this can be accomplished depends upon all members of the nation regardless whether they are the rulers or the ruled. Poland cannot count upon the rise of a miraculous government, for in the last sixty years it has tried several, always ending in failure.

And what can the nation do about it? Should it cultivate only the virtues of survival, existing on the fringes or in the underground, or should it rather try to mould the government, so it would be composed of competent and knowledgeable politicians able to advance the state's strength in a rational way? The most urgent task ahead of the Polish nation, I believe, is to create such a mechanism of selecting the rulers so that they do not come to power just by a process of counter-selection.[...]

The Northern War already revealed the weakness of the Poles in determining their fate. This weakness persists to this day. In my opinion, then, the Poles should not engage in futile discussions, but rather should get down to systematic development of the non-political elements of their strength which would safeguard their future.[...]For the political significance of any nation is in direct proportion to its ability to develop material resources. Only that nation which demonstrates this ability in material production, in technical and scientific skills, in creativity in arts and thought, and in morality, and uses them in the steadfast defence of its rights, can calmly look toward the future.

I should be only too pleased if my pessimistic assessment of the past and the present conditions of the Polish nation, as well as of its prospects of securing for itself a better future, were to be proven wrong.

Warsaw 1979.

## X

## A COMMENTARY ON THE SITUATION*

### Stanislaw Stomma

I should like to confine these remarks — in effect a commentary on the existing situation, to a few selected observations. There is no need to reiterate the well-known and widely accepted facts, but rather what is needed is to focus on those aspects of the Polish crisis to which little attention is being paid or which are even completely ignored.

I shall concentrate especially upon the objective character of the historical conditions and processes, but I should like to emphasize that this does not mean ignoring those elements inherent in the emotional layers of the national consciousness. These also are factors contributing to reality. The dynamics of emotion, anger, despair and hope cannot be replaced by just disembodied reason. These elements of reality must not be forgotten in searching for a Polish *raison d'état*. In evaluating the events in the "Polish crisis" from August 1980 to December 1981, they must also be kept constantly in mind.

\* \* \*

I should like to start by observing that at the time when the struggle to change the political system in Poland took place — from August 1980 to December 1981 — the political situation was in many respects especially favorable for us. The tragedy is that the great and *real*

---

*"Komentarz do sytuacji", an address delivered to the Primate's Advisory Council in April, 1981. Mimeographed. Italics by the author.

opportunities existing at that time, which could have been exploited, were wasted. I repeat, the *real* opportunities.

These opportunities stemmed from the following favorable circumstances:

i/ The international Communist movement faced, and, in fact, is still facing, a difficult situation;

ii/ The Polish Communist party, i.e. The Polish United Workers' Party, was put on the defensive and has largely disintegrated;

iii/ The workers' movement born in the shipyards in August 1980 displayed an impressive moral stance and political wisdom because it combined *dignity* and *prudence*. Boldness and determination went hand in hand with realist moderation. These were surprising and admirable phenomena, largely unprecedented in Polish history. Precisely because the situation was so novel it appeared that this time the "Polish revolution" would succeed.

But here we come to the objective limits of the changes. Because of the difficulties with which it was faced our "protector" was agreeable to expanding the limits of Polish sovereignty, as it did in 1956. Let's not forget that at that time we accomplished a lot. We widened our sovereignty by removing our ministries from direct subordination to those in the Soviet Union - since then the directives have been sent exclusively to the top party authorities. The composition of the army was transformed. Compulsorily introduced collective farms were disbanded. Victims of political persecution were rehabilitated. Many deportees returned home from the USSR. The Primate resumed his office. Relations with the Church improved.

In 1980 the "protector" could have accepted new changes, but only up to a certain point and within certain limits. To be precise, the reforms had to stay *within the limits of the existing political system.* It was the "socialist system" thus which determined those limits. But the term "socialist system" is quite vague. What did it exactly mean during the Polish upheaval in 1980-81?

The limits of the system became blurred. The economic crisis, bordering on catastrophe, in itself was propelling far-reaching changes. By necessity some elements of the free market economy had appeared in the so-called socialist states. We could observe this happening in the GDR as well as in Hungary. In Poland this process could have gone further, for Poland has traditionally enjoyed greater autonomy.

The monopoly of power by the Communist party also became unclear. The party, which in accordance with the Constitution is supposed to be the leading power, was in fact losing control over the state. It was precisely for this reason that the army had to step in.

Thus, what was meant, in the concrete conditions in 1980-81, by "the limits of the system"? I believe that the definition had two elements. First, loyal participation in the socialist camp, which in practice meant that *power in Poland had to belong to a political party which enjoys the confidence of the Soviet government.* Second, restricting of the economic and political changes within such limits, that the new situation could still *be characterized as a "socialist" one.* One can say, thus, that the limits were semantic. That it was necessary only to remain within the limits of a broadly "socialist" terminology. These were quite broad limits, but they also determined finite boundaries.

Such were the historical realities which posed the barrier to progress. One had to understand this and act accordingly.

So the workers' movement Solidarity from the outset was faced with a dilemma: either it had to restrict its program within the limits of the system as characterized above, or it had to press on, trying to overcome the inherent barriers. One could say that the Solidarity leadership did not make a conscious choice here, but rather, the movement spontaneously embraced an uncompromising struggle for sovereignty.

The national current which Solidarity represented had great potential and strength. Used internally this strength could have accomplished a great deal, but it had to be firmly directed by what, in turn, required conscious leadership and great discipline. At first it appeared that this was exactly what was happening. This was an opportunity bordering on the miraculous.

One could use the following metaphor: the awakened Polish workers' movement, channelled properly, could have driven the turbine of national development. Unfortunately, it was not so channelled, but instead stormed the existing dams, trying to sweep them away. It was for this reason that we have suffered yet another national defeat.

* * *

It is already possible to look at Solidarity from a historical perspective. One can see that Solidarity's defeat does not detract from its historical significance. The movement has been a challenge to the entire world and will continue to serve as a source of inspiration to the different people in Europe and outside.

Such words are moving. We find in them the echo of our old upheavals — reminiscences of our messianism: the sacrificing of ourselves in the name of great universal values.[...]

The universal consequences of the Polish events are natural and inevitable. But what universal effects should we like to bring about? What does the world expect from us, and what can we offer? Messianism is a serious and a profound idea. But what does it mean?[...]

Polish messianistic suffering is not needed at present. On the contrary it can only produce international complications. It could be an element in the international political game, but only briefly.

It is popular nowadays to strive for a lasting peace and a secure and stable life. Hence the great mass appeal of the idea of East-West détente. One can dismiss it with contempt as mere dreaming by consumer societies egoistically concerned with just themselves. Yet, in the final analysis, well-being and peace are legitimate strivings for all of mankind. And the opinions of the people who have managed to attain these conditions should not be lightly dismissed.

Poland as a source of potential conflict enjoys a very specific popularity, often mixed with pity (to observe this today, it suffices to read the West German press). Of course, honest and sensitive people will always be on our side. But these are merely voices of protest, and are countered by those coming from the opposite side. A Poland defeated and suffering offers no inspiration to the world. Messianism in its defeatist and suffering form has no political value — it carries with it no promise for the future, but simply marks a closed chapter.

Our real success should have been entirely different: the implementation in Poland of peaceful reforms which would have contributed to the humanization of socialism and brought it closer to Europe. *These were the reasons for our popularity.* The proof of this was in the admiration for Walesa and Solidarity, which were viewed as the harbingers of an *evolutionary,* and I stress, *evolutionary,* transformation of socialism. The attainment of such a goal required *a strategy of small steps.* The small steps could have led to a great success. The revolutionary movement has eliminated those hopes.

Let us remember one very important fact which, unfortunately, we often tend to ignore. Cardinal-Primate Wyszynski was a very real candidate for the Nobel Prize. He was supported by many groups abroad. And this would have been a prize, not for suffering, but, on the contrary, for his great success in the difficult task of promoting peaceful coexistence among the people belonging to the different camps. It was to be a reward for his attaining true freedom for the

Catholic Church in a Communist state and advancing the state's gradual evolution toward humanism and pluralism. Along the same lines, and stemming from the same motives, there were rumors of a possible Nobel Prize for Lech Walesa.

Let us underline one more fact of great importance. The choice of a Polish Pope was received with great enthusiasm for it affirmed mankind's hope for peace. For the same reason John Paul II's pilgrimage to his native land — a Catholic country, yet *ruled by Communists,* produced such a great response. It was received almost as a sensation, and one inspiring hope and optimism.[...]

\* \* \*

The political thinking of the Poles! What a truly tragic problem!

A problem deeply tragic because a nation deprived of its sovereignty, fighting for its freedom and condemned to repressions like those we are undergoing today, is not able to think objectively, and instead is repeatedly driven to protest. In such circumstances emotional and spontaneous reactions are natural for they are simply defensive reactions. One can understand and justify this; yet, it is *no excuse for a lack of rational political thinking.* No such excuse can exist. Each departure from political rationality sooner or later rebounds, and with a vengeance.

It the period between August 1980 and December 13, 1981 it was said that we were passing through a revolution; that it was an avalanche which could not be stopped until it had run its course. So the attempts to counter extremism were infrequent and ineffective.

Could it have been otherwise? I do not know whether this current could have been steered, but it was necessary to try. For one ought not to accept fatalism. Compare the attitude displayed in the shipyards in August 1980 with that at the Solidarity Congress in the autumn of 1981. The differences were great, in fact diametrical. The developments could have gone either way: but the difference in outcomes between the shipyards in 1980 and the Congress in 1981 was fundamental - it was the difference between success and defeat.

\* \* \*

On December 13 a historical period began — a new chapter in the Polish drama. And, once again, we see how spontaneity spreads and a new Polish fatalism is bred.

The government's turning to coercion has deeply offended the society. A new wave of enmity is rising — one can see with the naked eye how it mounts. And despite the success of the military operation on December 13 the situation remains uncertain. The government feels insecure and we hear threats of more repression. And this would only lead toward more enmity. Where are we heading?

Our postulates toward the government are open and clearly formulated: we demand the end to repression and the lifting of martial law.

On the political scene the society has remained the main actor. Fortunately, it cannot either be paralyzed or put to sleep. *Despite all the appearances to the contrary it is the nation, and not the government, which is strong.* So the role of the main actor on the national scene still remains open. For the time being it is deprived of initiative, but in the long run it is the society which is going to be of decisive importance. It is for this reason that influencing public opinion is so crucial. It is important that at least the leading intellectual circles evolve some rational political program.

For the time being public opinion has no program and its mood is characterized by mere negation, more and more mixed with hatred. An intensifying of this situation will only lead toward a new, tragic confrontation. The possibilities of staging such a confrontation have diminished, but they have not disappeared.

It is even more important, then, to evolve a new realistic program to find a way out of the existing crisis. After the December 13 confrontation this is not an easy task, for on the government side the success of that operation has strengthened those who would like to suppress national aspirations altogether, and on the side of the Polish society it has produced emotional complexes and blind negation. It is extremely urgent, then, to counter these postures with convincing, realistic and constructive solutions.

And in doing so one has to accept *a priori* certain general and overriding principles.

Only an internal compromise represents a constructive solution.

A spontaneous and uncontrolled wave of enmity would only lead towards new upheavals and misfortunes. It would be a tragic illusion to count upon an overthrowing of the existing system and to try to get rid of dependence. Similarly, the roots of a tragedy could lie in the calculations, still active among the rulers, that they will succeed in suppressing social resistance and introduce in Poland the calm of a cemetery. Reason dictates that the only solution for both sides is a compromise. At least in the next few years.

Hence an appeal to the Polish political thought to profoundly examine and to urgently search for practical solutions. The difficulties are great and disillusionments are inevitable. Yet, one cannot be deterred, but must continue to search, to propose, and to fight. For attaining peace in Poland is a categorical imperative.

# XI

# THE INTELLIGENTSIA, SOLIDARITY, THE GOVERNMENT*

## Andrzej Walicki

The reader of the following remarks ought to accept as a point of departure that while the existing system in Poland is bad, and perhaps even terrible, yet it could either improve or worsen, and, thus, is not an absolute evil in all aspects. For to reject this assumption is to imply that within the limits of the present system the Poles have nothing to gain or to lose, and that the only alternative open to them is to try to overthrow it.[...]

We have a state, but it is not sovereign. We do not even have purely internal sovereignty, such as exists in Finland. What are the consequences of this?

We can emphasize, that after all, it is a state, so it is more than just an autonomous region. We are recognized as a state in the international sphere, and this is important too.[...] Emmerich de Vattel has pointed out that the law of nations includes the "vassal states" bound by unequal alliances, but not the nations which have no state.

Or we can stress that, despite having the formal attributes of a state, in fact, we have no internal autonomy for we cannot decide for ourselves even our internal affairs. This is also true. On the one hand we have more than an autonomous region, but on the other hand we do not fully have even internal autonomy.[...]

---

*Andrzej Walicki, "inteligencja, Solidarnosc, wladza", *Aneks*, 35/1984 pp. 82-104. Italics by the author.

We can adopt the following line of reasoning: its non-sovereign status makes the state not ours and the Polish government is just a tool of a foreign power, so we should observe the same rules and modes of conduct as in the times when Poland did not exist. Or we can draw an opposite conclusion: the government is not sovereign, so it is not responsible for things which are beyond its control. It is a dependent government, but we have no proof that within its limits it is not willing to act on our behalf; and, moreover, despite that it is non-sovereign, it still has considerable autonomy which it can use even better as it grows stronger and broadens its popular support.

The first line of reasoning leads to the conclusion that cooperation with the government is just "collaboration". The second, in contrast, points to the fact that while one cannot expect the Polish government to do things which are impossible, nevertheless its alienation from the society is advantageous for neither side.[...]

The autonomy of the Polish *society* is restricted, but the autonomy of the *government* — supported by the attributes of the state — as far as the conditions of "real socialism" permit, is substantial. It is owing to this situation that we have enjoyed all the Polish "specificities", such as the existence of a politically powerful Church, the non-collectivized agriculture, and the quite considerable — at times almost amazing in comparison with the other countries of "real socialism" — freedom in education and culture.

It follows that the political autonomy (though not a political sovereignty), constitutes an umbrella, a sort of shield, which can be used to protect the small, restricted and essentially non-political, yet nevertheless quite tangible, specificity of our society. The recognition by the USSR of the autonomy of our party-government, could become the vehicle to expand the autonomy of the society. Yet, this can be true only when the government derives some benefits from such a development too. Expanded social autonomy, then, by widening the bases of the governments social support, should strengthen and not weaken it; and economic successes in particular, by enhancing its prestige, should improve its position vis-a-vis its Soviet master.

* * *

The ideal model of rational conduct, thus, ought to be an optimum widening of the autonomy of the government, in order to expand the autonomy of the society. This would involve: 1/ the government's understanding of the social and national aspirations, and, within the limits of *courageous* political realism, trying to advance them; and 2/ optimum social support for such a government, while at the same time watching over it, so that the narrow interests of its members (which exist in any system) will not get the better of them.[...]

One way or another the enlightened, strong and socially acceptable party leadership in Poland has proved to be a chimera. It has been necessary, thus, for the social elites to assume the initiative. Such an activity, however, could have been conducted in two different ways:

1/ Pressure could have been exerted upon the government to manipulate it and to secure the selection of better leaders; without, however, antagonizing and compromising it, for a weak government would inevitably fall prey to the opposite pressures from the USSR and from the hardliners in its own ranks.

The objectives of such a tactic should have been: a/ to secure the victory of the rational pragmatists over the hardliners in the political leadership; and b/ to exclude some spheres of life (the cultural activities, the social associations, non-political trade unions, and, partially, even some economic undertakings) from political supervision, and this way to secure their autonomy. In other words, the goal should have been to replace the *centralized* power with one which would be enlightened, responsive to social pressures, and *limited* in its scope by the exclusion from its authority of some spheres of social life.

A pre-condition for such a tactic would have been an effective mobilization of social life, without, however, its polarization, and without isolating the government by cutting the "transmission lines" through which the extra-systemic opposition (and also the West) could mobilize the intra-systemic opposition. And this, in turn, could have helped the various advocates of "organic work" in the party, as well as strengthened the position of the "liberals" versus the hardliners in its ranks. Supported by moderate, and non-provocative strikes, such a development could have created a situation where both the hardliners in the Polish party, and their Soviet protectors, would have had no choice but to accept a compromise.

2/ The other way that the social elites could have acted was to stage a political confrontation: to polarize the society and to antagonize the government. It would not be a struggle for a victory of the most sensible people in the party elite, making them largely dependent upon non-party backing, but a struggle for direct participation in the government: a "participatory-autonomy" rather than a "freedom-autonomy". True, there would have been no direct attempt to take over power, but there would have been attempts at participating in it: mere influence over the ruling elite, restricting its scope of power, would not be enough.[...]

It was this way which was followed in practice, with the following results:

- Resorting to naked force has deprived the government of all chances of legitimization and social support, and has made it more dependent upon the hardliners and their foreign protectors.
- The society has sank into apathy, or what Janusz Reykowski has called "a state of destructive conflict", making it impossible to overcome the dramatic economic crisis.
- The West has lost the opportunity to influence Polish events in a constructive fashion. The economic sanctions have hurt the population, but they have failed to win any concessions from the government of People's Poland.
- "The transmission lines" have been cut and the influence of the moderates has been reduced. They have abandoned their mediating roles: some joining the government and some the opposition, while still others, after some symbolic protests, have simply withdrawn from politics.
- Isolation of the government has been effectively accomplished, but this also means that society's influence over it has been reduced; for by definition such influence can only be exerted when the government is *not* isolated.
- Furthermore, the recent experiences for many years to come will make the government unresponsive to social pressures.[...] For it cannot be denied that no Communist government ever offered more concessions than the Polish one in 1980-81 (ranging from the recognition of the free trade unions, and to some extent even their political role, to the conducting of elections at the party Congress by secret ballot); but even all these steps did not avert the declaration of war against it by virtually all of politically active Polish society.[...]
- The need for ideological rationalization of its conduct has made the party immune from social influence. Many people in the government have adopted an attitude similar to that of Aleksander Wielopolski, who declared that: "one can do something for the Poles, but never with the Poles". This deeply damaging slogan, moreover, offers the possibility of presenting martial law as a heroic act aimed at containing the stupidity of the Poles, and even at defending from them the peace in Europe!

In short, for quite some time to come now the opportunities to realize the "manipulative" alternative of the social opposition, have been wasted.

And the possibilities for such an alternative were quite real. Many different people deliberately followed the principle that, since the system cannot be overthrown, it should be at least "humanized", "democratized", adjusted to the social traditions and aspirations; in other words, that the opportunities for positive developments inherent in it should be optimally pursued. It was to be a struggle for victory over the system by co-opting it to the society.

The determined opponents of the system are right in reminding us that such a development would carry a price tag, for it would have meant an accommodation of the society to the system, and, therefore, its greater legitimization. This is true, but considering that there was no alternative, that was a price worth paying. And, anyway, even in the conditions of optimum social influence, had there arisen an opportunity to repudiate the system, we would have done so. And, last but not least, if within the limits of the existing system we would have achieved a higher level of culture, greater economic efficiency, stronger social discipline, better education and historical knowledge, etc., then we would certainly have been better equipped to change the system, than we are in the conditions of the deteriorating quality of work, universal demoralization, the growing (at least in relative terms) backwardness, and the general national frustration.

* * *

I am well aware of the fact that the mass movement developed spontaneously, and that in general it is useless to argue rationally with revolutionized masses. I am also conscious of the great values which were inherent in this movement and the great opportunities which it offered. The mobilization of such vast masses of the workers made a profound impression upon the political elite and the party members at large. It both frightened them and appealed to their consciences (at least in the case of those who have consciences, and it would be demagogic to claim that all the party members are devoid of one). It was, then, a unique combination of physical pressure through the strikes, and appeals to the myths of the proletariat as well as to national solidarity, both of which had been so strongly emphasized during the Gierek period.

Establishment of the free trade unions was an unprecedented accomplishment in a country of "real socialism" and it was imperative to do whatever could have been done, to make them a permanent feature of the system. Instead, everything possible was done to transform the trade unions into a battering ram to destroy the political system.[...]

I shall not try to analyze the entire tactics of Solidarity; there were many different currents in it, and to describe them all would require a book. So I shall limit myself here to pointing out three episodes in its history:

1/ Developing Solidarity's organization along geographical lines. [...] The adoption of such a structure made it inevitable that the specific, professional interests would become subordinate to the overall objectives, and that it would become the battering-ram in the political struggle; and, moreover, it was obvious that once such a struggle was launched it would be unstoppable.

2/ The Bydgoszcz incident in March 1981. The film showing Solidarity leader Jan Rulewski talking with the militia officer has clearly revealed the demogogic nature of Rulewski's position. Had he wanted to, he could have left the room with dignity, and he *should* have been aware of the dangers inherent in his refusing to do so.[...] The Solidarity leaders in Bydgoszcz went beyond the terms of the existing agreements and Solidarity's own by-laws. One, then, should not claim that it was only the government which did not respect the agreements and that it was not provoked. It was imperative to avoid provocations and, unfortunately, in Bydgoszcz the provocations were not just confined to the beating of the Solidarity activists by the militiamen.[...]

3/ The resolutions adopted and the statements made at the Solidarity meetings in Radom and Gdansk at the end of 1981. The proposals for a referendum to express confidence in the government and for free elections, and Solidarity's offer of guarantees to the Soviet Union (which from the USSR's point of view was both ridiculous and provocative), and, finally the announcement of a general strike on December 17. The implementation of all these plans would have posed a real threat to the government. Why, then, it was thought that the government would not defend itself? To really believe that "no Pole would turn against fellow Poles", would have had to be a curious mixture of revolutionary fervor and incredible political innocence.

It seems to me that such maximalism combined with such naiveté would have been impossible had it not been for some theories put forward by Solidarity advisors from the intelligentsia. We had here a situation where the intelligentsia saw confirmation of their wishful thinking in the workers, and the workers saw theirs in the intelligentsia. On the one hand there was the conviction that "we are invincible because the masses are on our side"; and on the other hand there was the belief that "we can proceed boldly for wise men are with us". How tragic this momentary super-optimism has proved to be!

\* \* \*

The intelligentsia advanced three theories encouraging Solidarity to move forward along the road of "peaceful revolution", which amounted, despite all its façade of a peaceful dialogue, to the road of political confrontation.[...]
1/ The theory of evolutionary changes, which, however, were to be brought about through political confrontations. In contrast to the old "revisionism", this theory propounded that there are no forces inside the Communist party which deserve more support than the others, and, thus, that there is no sense in trying to establish cooperation between the moderate wing of the party and the outside opposition. For, it was claimed, the party elite is entirely uniform and concessions can only be "forced" from it by outside pressure. There are several errors inherent in this theory:

- The erroneous analogy with the situation in the international sphere. It is possible to argue that in international politics pressure upon the USSR is more effective than are the efforts at reconciliation with it (détente). But it does not follow that the opposition in Poland can "force" concessions from the Communist government in the same fashion that the United States can win concessions from the Soviet Union. For the United States has at its disposal military force, while the Polish opposition has no such means with which it could back up its demands.[...]
- One who has no physical power should try to manipulate and not to "force" his opponent. In the early 1980s the Polish opposition had at its disposal a powerful means of pressure, namely, the strikes. Yet, it was necessary to decide whether the strikes would be the means toward an evolution or a destruction of the system, and if it was the former, then they should have been accompanied by efforts to manipulate the adversary.[...]
- The most powerful element of manipulation should have been to try to split the adversary by constantly emphasizing that the struggle was not aimed against the party and the government, but only against the hardliners in its ranks. Yet, the theory proclaimed that among the ruling elite there are no differences. As such it contributed to the general conviction that "there is no sense in talking

with the Reds'', and that there is no chance to improve the system. It did not address, however, the key question: how can one get rid of the Reds and the system?

- The instrument of ''forcing'' the changes apparently was to be the mobilization of the society to show who commands the majority. Yet, what was not taken into account was the fact that the ''majority'' argument could be used only where there is agreement that the minority must abide by the will of the majority. But, as is well known, the Communists do not subscribe to this principle. And, as is also known, even if the Communists in Poland would have liked to subscribe to this principle, they would not have been permitted to do so by our neighbors; and if they had done so they would have been in effect signing their own death warrants.[...]

- This does not mean that the Communist party did not want to widen its social basis and to have its rule legitimized by both the workers and the nation. This desire opened up great opportunities for political manipulation: possibilities of partial and gradual ''legitimization'', the offering of conditional support, etc. But the theory which proclaimed the entire party to be an enemy from whom no meaningful concessions could be expected, stood in the way of such efforts. It overlooked, and even negated, the opportunity to try to exert *moral* pressure upon the party — for you cannot exert moral suasion on someone whom you regard as immoral in the first place.

- And, finally, there was a major psychological error inherent in this theory, for it is necessary to allow your adversary (especially if he is still powerful) to retreat with grace. A confrontationist style of winning concessions, and emphasizing that all of them are ''forced'' (even when this is true), humiliates the other side and makes it close ranks and seek revenge.

2/ The theory of the ''self-governing Republic'' which posited retention by the Party of control over all the crucial defence and economic matters, thus assuring protection of the basic Soviet interests and deflecting the accusation of an attempt to take over the government. [...] It was tactically a clever theory for mobilizing and directing the masses. For it enabled its proponents to refute the charges that they wanted to take over the government, while at the same time it led to a politicizing of the conflicts with a view to subverting the government ''from below''. True, it was not a frontal assault on the government in the Leninist sense, but nevertheless it was an attack against the central authority because it was aimed at the very foundations of the system, which rests upon the principle of government "from above". It stemmed from recognition of the fact that victory in battle against the main forces of the adversary was not attainable, and, instead, it proposed the dispersal of its own forces so they could wage successful guerilla warfare.

To support this theory its proponents invoked the concepts of Edward Abramowski [a socialist thinker of the early 20th century] who proclaimed a program of organizing social forces outside the state. But Abramowski lived at a time when the economy was not centralized and nationalized, so his idea oi a "cooperative Republic" was less utopian than that of a contemporary "self-governing Republic". It is rather embarassing to note that without a major economic decentralization — which would have transformed the entire system anyway — there is at present no possibility of organizing social forces outside the state.[...]

It seems to me, thus, that the advocates of this theory really treated it as just an instrument in the political struggle. On the one hand they did not want to go to the barricades, and on the other hand they did not want to pacify the public, so what they strove for was an inter-mediate course, namely, the maintenance of the mobilization of the masses and the using of them to gradually erode the government "from below". In the fall of 1981 they openly admitted that the "self-govern-ing reform" would not salvage the economy, but *on the contrary* (sic!), through striking at the managerial class, it would pave the way toward a political struggle, and, thus, a "gradual Finlandization" of Poland.

The basic error in this theory, as it turned out, was overestimation of the stupidity of the enemy and underestimation of its determina-tion and capability for self-defence.

3/ The third theory was that of "self-limiting revolution". It admitted that the process of "renewal" was, in effect, a revolution, but it was supposed to be a self-limiting revolution, and, as such, it conformed with the tenets of political realism.[...]

The circumstances in which this theory came into being were typically Polish. The moderates, who should have done anything they could to prevent the revolution, responding to moral pressure, joined it, then tried to do whatever they could to prevent the revolution from being too revolutionary (forgetting Adam Mickiewicz's warning that "in a revolution you must act like a revolutionary"). So the radicals at first frustrated the plans of the moderates, and then the moderates became a hindrance to the revolution which they joined. It was an exact repetition of what already happened in 1863! Why cannot we learn from our history?[...]

There were people who had no illusions, who had expected the tragic ending, and yet still joined the movement.[...] Many intellectuals, including some most prominent ones, acted in this way because of the alleged moral imperative. I respect this moral posture, but I cannot accept it as a substitute for a political action. For politics is "the art of the possible": its objective is to achieve concrete results, and it is not a stage where one merely displays moral postures. The only exception would be in the case of some great symbolic gesture which would influence the views and aspirations of the next generation. But, then, one should carefully consider the price which the generation living *today*, and wanting to live better tomorrow, would have to pay to make it.

* * *

I believe that what I have said so far reflects more or less accurately the views of substantial segments of the Polish intelligentsia. Only our notorious lack of civil courage prevented these views from being articulated more boldly in 1980-81.[...]

What I want to say now is less popular. The dominant political stance of the Polish intelligentsia fits into the democratic-socialist tradition, while I am closer to the ideals and values of classical liberalism, which — despite all the claims to the contrary — is little known in Poland, and is wrongly identified there with just political democracy. To put it in another way, the democratic ethos, like ethos of socialism and patriotism (or nationalism) — if it is not *restricted* by the liberal concept of the individual's rights — is a collectivist one; while the ethos of liberalism is decidedly anti-collectivist.

A widely accepted view is that Solidarity was a powerful movement for a national liberation; many writers see it, in fact, as a continuation of the old romantic struggles for independence within the context of a persistent Polish "national question". It seems to me that this is only a part of the problem. The patriotic phraseology (at times smacking of just the "God and the Homeland" slogan), was mainly a tactic to employ against the adversary.[...]

Solidarity had many beautiful and admirable features, especially in its early stages when it was a genuine movement of the workers' elite. Once it became transformed into a mass movement, however, it became more representative of the average social mentality shaped by "real socialism". I shall try to demonstrate what I mean by this.

1) Socialism implies a faith in the magic power of political decisions. The government produces, and provides for all of us — in effect it can do anything. If this is so, then, let's press the government to look after us still better. This attitude, unfortunately, was typical for the majority of the Poles.

Solidarity *in theory* supported the market mechanism [...], but in practice did not attempt to distinguish between economics and politics with a view to restricting the omnipotence of politics. On the contrary, there were constant demands to determine prices through political decisions.

2) There was also no effort to oppose sovietization in the work culture. If sovietization means the right not to strain oneself, equality conceived as reducing everyone to the lowest common denominator, as inefficiency, sloppiness, or even theft — then, unfortunately, in these efforts our nation has caught up with the Russians. Indeed, in some respects we have even surpassed them, for in Poland there has been less fear and a more permissive attitude on the part of the government. Almost African corruption has not been confined to the ruling elite — everyone given the opportunity has voluntarily participated.[...]

The responsibility for this situation is attributed to the system and the government. Yet, for quite some time now the system has not been just something external, the society has been an integral part of it, succumbing, and quite willingly, to its various temptations. And, furthermore, if the system absolves us, then we also have to absolve the system, for, after all, a systemic determinism affects first of all the rulers.

I would not have taken this subject up had Solidarity not presented itself as a movement of "moral renewal". No doubt, there were such elements in its program too.[...] Yet, if criticism is to serve the "moral renewal", then one should begin it with oneself. Personally, I believe that Solidarity's moralizing contained too little self-criticism, and too much self-adulation and self-gratifying national flattery.

3) Solidarity's ethos was one of anti-individualism and anti-liberalism, which also stemmed from "real socialism". Solidarity's program include ' a demand to establish an "acceptable social minimum". This amounted to a governmental right to take away from the individual anything that would exceed the "acceptable minimum", regardless of whether the accumulated wealth was legally acquired or not.[...] This most far-reaching of Solidarity's social demands clearly reflects the characteristic thinking of the compulsory-distributive system, in other words, "real socialism".

Thus, if socialism, i.e. "real socialism", means:
- egalitarianism and collectivism;
- acceptance of a priority of politics over economics, ignoring the market laws, believing that the political authority can and should regulate the entire social life;
- faith in *unlimited* authority which is dangerous even if it expresses the will of the majority;
- subordination of private to public law and turning the latter into an instrument of social policy;

then, Solidarity must be seen as a *socialist* mass movement that aimed to participate in the government, perhaps even taking it over, but not restricting it in the name of individual liberty. It was striving not to separate economics and politics, but just to democratize political control over the economy.

As such, Solidarity was a democratic, but not a liberal movement. It was opposed to authoritarian, bureaucratic collectivism, not in the name of individualism, but in the name of democratic collectivism of the masses. It strove to divide and to decentralize political authority, but it was not sufficiently aware of the need to *limit* all political authority, including the democratic one. In this sense — despite its verbal condemnation of all brands of totalitarian systems — the Solidarity leaders, not to mention its broad membership, were contaminated by socialist totalitarianism.

I also planned to review here the current political consciousness of the Polish intelligentsia, but this essay has already grown too long, and, in any case, my views on this subject are implicit in what I have already said. My major reservations about it concern its auto-heroism, anti-intellectualism and persistent wishful thinking, and, above all, its hiding behind the national taboos: which lead to intolerance of all opposing views, and moral condemnation of all who do not share the widely accepted — the herd-like emotions and opinions.

Over a decade ago "heroism" was widely ridiculed, and, indeed, not to reject this view — since it was propounded by the "partisans' " faction in the Communist party — was regarded as suspicious. Yet today no one would dare ridicule Solidarity: the national flags marking each strike, the picture of the Virgin Mary in one's lapel, or even the clamor at its Congress when the news arrived about the cigarette price increases! If even serious criticism is inadmissible, how could one dare to revert to satire?[...]

The major positive aspect of our renewal has been that it has offered us valuable experience. Not a legend for future generations, but actual national *experience* which should help us next time to act more effectively and more wisely (and in this respect the Communists have much to learn too). Yet, a pre-condition for profiting from this experience is its critical evaluation. It must not be wasted in just the erection of new national altars and the founding of new romantic legends.[...]

# XII

# POLAND: AN ENDANGERED SOCIETY*

## Aleksander Gella

The Polish Society is now threatened in three ways:
1. There is a political and economic threat that may lead to an interruption of the Polish statehood;
2. There is a social threat which may lead to a gradual transformation of the Polish nation into just an ethnic community.
3. There is an ecological threat that may lead to a deterioration of the environment and of the health of the Polish nation.

Although this paper specifically addresses these dangers to the Polish society, I should like to review first the threat to the Polish statehood. For it would be totally irresponsible to separate the progress of the nation from the existence of the statehood.

We did survive over a hundred years of partitions, yet let us remember that the price which we paid for this was extremely high. Our influence in the east and the west was curtailed. Our participation in international scientific and cultural progress diminished. And almost every generation suffered a great loss of life.

The Poles went to believe that Europe needs us and that, in fact, we are its heart.[1] Yet, let us remember that Europe flourished when its heart was dismembered — when Poland's aspirations toward unification and independence were brutally suppressed.

---

*Excerpts from a paper presented at the Congress of Polish Culture held in London September 14-20, 1985.

199

During the years that the Marxist ideology has been imposed upon the Polish nation, despite of all of our resistance, we have become somehow infected by it. And in our position this is a dangerous infection. We have begun to conceive the state in Marxist terms.

We have become used to seeing the state as merely an instrument of oppression by the ruling class, which in our case is the Communist elite. This definition, of course, is partially true. Yet, there are other ·definitions. The state is composed not only of the government, but also of the population and the territory. So, as a result of Marxist thinking, while opposing the oppressive Communist government, we have tended to forget about protecting the Polish state.

Occasionally we even hear bitter arguments: "Better to have no state than the Communist one"; or: "Better we should be under a foreign occupation than to have a pseudo-independence". Yet, such statements merely reflect political rage and not political reasoning. For one can oppose the government without at the same time opposing the state. A government can be changed or limited without necessarily destroying the state.[...]

Since 1945 the great majority of the Poles have regarded the Polish People's Republic as a creature imposed from outside, and, consequently, they tend to identify the government with the state. Yet, in the last forty years already two generations have matured who know no other reality than this post-war-one. And gradually it is seeping into the national consciousness that this situation cannot be changed because the status quo in Europe is guaranteed by the two superpowers.

In these circumstances many thinking Poles have started to distinguish between the struggle against the government, the political system and the foreign ideology, and the necessity to preserve the state, even one with a restricted sovereignty. We must not forget that in our location it is easier for us to be erased from the map of Europe than to return to it. We have enough historical experience in this regard.

It is interesting to observe that among the political scientists of Polish background at the western universities there is virtual agreement that it would not be expedient to try to use Poland as a detonator in the political system of Eastern Europe. Notably, Zbigniew Brzezinski subscribes to this view.[...] Yet, in the present highly emotional atmosphere, both at home and in the emigration, any attempt to salvage the state's existence is interpreted as indirect support of the present government.

The Poles, as Piotr Skarga noted in the 17th century, in disputations always prefer trumpets to reason. Individuals whose whole lives prove their uncompromsing patriotism, are today strongly denounced by the zealots of the opposition. People who have the courage of critical and rational thinking are being labelled as "lice". And those who do not share in the syndrome defeat and dare to talk or write about the mistakes of the opposition in 1980-81 are particularly vehemently condemned. This is a sad testimony to the victory of Marxism over the old tradition of Polish tolerance.

The existence of the Polish state is threatened not only by the prevailing situation in Europe, but also by the economic crisis devastating the social life of the country. We are witnessing the peaceful reemergence of Germany. Its economic successes and the growing cooperation between its two parts may lead to a situation where its patrons may be tempted to transform that country (once the most powerful in Europe) into their ally.

To that end the U.S.S.R. might even play its trump card — the Polish western territories. The argument could be used that since the Poles have failed to properly utilize the lands which once were the granary of the German Reich: and since they have not been able to exploit the industrial potential of Silesia (which after the Ruhz and the Donbas is the third most industrialized region on the continent), then it would be advantageous to Europe as a whole that these territories should be returned to Germany. The nightmare of a Poland restricted to the Duchy of Warsaw, and even more dependent upon its neighbors than it is today, would then become reality.

There is also the danger of a gradual, phased but systematic, incorporation of Poland into the Soviet Union. To a large extent the realization of this scenario is up to us. Are we going to facilitate it for our powerful neighbor in the east? Are we going to repeat the errors of the Poles of the 19th century, who by their blind loyalty to Napoleon precluded any political maneuver on their part at the time of the Congress of Vienna? And of those who in 1830 lost the chances for gradual expansion of Polish autonomy in the Congress Kingdom? And, finally, of those who in the heroic, but insane, insurrection of 1863 even forfeited the rights to Polish language, education and social organization.[...]

\* \* \*

I would not expound so Cassandra-like, and I would leave the entire problem to the political scientists, were I not convinced that the political crisis which started in the late 1970s by now has expanded into a major economic and social crisis. It all began with the massive credits extended then to Poland by the West. These loans amounted to an unintended and a belated Marshall Plan for Poland though they were badly conceived and utilized. They did provide the Poles, however, with at least a breathing spell. They allowed Polish people some relief from simple human misery. Yet at the same time they brought about a relaxation of political oppression, which contributed to the rise of many opposition groups.

In those conditions there emerged the first, indeed, the only non-totalitarian mass movement in 20th century Europe: Solidarity.[2] It started as a free trade union, but it was soon transformed into a kind of peaceful insurrection in which the entire nation mobilized around goals which far exceeded those of any ordinary trade union.

I do not intend here to dwell upon Solidarity's achievements, which are well known, nor upon its less-discussed mistakes. I should just like to point out that after its defeat on December 13, 1981 there ensued a multi-layer diversification of the Polish society. The defeat syndrome, which was more emotional than political, and as such was natural among the suppressed youth, also affected the opposition leaders to the point of driving some of them underground.

Since that time the economic crisis has deepened, aggravating the social crisis too. The Polish society has been living not only on credit, but in an unreal world. We have been pretending that we work, carry out reforms and strive toward a national reconciliation. And what we have accomplished in reality? We have produced highly politicized but poorly educated youth. We have created a class of prematurely retired people. And, taking advantage of a freedom of expression unprecedented since 1945, we have been preoccupying ourselves with legal or illegal manifestations which merely serve to provide an outlet for our political emotions. Last but not least we have led many young people, who have lost faith that their work and their courage are needed in Poland, to go abroad.[...]

And, above all, we pretend, or rather we delude ourselves, that we do not see the approaching total catastrophe. We take to the streets when faced with price increases, yet we are unable to cope with the major social ills. We have failed to prevent the drastic increase in infant mortality, the glaring deterioration of conditions in the hospitals, the spread of drug addiction among some 200,000 young people and the deeply damaging changes in the system of education. We did not even protest when the parliament informed us that the ecological deterioration is evident in areas inhabited by no less than 30 per cent of the population. We do not object to the disintegration of our ancient cities. Indeed, we stay silent when, instead of drinkable water, an undefined yellow liquid flows from the taps in most Polish towns.

The feeling of helplessness, lack of initiative and interest in anything, stems in the first place from the disintegration of social infra-structures. It makes it impossible for the people to cooperate even in the small, local communities. Instead of addressing themselves to those problems which should be resolved immediately, the Poles keep waiting for independence, for a collapse of the Soviet Union, or (alas!) for Poland's joining as the 51st state of the United States. It is in this feeling of helplessness, ironically called the "Polish impossibility", where the roots of the present tragic situation are.

It has not always been like that. In the past, while opposing the Communist government and ideology the Poles have quietly formed various informal social structures independent of the Communist party. These structures were various in character and operated at different social levels. The strongest, of course, was the Catholic church. But important roles were played also by less visible social structures. They existed among the academics, engineers, lawyers, physicians and, most importantly, among the workers. Their members were linked by similar views, interests and, above all, by mutual trust. Indeed, without those informal structures the rise of Solidarity as a mass and peaceful movement would not have been possible.

I do not forget, of course, that the emergence of Solidarity also would have not been possible without the historic event which took place on October 16, 1978.[...] The fact that a Pole ascended to the Throne of St. Peter (even if he had not had the charismatic person-ality of Karol Wojtyla), would have intoxicated the Polish nation. Subsequently, John Paul II by his calm has contributed much to salvag-ing Poland from fratricidal civil war and its tragic consequences.

It is by no means the Pope's fault, however, that the Poles, so addicted to political thoughtlessness, have also used his position in another fashion. To their dreams of help from the United States they added yet another delusion, namely that salvation was now to come from the Vatican. And they reduced the old Christian principle: *ora et labora* (pray and work) to its first part only. Let us pray intensely, but let us also remember the wise counsel of Reverend Piwowarczyk who stated: "There are no miracles, one must work".[3]

Expanded freedom during the Solidarity period led to the rising wages, the adopting of the five day work week and the postponing of the price increases. But these were illusory successes. Their harmful effects have been aptly evaluated by the economists [...] My task is to point out their no less detrimental social consequences.

The price increases were confined to those groups which are directly linked to the obsolete economic system, i.e. to those whose satisfaction, or at least whose appeasement, is of crucial political significance to the government. And yet, it all comes from the same pie, and a decreasing one, so when some receive more, others receive less. Thus the old and the weak — in an ostensibly Marxist and in reality a Catholic country — have become unwanted and poorer.

And free Saturdays have been introduced in a society which does not know yet how to use free time. As a result there has been an increase in the consumption of alcohol. The second-hand pop culture — so eagerly embraced by the Polish television — has also spread.[...] Free time, thus has contributed to the lessening of social discipline and consciousness among the young Poles, transforming them into a highly combustible mass which could be easily ignited by anybody wishing to do so.

The great hopes and the subsequent equally great disillusionments have contributed to the radical changes in the Polish society.[...] The crucial line dividing the Poles today is between those who stand for the salvation of the nation and the country and those who give priority to the struggle against the Communist ideology and system which have been imposed from the outside and affirmed by the existing international situation.

We must not ignore the fact that from the outset commitment to the Communist ideology only ever affected a very small segment of the Polish society, and after 1956 as been abandoned by virtually the entire nation. At the same time it should be remembered that we cannot shake off the existing political system, which is rooted in the division of Europe and the world, and accepted by both superpowers.

Each Pole then must decide for himself what is more important for him: rescuing 37 millions of his compatriots whose very survival is at stake, or assuming a posture of a lonely hero attempting to overcome the present division of Europe and the world. We can declare, after Pilsudski, that "we cannot live in a latrine", and either go underground or emigrate. Or we can undertake an even more difficult task of trying to protect the nation from its imminent catastrophe.

* * *

The Polish society is more aware of the political and economic threats than, despite the fact that it endangers the very basis of their national existence, the ecological one. For quite some time the Poles at home and abroad have been aware of the fact that Poland is located in the greatest danger zone of a nuclear war. Yet, only recently have they noted that ecologically Poland is also the most threatened nation in Europe. This is so because on the one hand the country cannot rapidly transform its present industrial structure, and on the other lacks the financial means to acquire the necessary installations to prevent industrial pollution of the environment.[...]

On February 28, 1985 a committee attached to the Presidium of the Polish Academy of Sciences submitted its prognosis for the long-term developments in the country called: "The Polish Society at the Turn of the 20th and the 21st Centuries". We know of the substance of this report from a summary of the discussion on it prepared by the Committee's chairman and the Academy's Vice President, Professor Wladyslaw Markiewicz.[3][...] We learn there what the Committee members, who are the best informed scholars on this subject in Poland, think of the country's prospects. It is a bleak assessment:

- it is necessary to realize that the country is faced with three profound problems: the shortage of energy, and of raw materials, and the threat to the environment;
- we must admit that as a nation we find ourselves at the threshhold of a general catastrophe and that there is no possibility that we can resolve all the accumulated problems before the end of the century;
- there is a need for profound changes in socialism to release the internal energies of the nation. This is not sufficiently accentuated in the report, but this is the only chance for progress, for overcoming the impasse and avoiding the catastrophe with which we are faced.[4]

The social progress and the survival of the nation, thus, depends upon colossal and most prudent efforts from all of us. Should we not be able to find ways of overcoming the political crisis which is at the root of the present impasse, and should we not be capable of mustering all our intellectual and moral resources to reconstruct the economic and social life, some time in the near future (according to the most knowledgeable Polish scholars) we shall suffer a horrible catastrophe. And this will be caused, not by our external enemies, but (alas!) by the internal forces in the country.

We are threatened with, not just temporary, but permanent drought. The water table has been lowered in many areas of Poland. This is due to the excessive use of water by heavy industry and the simultaneous progressive destruction of forests by industrial pollution. Early this year the Warsaw papers reported that only 8 per cent of water in the Polish rivers is drinkable.

The threat to the environment constitutes a danger to the health of the population. Reportedly, in accordance to the parliament sources, 10 per cent of the Polish population inhabits regions where deterioration of the environment has reached the level of an ecological disaster.[5] Yet, from the same source we learn that the measures undertaken to cope with this situation can at best stabilize it by 1990, and may reverse it only in 1995.

Ecological catastrophe, of course, threatens the entire globe.[...] So in this respect we are not isolated. Yet, if we do not want Poland to become the first victim in a chain of such catastrophies, if we want at least to mitigate its scope, then we must use the existing system of central planning and management not just to improve the present standard of living, but first of all to secure the survival of the future generations. And those of us who would shirk this duty of engaging in a dialogue and achieving a national reconciliation — regardless whether they are in the government or the opposition — accept a grave responsibility.[...]

* * *

The greatest responsibility rests on the government. This is beyond doubt. Yet, at least a part of this responsibility is shared by the opposition — both open and clandestine. For it must be clearly stated that, faced with the active or passive opposition of almost the entire society, no government feasible in Poland's international situation today could carry out a meaningful program of reforms on its own. The responsibility for the future of Poland, thus, rests with all of us.[...]

After each national defeat it is the moral duty of every patriot to return to the organic work. This means concern about what is essential for our national existence: biological survival, salvaging the youth, and the slow, but persistent, rebuilding of the infrastructure of our social and cultural life.

We have too many urgent, yet resolvable, problems to go about attacking those problems over which we have no control. We cannot demand from our people that they challenge the political situation guaranteed by international agreements in which the Polish nation has no voice.

At the present stage of great danger the Polish society is divided, not only between the governing and the governed, but within each of these two groups. The rulers are split into various factions. There are divisions among the opposition — some of its members operate clandestinely and some in the open. And, then, there is the silent center, ridiculed by the opposition activists.

As a nation with a great tradition of romanticism in poetry and politics, we are divided into the defenders and the opponents of this historical legacy. Unfortunately, both of these groups abuse the old patterns and postures. The policies of the great powers, as always in the past, are guided by realism, i.e. machiavelism. In an era of parliamentary democracy, however, their *raison d'etat* is often masked by declarations about freedom, justice, equality and peace. These serve as a disguise for the machinations of the politicians and at the same time as narcotics, stupefying those who are just pawns in their political games. No wonder, then, that our idealism and romanticism, which we so lightly transplant from literature into politics, have been so often exploited by Poland's enemies.

It is worth remembering that in our position of fighting for national survival we ought to preserve the idealism and romanticism of our aims, but at the same time to think in a realist fashion and to work in a positivist tradition. In defending our nation we need great realism — respect for the principles which revitalize social life and protect the nation's infrastructure, but at the same time contempt for those practices which lead to both fragmentation of the society, as well as those aimed at its homogenization and cultural impoverishment. Unfortunately, today the Poles are not inclined to follow such realism, for the entire nation is permeated by intense emotions. But, we should remember the advice of Talleyrand that there is no room for emotion in politics.

---

[1] Poland was labelled as the heart of Europe by Norman Davies in the Title of his book: *Heart of Europe, A Short History of Poland,* Oxford, 1984.

[2]. See Aleksander Gella, "Solidarity - the first non-totalitarian mass movement in 20th century Europe: Socio-Historical Factors in Its Growth", *Studies in Soviet Thought,* 26 (1983).

[3]. Wladyslaw Markiewicz, "Notatka z dyskusji nad raportem 'Spoleczenstwo polskie na przelomie XX i XXI wieku' ", *Kultura,* July-August 1985.

[4]. *Ibid.*

[5]. *Tygodnik Powszechny,* April 30, 1985.

# XIII

## THE CONSTANT: RUSSIA*

### Aleksander Hall

Our attitudes toward Russia and Germany constitute problems which must be constantly re-examined in Polish political thought. And it is no less important to develop in our society ways of thinking about these two most important neighbors of ours in a rational and realistic fashion. Much needs to be done here. In this essay I shall focus upon Russia.

Between August 1980 and December 1981 the Polish society and the Soviet leaders played a Great Game. It ended in a defeat for the Polish side. It is difficult not to note that we contributed to this outcome through our own mistakes. Of course, it is impossible to say what would have happened had it been otherwise.[...] Yet, it is virtually certain that we were not prepared to exploit the historical opportunity which arose in August 1980. We played the Great Game with Russia poorly.

In the realm of high politics the only things Solidarity produced were the declaration confirming our commitment to the existing alliances and the Appeal to the Nations and Workers of Eastern Europe. The political and intellectual elites of the movement, however, failed to come out with a realistic and long range program for our relations with Russia. Some members adopted a purely pragmatic attitude of just muddling through the successive crises, while others

---

*Aleksander Hall, "Czynnik stały: Rosja", *Polityka Polska*, No. -2-3, 1983. (Mimeographed)

succumbed to the temptation of embracing visions which totally ignored the realities of time and place, and confused the long range and short range goals.

Among the rank and file of the movement's members (which in practice included the entire Polish society) the prevailing tendency was to follow the course of least resistance: to shout loudly about everything that so far had been prohibited, and to give vent to emotions and sentiments. Hence the popularity of many of the publications which dwelt upon the injuries inflicted upon Poland by Russia and the cartoons presenting Brezhnev as a Russian bear, and also the biting satires about the USSR presented in the newly uncensored cabarets. All of these were quite spontaneous. The Poles were intoxicated with their freedom and guaffed it deeply without limit. Psychologically this was perfectly understandable, yet politically it was deeply damaging. It pushed the adversary toward confrontation and provided it with valid propaganda arguments. The fact that the Polish society could not control itself, and that it failed to perceive the danger inherent in such conduct, was one of the major blunders it committed between August 1980 and December 1981.

* * *

What then is the attitude of the Poles toward Russia and the Russians? No doubt, it is primarily characterized by enmity accompanied by a large dose of contempt. The reasons for this are natural. They stem from the past and present pattern of Polish-Russian relations. Since the beginning of the 18th century, when the pendulum swung against them, it has been the Poles who have been systematically hurt by the Russians.

This historical record is further aggravated by the present situation. Dependence upon Russia is the major reason why the Poles cannot freely develop their national life in a way that would express the sovereign will of the nation. December 1981 was most recent of successive manifestations of this painful truth. Our patriotic ethos has been affected in a major way by our struggle against Russia. Our contempt toward Russia and the Russians has also been influenced by these past and present experiences. We have not appreciated what in Russia is great and deserves respect, as we have been exposed only to its cunning and brutality.

Differing types of civilization and patterns of communal life have been another element dividing the two nations. Yet, this has also performed a useful role for us. It has protected us from russification, and then sovietization, and it has helped us to preserve our separate identity and spiritual independence as a nation. Thus, it has been a positive element, especially at those times in our history when our national survival has been at stake. Yet, when opportunities for a dialogue with Russia have arisen (although in the last two hundred years these have been very rare), our anti-Russian sentiments have complicated them, or have even altogether prevented us from exploiting them.

Still another element of our attitude toward Russia has been our profound ignorance of the developments there. The most frequent error is our tendency to identify the USSR with the old Russia, neglecting the multinational character and the strong ideological component of the Soviet state.

Do the Poles appreciate Russia's power? Do they fear it? Before August 1980 my answers would have been affirmative. But after sixteen months of Polish freedom I would find it difficult to answer unequivocally.

The experiences of Polish-Russian struggles should have made us appreciate Russia's power. We have managed to preserve our national identity and our aspirations for independence, and we have averted both russification and sovietization; yet, despite all our upheavals and sacrifices we have failed to free ourselves from the Russian domination. Independent Poland was just a historical episode which lasted for twenty years. A non-sovereign state is clearly better than no state at all, but it certainly does not meet the Polish national aspirations. The awareness of Russian power and the international realities which emerged at the end of World War II certainly contributed to the restraint with which the Polish society has struggled against the Communist government. It circumscribed both our means and our ends.

Prior to August 1980 among many segments of the Polish society this situation still had paralyzing effects. The arguments were often heard: "We cannot do anything because Russia would not permit it"; or, "Even if we did succeed in carrying out major changes in Poland it would only lead to a national catastrophe, namely, Soviet intervention." Many people used these arguments — a peculiar ideology of fear — merely as justifications for passivity and conformism. But many genuinely believed them.

Yet, curiously, these was also a lot of wishful thinking. At a time when the entire world respected Russia as one of the two superpowers, there were many Poles — often serious and highly regarded — who argued that Russia is just "a colossus with feet of clay", and, in fact, was on the verge of collapse. And many segments of public opinion shared this view, probably because people often accept as true what they would like the truth to be.

During the period from August 1980 to December 1981 there were important changes in the Polish society. At first we feared the Russian reaction to these events. The apprehension was perhaps less visible in Gdansk and Szczecin, but it was quite tangible in Warsaw. The danger of the Soviet threat, no doubt, contributed to the realism of the strikes and the moderate nature of the accords which emerged from them, and especially to the workers' acceptance of the political system in People's Poland, including the dominant political role of the Communist party.

As time went on, however, and Solidarity scored more and more successes, the awareness of the external threat, among both the masses and the elites, declined. The more distant August 1980 became, the greater was the self-assurance. The view prevailed that "since they have not invaded so far, they never will". By the fall of 1981 most people did not expect a confrontation. It had taken little more than a year for the people to forget the past.

\* \* \*

There are times when no realist course is open at all, and, then, all that remains to be done is to protect the national consciousness and identity. Such a situation emerged in Polish-Russian relations after 1943. Stalin's Russia did not want an accommodation with Poland, even one that would be most advantageous to it. It was not interested in Poland as a partner, but it simply wanted to have a satellite, which would be subordinate to it politically, ideologically and economically. The constellation of forces — the striking discrepancy in power between the Polish and Russian nations — precluded any room for maneuver on our part. And this was especially so, once the western allies gave Stalin a free hand in Eastern Europe. We kept fighting, for we had to fight, but without any prospect of a political success.

The reality of Polish-Soviet relations has adversely affected our post-war political thought. For a viable political thought must not only determine the long range political goals, but must also indicate how they can be attained. It must be rooted in reality: to map plans for the future with regard for the changes already under way, or those which are likely to take place soon, and not just to indulge in wishful thinking. And yet, our political thought has remained confined to pointing out the long range objectives, while failing to indicate how they can be realized.

This approach was apparent among most of the people at home as well as among the emigration. It continued to permeate the programs of the 1970s and the early 1980s of such political movements as the "Ruch", the Defence of Human and Civil Rights Movement and the Confederation of Indpendent Poland. Their arguments were as follows:

1/ The blame for all our misfortunes, and especially for the denial of our national independence, rests with Russia (the USSR).

2/ No compromise with the Soviet system is possible.

3/ The USSR is the last colonial empire in the world and like all the other empires is doomed to collapse. The nationality problem is its Achilles' heel.

4/ Our struggle for independence, thus, is inseparably linked with the struggle of the non-Russian peoples in the USSR, and especially those who have had historical ties with the ancient Polish Commonwealth.

5/ We shall fully attain our goals only when the Russian empire disintegrates.

This line of reasoning, of course, is deeply rooted in our insurrectionist, anti-Russian tradition; it reverts to the slogan "for our freedom and yours", and to the legacy of the old multinational Commonwealth. Yet, it has two major shortcomings:

1/ It condemns us to a permanent antagonism with Russia, regardless of any changes there, and excludes any accommodation with that country;

2/ As a precondition of our independence it assumes a complete change of a political situation in Eastern Europe, and, indeed, the emergence of a novel world system where there would be no place for Russia as a great power [...]

What conclusion can one draw from the above considerations? It seems that the Polish society is well equipped to withstand the threats of russification and sovietization and it will persist in its resistance against them. It has preserved its strong consciousness of its legitimate international rights. And there are enough people and groups who will continue to remind us of our right to independence in the future. Yet, the Polish society is not sufficiently equipped to engage in a political game with Russia; it cannot perceive Russia in realistic, rather than just emotional, terms. It is unable to advance Polish-Soviet relations in a constructive fashion, even when the external circumstances are conducive.

\* \* \*

In our thinking about Russia we tend to fall into two extremes. On the one hand we tend to think of the Soviet Union just as a continuation of Tsarist Russia. This approach assumes that the main lines of Soviet internal, and especially external, policies are inherited from the Tsars; that Stalin and Brezhnev were in effect the uncrowned successors of Ivan the Terrible, Peter the Great, Catherine II and Nicolas II. The Communist ideology is seen just as an instrument of Russia's imperialist policy; in other words the USSR is just the Russia of today.

The second approach (which has been best formulated by Alexander Solzhenitsyn) posits that there was a total break between the old Russia and the USSR. It is Communism which is evil and the Russian nation was its first victim.

It seems to me that truth lies somewhere in the middle. The historical model of the Russian state and its collective life has undoubtedly facilitated the Communist experiment in that country. Many Soviet policies indeed represent continuations of those from the Tsarist period. The USSR is a new and transformed form of the Russian state. This is precisely the reason why I refer to this state interchangably as the USSR or Russia.

One does not understand the Soviet Union, however, if one fails to see that it is also an ideological state with all the consequences flowing from this fact. Ideology offers legitimization for the ruling elite to stay in power; it is also a crucial element in holding together the Soviet multinational state, as well as its system of satellite states. Last but not least it makes Moscow the main center of the international Communist movement. Owing to its ideology the Soviet Union has many influential allies not only in the Third World, but also in the West.

It is not important whether the Soviet leaders really consider themselves true disciples of Marx, Engels and Lenin, or whether the party leaders in the satellite countries honestly subscribe to the slogans of internationalism and moral unity with their "Soviet comrades". What is important is the fact that without those ideological ties the present imperial system — at least in its present form — would come to an end. This would not necessarily mean a permanent collapse of Russia, but it would probably imply serious convulsions for it.

For the Poles the ideological character of the Soviet state is a major drawback. It makes achieving any accord between the two nations, based on situations where the Polish and Russian interests coincide, much more difficult. It also precludes the possibility of the USSR accepting a non-Communist government in Poland — even if it were pro-Russian and respected Russia's national interests.

* * *

There are reasons to believe that Soviet power will decline, or perhaps even that the Soviet state will collapse. The crisis phenomena are there and are multiplying. Some of them are as follows:

- economic difficulties and the growing technological gap with the West;
- an anachronistic political and economic system where the obsolete structures and mechanisms of power are hindering the adoption of indispensable reforms;
- the growth of autonomous aspirations among the non-Russian peoples in the USSR, accelerated by demographic trends adverse to the Russians;
- the aspirations toward greater freedom and independence among the various states in the Soviet sphere of influence.

Yet, there are few signs that all of these developments — barring a world-wide catastrophe — will lead soon to a sudden collapse of the Soviet empire. On the contrary, these are clearly long term processes which may take many years to come to fruition, and may even diminish in their significance. And most importantly, their outcome is by no means predetermined; some of them may be even overcome through — not very probable, but not impossible — systemic reforms.

In any case those who already see the "death throes" of the Soviet empire are guided more by their imagination than by objective analysis. They see there what they would like to see. Today, tomorrow, and probably still the day after tomorrow, the Soviet Union will remain a great power influencing not only the fate of Poland and Eastern Europe, but of the world as a whole.

One can put it this way: as long as the Yalta system remains binding in Europe and the Soviet Union stays an ideological state, the maintenance of the Communist government in Poland will continue to be of a crucial significance to the Soviet leaders. On this account we should have no illusions. The only government in Poland acceptable to the USSR is a Communist government. And no other form of Polish government, however willing to respect Soviet interests, could fulfill this role.[...]

* * *

Only the Poles (and not even all of them) are ready to sacrifice and die for Poland. For only to them this is a matter of decisive importance. The governments and the people in the so-called free world may sympathize with Poland, and offer it their support, but they will not risk their own interests for it. For the West, the Polish question has always been a part of the international game. The players in it, moreover, have not been equal. The West can treat us fairly and honestly, or just as an instrument, or even as a bargaining chip which can be traded away, as happened at the end of World War II.[...]

Even from the most sympathetic western politicans we cannot expect Polonocentrism. There is no reason why it should be otherwise, and we must accept it as it is. If one day the United States should use the Polish question as a pretext to go to war against the Soviet Union (a highly improbable development), it will be only because they judge such an action to be in their own interest.

The conclusion from this is quite simple: we must count above all upon our own strength and we have to assume the responsibility for our own policies.

One may dislike Russia, or even hate it, but those negative feelings should not outweight one's love for Poland. I underline this, for occasionally one gets the impression that there are Poles who would be willing to risk the existence of their own nation, in order to contribute to the collapse of the Soviet Empire. Such reasoning must be categorically rejected. The Polish question is not a part of any broader issue for which it could be sacrificed. The cardinal precondition of our thinking about Russia must be the repudation of all those concepts which advocate sacrificing Poland in the name of freeing mankind from "Red Tsarism".

Russia today is ruled by the Communists and they determine its policy toward Poland. And nothing suggests that this situation will change soon; in fact it may still continue for decades. Yet, it is also true that ideologies and parties come and go, while the nations stay. Regardless of the future of Communism, thus, Russia and the Russian nation will stay, and Russia — white, red or any other color — will be a permanent and important element in our part of Europe.

One cannot work for reconciliation with the Russian nation and any future Russia, and at the same time try to use Poland as an anti-Russian Piedmont; as a base for liberation movements there. A choice must be made here. No Russia could come to terms with a Poland aiming at its dismemberment. The dilemma with which we are faced here is as follows: either we try to promote an agreement which will respect our present eastern boundary and the great-power status of Russia, or we should give up all efforts at reconciliation and link the future of Poland inexorably to the hope for the collapse, or at least the decline, of Russia.

In the present circumstances it is not possible to achieve either Poland's independence or true reconciliation between the Poles and the Russians. Yet, both of these objectives could be already prepared for today. And in those efforts there should be no mistake about the fact that the independence of Poland is the end, and the reconciliation with Russia is the means.[...]

How can this end be promoted?

* * *

Our basic task is to maintain our national identity and to expand as much as possible the autonomy of life for the Polish society. This can be attained only through a continuous struggle: the tug-of-war between the Polish people and the Communist system. The paradox of this struggle is that until the external circumstances change we cannot, and in fact we do not want, to win it; so we are condemned both to struggle and to coexist. Yet, the fact that our country is ruled by the Communists does not preclude the expansion of national and civil rights. They have changed in the past and they will continue to evolve in the future.

The situation which was created on December 13, 1981 has posed us the challenge of regaining the lost territory: the expansion of our sphere of activity independent of the government. I believe that there are no predetermined boundaries for the internal sovereignty of a society. It is up to the society to determine them. And, in turn, the extent of its internal freedom determines Poland's position in the Communist bloc. It is in our interests that through internal pressure the Polish society should compel the Soviet Union to accept the Polish differences and to tolerate in our country the specificities which are not accepted elsewhere.

We have to try to correct those errors and faults of ours which came to the surface so clearly during our seventeen months of freedom. For they contributed in a major way to our defeat in December 1981. The greatest weakness of the process of renewal, led by Solidarity, was its political immaturity.

To a large extent this weakness stemmed from the absence of social-political elites and strong conceptual centres. It is crucial, then, to create such strong elites that they, in turn, can influence the masses. This is a matter of crucial significance for it will determine whether in our next encounter with history we shall once again be taken by surprise, or whether we shall be able to determine its course.

Among the most important tasks ahead is to find programs which would be acceptable to the society, and at the same time would express in a realistic fashion the national goals. In the long run they have to map the road toward Poland's sovereignty. Yet, they will not serve this purpose if they are confined to vague generalities and ignore the problem of relations with Poland's neighbors. It is necessary to recognize that what is needed, even if society resents it, are rational proposals, and not slogans, however appealing. Thus, we simply cannot afford to ignore the Russian problem.

\* \* \*

Concerning the Russian problem it would be desirable to evolve one common Polish program. In this matter the political elite and all the main currents of public opinion should arrive at a concensus. Such a program should, if effected, become our offer to Russia. Its realization, however, would have to wait until appropriate changes were to take place for our offer to be acceptable to the Russian side.[...]

I expect no cataclysm in which the Russian nation will be obliterated; on the contrary, I believe that Russia will remain our most important neighbor and that the Russian nation will continue to be the most powerful country in Europe.

Still, the Russians should know that:

1/ The independence of our state and the complete freedom to determine our internal political and social system are the cardinal Polish goals, which we will not abandon. This does not mean that these goals have to be attained all at once; they could be realized gradually.

2/ Poland's independence means that the center of political decisions has to be in this country and has to be established by the Polish nation itself. This does not mean that such a center should follow a "lunar policy"; on the contrary, it should be guided by our national interests, which will take into account the realities of Poland's geopolitical position.

3/ These realities should contribute to "good-neighbor" relations with Russia along the existing boundary. We know that this boundary was established as a result of the Hitler-Stalin pact which was aimed against Poland. Yet, even though it came into being by conniving and force, questioning it is useless. What we would expect from the Soviet Union, however, is respect for the national and cultural rights of the Poles remaining in the former Polish eastern provinces, and preservation of the Polish national heritage in those lands.

4/ Poland would not interfere in Russia's internal problems and the way it might resolve its nationality problem, although this would not detract from the Poles' sympathy for the right of all nations to self-determination and for their efforts to preserve their national identities.

5/ There are many problems in Europe where the Polish and Russian interest coincide. A genuine partnership between them, then, based upon real political, economic and cultural cooperation, should be mutually advantageous and more constructive than the type of relations which exist between them at present.

In order to accomplish the above sketched program, however, the attitudes of the Poles toward Russia must also undergo a profound change. This is a delicate problem. For in the past the Polish attitudes have protected us from spiritual bondage — they have been the effective antidote. And this we must not forego.

It would be preferable, however, if our national identity were manifested not through animosities — even if justified ones — but through positive values. And these should include: an awareness of our rights, the preservation of the tradition of Poland in the European community of nations — which even if it cannot be realized today should remain our ultimate goal — an, last but not least, an ability to think rationally about relations with our neighbors.

The indispensable precondition for all of this is for us to develop respect for the Russian nation — to stop seeing it as composed of cunning and brutal Asian barbarians whose influence rests exclusively on force.

This should be facilitated if we remember that by far the most numerous victims of Communism have been Russians. Many millions of people perished before the system became consolidated. We should also be cognizant of the great and diversified Russian culture and the Russians' exceptional readiness to sacrifice for their country and the nation.

At the same time we should entertain no illusions about the facts that the Russians are, and will remain, very different from us. They are Europeans, but of a different kind. Except for a short period in 1905-17, and especially between March and November 1917, they have never been exposed to democracy. And there are no signs that they will follow the road of the western democracies today. Their road of political development will probably remain quite different.

We have also to keep in mind that through their history the Russians have been doomed to struggle against various peoples who have been absorbed into their empire and have striven for national determination. And there is little prospect that this problem will be resolved in a satisfactory fashion in the near future.

Last but not least there is also the devastation and the depravity in the Russian national psyche which has been brought about by Communism. Even if Communism were to collapse tomorrow its sad impact would endure, and it would be many years before it could be fully overcome.

While taking into account all of those differences, and remembering the disparity in injuries inflicted upon each other, we nevertheless ought to make the effort to bring the two nations closer together and to strive for their reconciliation.[...]

The success of those endeavors, of course, will not depend only upon the Poles. It will also depend upon whether sufficiently influential forces emerge in Russia which are willing to enter into the Polish-Russian dialogue. And this would require on their part the recognition of the principle of Poland's independence as well as the admission of the profound injuries inflicted upon Poland by Russia in the past.

Will such forces come into existence in Russia? There is no way to know this today. Yet, whatever one can say about the Russian policies it cannot be denied that they have always been flexible and realistic: rooted in the concrete existing conditions. One can only hope that this realism will also lead the Russians to change their future policies toward Poland.

Should this not be the case the two nations will be doomed to lasting enmity. And neither side will benefit from it.[...]

# XIV

## JUBILEE HOMILY AT JASNA GORA*

### John Paul II

I have come here as a pilgrim to praise God Eternal in the sanctuary of my homeland, where the Madonna of Jasna Gora as the Servant of the Lord gives to the Holy Trinity all respect and glory, and all the love and gratitude which she herself is being offered here.

I thank God that I can be here in the Jasna Gora sanctuary, in this other *City of God*, where - to borrow the worlds of Cyprian Norwid - *one has only to cross the threshold to breathe God.*[...]

In Cana of Galilee Mary said to the servant at the wedding reception: *Whatsoever he tells you to do, do it.* Since 1382 Mary has addressed the same words over the generations to the sons and daughters of this land. And accordingly Jasna Gora has become a place of special evangelical significance. The Word of God has here acquired unusual relevance, for it has been transmitted by our Holy Mother. Jasna Gora has contributed, to the history of the Church in our land, and to all of Polish Christianity, this special maternal message which originated in Cana of Galilee.[...]

Christ, present with his Mother in this Polish Cana, has placed before us, generation after generation, the great cause of freedom. Freedom is given by God to man as a measure of his dignity. Yet, it is also an obligation. As Leopold Staff said: *freedom is not only*

---

*Papiez Jan Pawel II, "Homilia podczas jubileuszowej Mszy swietej, Jasna Gora", June 19, 1983", *Crzescianin w swiecie,* June-July 1983. No. 7-8, Vol. XV. Pp. 118-119. Italics in the original text.

*the relief, but also the burden of greatness.* For freedom can be used by a man rightly or wrongly. He can use it either to construct or to destroy.

The Jasna Gora evangelical message calls God's children to their heritage. It is a call to life in freedom. And to make good use of freedom. For constructing and not for destroying.

This Jasna Gora evangelical message, to live in freedom, as befits God's children, has a long, six-century history. In Cana of Galilee Mary cooperated with her Son. The same has happened at Jasna Gora. How many pilgrims have passed through this sanctuary over the six centuries? How many have been reconverted here: moving from bad to good uses of their freedom? How many have regained their dignity as God's adopted children? How much could the confessionals in this basilica tell? How much could the Way of the Cross and its walls reveal? — This great chapter in the history of human souls! This is probably the most crucial aspect of the six hundred year jubilee of Jasna Gora. It has been preserved, and is still being preserved in the people who live today, in the sons and daughters of this land, when God sends the Holy Spirit into their hearts so that with their entire, essential being they cry: Abba! Father!

The Jasna Gora evangelical message of freedom has yet another aspect: the dimension of a free Nation and a free Homeland, restored to the dignity of a sovereign State. The Nation is truly free when it can develop as a community which is determined by the unity of its culture, language and history. The State is truly sovereign when it governs the society, but at the same time serves the common good of the society and permits the Nation to realize its own sovereignty and its own identity. This involves the establishment of appropriate conditions for development in the spheres of culture, the economy and other aspects of the life of the social community. The sovereignty of the State is inseparably linked to its ability to advance the freedom of the Nation; to create conditions which enable the Nation to be sovereign through its State.

These elementary truths of moral order have been dramatically manifested over all of those centuries that the Portrait of the Madonna at Jasna Gora has testified to the special presence of the Mother of God in the history of our Nation.

The beginning of this presence coincided with the transition from the Piast to the Jagiellonian dynasty. One might say that it anticipated the best period, the "golden age", in our history. Today we should be thankful for these centuries of great development and success. The historical experience, however, also points out that the Mary depicted in the Jasna Gora Portrait was given to us, above all, for difficult times.

They started in the 17th century with "The Deluge" (as we know so well from the novel by Henryk Sienkiewicz). After Jasna Gora defended itself from the Swedes, and, following its example, the entire country freed itself from the foreign invaders, a special relationship developed between the Jasna Gora sanctuary and the increasingly stormy history of the Nation. By pledging our nation to her, John Casimir declared the Mother of God to be also the Queen of the Polish Crown. Subsequently, the Day of the Queen of the Polish Crown who was *given to the defence of the Polish nation*, became the same as that of the Constitution of May 3, 1791. And in this Constitution was confirmed beyond all doubt our will to preserve the independence of our Homeland by the introduction into it of appropriate reforms. Unfortunately, almost immediately after the adoption of this Constitution Poland was deprived, succumbing to the greater power of its three neighbors, of its independent existence. Thus the basic rights of the nation, and the law of moral order, were violated.

During my previous pilgrimage to the Homeland in 1979 I said at Jasna Gora: here we have always been free. It is difficult to express in any other way the symbolic significance which the Portrait of the Queen of Poland acquired when Poland was erased from the map of Europe as an independent state. And Jasna Gora has inspired the hope of the Nation and its persistent efforts to regain independence, so well expressed in the words: *We place a plea before Your Alter; God return unto us our free Homeland.*

Here we also have learned the basic truth about freedom: the nation wanes when its spirit is depraved; and the nation waxes strong when its spirit is purified — and then no outside power can overcome it!

We celebrated the Millenium of the Baptism of Poland already when, after 1918, Poland was restored as a state on the map of Europe; we celebrated it after the horrible experiences of World War II and the occupation. The Six-Hundred-Year Jubilee of the Portrait of Jasna Gora represents an indispensable supplement to this. It is a natural conclusion of our great cause — the cause which has been essential to the history of the people and the history of the Nation.

The name of this cause is The Queen of Poland.

The name of this cause is Mother.

We have a very difficult geopolitical position. We have had a very difficult history, especially in the past few centuries. This painful historical experience has enhanced our sensitivity to human and national rights; and especially to the right to sovereign existence, to freedom of conscience and religion, and to the rights of human work.[...] We also have some human weaknesses and faults, as well as sins, even grave sins, which we have constantly to keep in mind, and constantly to try to free ourselves from.

But dear Brothers and Sisters, my beloved Compatriots — amid all of that, we have at Jasna Gora our Mother.

A mother as caring as that at Cana of Galilee.[...]

We look around us and take into our hearts this sanctuary of Jasna Gora — our Polish Cana of Galilee.

We think of our future. And our future begins today. We are gathered here today in Anno Domini 1983.

Today we look into Your Eyes, Our Mother.

Oh Mary, You who knew in Cana of Galilee that they *had no wine*.

Oh Mary! You know everything that we are missing! Everything that pains us! You know our sufferings, our guilts, and our strivings.

You know what is in the hearts of the nation which was given to you for a Millenium, into *the motherly slavery of love* ...

Tell your Son.

Tell your Son of our difficult "today". Tell of our difficult "Today" to This Christ whom we came here to invite into our entire future. This futue starts "today" and depends upon what our "today" is.

In Cana of Gallilee when there was not enough wine you told the servants, pointing to Christ: *Whatsoever he tells you to do, do it.*

Say these words to us too![...]

# XV

# THE LEGACY OF NATIONAL DEMOCRACY*

## Aleksander Hall

In an editorial article in the first issue of *Polityka Polska* we declared our affinity with the tradition of the National Democracy. This declaration requires an explanation and an elaboration. What does it mean, "an affinity with the National Democracy"? Is the National Democratic political thought and ideology useful in any way in solving the contemporary Polish problems? Have we not tried to establish for ourselves an artificial historical geneology? And last but not least, is there any sense, considering that it is not very popular, in reverting to this tradition? These and other questions, then, require answers.

Let's start with two preliminary observations:

- Among most segments of Polish society knowledge of the National Democracy is negligible.

- And among the most influential groups of the intellectual elite (and also among those who pretend to this role), until recently the National Democracy has had a distinctly bad reputation.

The first phenomenon stems from a poor knowledge of Polish history and a tendency to replace fact with legend. And this legend is dominated by the person of Jozef Pilsudski — who, after playing a major role in regaining Poland's independnece, and subsequently in the inter-War period, served as our introduction into the 20th century. Legend-making has its own rules. Colorful, and surrounded

---

*"Dziedzictwo narodowej demokracji", *Polityka Polska*, No. 4, 1984. (Mimeographed)

by a romantic aura, the personality of the Marshal fits better into legend than do those of the founders of the national democratic movement.

It is also not accidental that the legend of Pilsudski has been revived in recent years. The time of the great awakening and the manifestations of the true aspirations and sentiments of the Polish people required appropriate historical symbols. Pilsudski was needed by the radical, pro-independence opposition before August 1980, and, then, by the Solidarity radicals who advocated a "quick march forward". He well personified the strivings for independence and the anti-Russian sentiments.

He also — regardless of the historical facts — subscribed to the view that "whatever one strives for, one can accomplish": that the nation by an act of will can overcome adverse external circumstances. That Pilsudski was also a politician, and a pragmatic and flexible one at that, was forgotten; what survived was the legend. And this, in addition to its positive patriotic value, also performed a negative role. It created a barrier preventing realist thinking on the part of the leaders and the activist of Solidarity.

* * *

The reasons for the second phenomenon, namely, the intellectuals' low opinion of the National Democracy, are more complex. I shall list only some of them here.[...]

Before the war the National Democracy had many adversaries. It represented a powerful political force and it was one of the major participants in the controversies over the nature of the new Polish state. For many years its main conflict was with the Pilsudskiites, but after the mid-1920s it was with the Left. The notion of the Left, of course, is imprecise. There were differences among its various factions, and especially between the Communists and the socialists. Yet, there were also elements common to all of them. One — and perhaps the most important in those years — was the conviction that internally the main enemy was the nationalistic Right, and externally "international fascism". And in the second half of the 1930s, the political struggle in this country was greatly accelerated.[...]

A conviction spread on the Left that the national democrats subscribed to the same political philosophy as the Nazis in Germany and the fascists in Italy. It was believed that there was in nationalist international, and that all the "progressive forces" had to oppose it in order to protect Europe and the world. It also appeared that the western democracies which had sprung from the Enlightment and liberalism were on the decline, and would be replaced by new forces which would determine what the new world would be like: that the choice was between Hitler and Stalin. *Tertium non datur*![...]

This is not to say that in the second half of the 1930s in the ideology, and especially in the political practice, of the National Democracy there were no elements which would have contributed to such an opinion. But they were grossly exaggerated and mythologized to the point of caricature. Why do I mention this? Above all, because in the post-war period, and especially in the immediate post-war years, those people who subscribed to this caricature had every opportunity to implant it in the social consciousness. They were the Communists who now ruled in Poland. To the first generation of Communist rulers the National Democracy represented a real and tangible enemy. In this respect they differed from their successors. They were motivated by a Jacobite fanaticism. As Communists they had been brought up in the atmosphere of the struggle against ''reaction'' and fascism.[...]

It is a historical fact that after the war the majority of leftist intellectuals supported the new system and participated in its consolidation. Their disillusionment and rebellion came only later. How can this be explained? It is not enough to dismiss it as resulting from opportunism, fear or fatigue — although in many cases these motives were there. But certainly not in all the cases. One should search for an answer, thus, into their views and experiences before and during the war. World War II only re-affirmed their opinion and after the war they still believed that: *Tertium non datur.*!

Did not Nazism ultimately compromise not only nationalism, but all the national values? Did not the western democracies, at first through their fearful appeasement of Hitler, and then through their eager cooperation with Stalin, confirm their weakness and decline? Did not the Soviet Union demonstrate by its victory its vitality and so prove that the future belongs to it? This was the thinking of the people who subscribed to historical determinism. They went along with what in their opinion fitted the laws of social development, and what was inevitable, and, therefore, right.[...]

And after the war the leftist intellectuals, alongside the Communists, took over many positions as professors and editors, and assumed the responsiblity for official culture. And so they also passed their complexes to the younger generation.

* * *

It would be unfair not to note that after 1956 the representatives of the Left played a significant role in the struggle for expanding the freedoms of the Polish society and for containing the totalitarian threats to it. They participated in its several important episodes: before March 1968 they helped to arouse the intellectuals and the students; and in the late 1970s they played a major role in the activities of the democratic opposition. They were there at the birth of Solidarity and later on joined its ranks.

Yet, in most of the cases they were not suddenly converted. One does not change one's ideas, one's *Weltanschauunng,* and one's political philosophy, overnight. On the contrary, the process of evolution and the searching for new ideas on the part of the rebellious Left advanced only slowly and often with reluctance. Many old complexes and stereotypes remained unexamined and unchanged. Among them was the distrust and fear of nationalist values.[...]

This type of reaction was visible abroad in the writings of Juliusz Mieroszewski, and at home those by Jacek Kuron and Adam Michnik. [...] After March 1968 Kuron and Michnik became the leaders of the "secular Left". And this group — intellectually alert and in the very forefront of the struggle for civil rights and democratic freedoms — exerted a profound influence over the younger opposition circles. The "secular Left", then, transmitted to the next generation a particular view of modern Polish history contributing to the "black legend" of the National Democracy.[...]

Negative attitudes toward the National Democracy were also shared by the most important Catholic groups around the weekly *Tygodnik Powszechny* and the monthly *Wiez.* This stemmed from both the origins and the ideological and political conceptions of these groups. The *Tygodnik Powszechny* was composed of people who before the war had belonged to the minority, anti-nationalist current in Polish Catholicism. [...] They strongly opposed the National Democratic model of a "Pole-Catholic" bringing together the national and the Christian values. They countered it with their model of "quiet work" by the Church, giving the Polish Catholicism an intellectual character derived more from French personalism and, later, from Vatican II.

This program was different from that espoused by the Polish Episcopate, and especially by Stefan Cardinal Wyszynski. The Polish Primate was open to the Vatican reforms and supported the intellectual deepening of Polish Catholicism, but remained an ardent advocate of the synthesis of religious and national values as embodied in the model of the "Pole-Catholic".

* * *

In recent years there have been some changes. Among the opposition and the intellectual circles there has been enhanced interest in the National Democracy and there have been attempts to look at its historical record more objectively. What has contributed to this development?

One of the reasons is the rise of a group of opposition youths who in 1977-81 in the samizdat publication *Bratniak* (which since 1979 has been the official organ of the Movement of Young Poland), undertook the task of defending the ideological heritage and the political thought of the National Democracy. These efforts, even if they were not especially profound, aroused interest in the stimulated discussions over the program of the National Democracy in the democratic opposition circles. [...] There also appeared an important text: "Conversations in the Citadel", written when he was interned in Bialoreka, by Adam Michnik. It revealed a substantial evolution of the views of the author. It represented the first attempt at an objective assessment of the National Democracy among the "secular Left".

I believe, however, that the basic reasons for the growing interest in the National Democracy go still deeper. They can be found in the present state of the "Polish question". For the past few years have greatly contributed to a more acute sense of national community, both among the broad masses and the intellectual elites. A profound common experience of the nation was shared during the two Papal visits, during the Polish August, during the days of Solidarity and, then, during the developments which followed December 13, 1981. We have lived together our difficult Polish fate; the unity of our basic aspirations and sentiments, both in victory and defeat. In the national community we have found a source of strength — which at first inspired us to reach toward what seemed impossible, and then helped us to survive bitter disillusionment.

It is of great significance that in his teachings in Poland, John Paul II has fully sanctioned the common national bond, revealing at the same time its religious dimension. There has spread a broad consciousness that we must shake off fear, and stop blaming ourselves for our national complexes. On the contrary, the Pope's statements confirmed that in the Polish context the close union between the struggle for civil rights and democratic freedoms and that for national values, give the national community a unique strength.

It has been natural that side by side with the growth of interest in the national community a search has been undertaken for those traditions in political thought which placed it at the center of the Polish national ethos. And there was the urgent need for new political thought. The period of Solidarity and martial law revealed the apparent lack of political reflection on the part of our political elites, which largely contributed to wasting of the opportunities which had arisen in August 1980. The style of politics that could be reduced to mere phraseology about independence, and which was not even entirely free from sheer demagogy, became largely compromised. It became obvious that in Poland's situation the slogan "everything or nothing" as an entire political program was useless. In those circumstances the political thought of the National Democracy had valuable insights to offer.[...]

The above remarks, however, still do not explain why in *Polityka Polska* we declared our affinity with the National Democratic tradition. It was because we believe that the National Democracy is a valuable part of the Polish heritage, and by ignoring it, or distorting it, we impoverish our knowledge of Poland, and, this way, also our knowledge of ourselves. [...]

Yet, the legacy of the National Democracy is not just of historical significance. In both its ideology and political thought there are important elements which remain valid today. They could be usefully adopted to deal with the contemporary Polish problems.

\* \* \*

The National Democrats saw the world through the prism of nations. They believed that the progress of mankind has been accomplished through the activities of different national communities, and also that service to mankind is realized first of all through one's work for one's own nation. And this should not be forsaken in the name of some universal human ideals, which, because they are so abstract, do not require tangible sacrifices; while, in contrast, the duties toward one's own nation are always concrete. The National Democrats, then, opposed the uniform cosmopolitan ideals, believing that they threatened the very basis of European civilization by striking at its essence, which is a synthesis of the values elaborated by individual nations. For Europe is composed of nations. We share this conviction with the National Democrats. If we are today undergoing the crisis of European civilization it is precisely because of the weakening of its own identity and its will to self-defence. [...]

The National Democrats also believed that Poland is an integral part of the Latin, Western European civilization, determined by the legacy of ancient Greece and Rome, and, above all, that of Christianity. Polishdom emerged within this civilization and an essential role in this process was played by the Catholic Church.

It is useful here to quote from Dmowski's pamphlet: *The Church, the Nation and the State:* "When we try to examine the elements in our souls which make us today a modern European nation, we can find their roots both in our ancient ethnic origin and the existence over centuries of the Polish state, as well as in our millenium-old Catholicism. Catholicism is not just an adjuct to Polishdom, coloring it in a special way, but is inherent in its very core and to a large extent constitutes its very essence. Any attempt to divide Catholicism and Polishdom, to separate the Nation from religion and the Church, then, strikes at the very essence of our Nation." — The post-war Polish reality has fully confirmed, and is still confirming, Dmowski's assessment.

Christianity is the essence of our identity, and the Church is not only the major institution in our national life, but also the leader of and spokesman for the Poles. At present, more than at any time in the past (including even the partitions' period), it is impossible to imagine Poland without the Catholic Church. The National Democrats, thus, as ardent advocates of a union between the nation and the Catholic values have been historically right.[...]

In the 1920s and the 1930s strong anti-parliamentary and autocratic tendencies appeared among the National Democrats. Yet, these never led them to adopt a class-criterion. The selection of national elites, which were to lead the state, was to take place without any regard to their origin and social status. In this sense the National Democracy always remained faithful to democracy.

The patriotism of the founders of the national democratic movement, and especially that of Dmowski himself, was intense, but free from any national megalomania. On the contrary, they never concealed the shortcomings and the faults of the Poles. Indeed, at times their criticisms were even exaggerated and unjust. *The Thoughts of a Modern Pole* was not just a patriotic manifesto, it was also one of the sharpest criticisms, denouncing without any hesitation the weaknesses of the Polish national character. Dmowski condemned the superficial patriotism manifested in lofty slogans, and consisting of "declaring what one would like to have, and protesting, either by word or deed, against what one does not want". He rejected sentimentalism and the temptations to evade reality by escaping into the world of delusions and wishful thinking. [...]

No one would find in Dmowski's writings, moreover, any attempt to place his own nation above others. His nationalism was exactly the opposite of those nationalisms which, as their essence, adopt an assumption of their own nations' superiority. To Dmowski true patriotism need not be based on a notion of superiority of one's own nation over the others; and, conversely, a feeling of inferiority in no way should detract from the nation's moral strength. In *The Thoughts of a Modern Pole* there is another passage on this subject to which we fully subscribe: "As a man accepts his obligations toward today's Poland in his own name and that of his generation, in the same fashion he accepts obligations toward all of humanity in the name of his own nation. Our nation has benefitted over centuries from the experiences, the accomplishments and the spiritual resources of other nations which have attained higher civilizational levels. In proportion to what we have derived from them, we have contributed very little to the humanity. Should not, then, our pride guide us towards the civilizational creative attainments from which in the future other nations can benefit, as much as we have benefitted from them in the past and we are still benefitting today? And is this not the most noble obligation owed to humanity?"

After their coup in 1926 the Pilsudskiites accused the National Democrats of not appreciating the importance of the state and of counterposing it to the nation. This allegedly was due to their nationalist ideology. This view still persists today. Yet, it is clearly rooted in misunderstanding.

The National Democrats attached a great role to the state, but they saw it in an inseparable union with the nation. In "The Foundations of Polish Policy" Dmowski wrote: "the national idea without the state is an absurdity". And elsewhere there he asserted: "The nation is the indispensable essence of the state, as the state is an indispensable political form of the nation. A nation may lose its state, but it will remain a nation as long as it does not abandon the tradition of its own state and its aspirations to regain it. [...] It is obvious that a politician who saw the role of the state this way during the partitions of Poland, would have regarded it as the main goal of Polish policy.

\* \* \*

Which of the above political concepts are still valid in present-day Poland?

Above, all the conviction of the indispensable need for Poland to possess its own state, and to regard its attainment as the major long-term goal of Polish policy. In the future an independent Polish state must be restored and, meantime, all our activities must be subordinated to this central goal.[...]

The contemporary Polish generation cannot accept People's Poland as its own state. It is not a sovereign state, but is dependent upon the USSR, and it is a party state. All of the post-war accomplishments of the nation, and all its struggles for freedom, were opposed by this state. The Solidarity period only confirmed this — it was a confrontation of the nation, organized into free trade unions, with an alien state.[...]

Dmowski's conviction that the state should be an emanation of the nation, and that only then can the masses identify with it, is still valid too. [...] But this does not mean that independence should always be a direct goal of political activities. Only in 1916 did Dmowski openly declare Poland's independence as his immediate political objective. Until that time the National Democratic movement had concentrated its efforts on laying down the foundations of independence, and had tried to advance it step by step. Nothing is more alien to the National Democratic political thought than the view that independence and sovereignty can be attained through just a single upheaval.[...]

The National Democrats believed that for Poland's independence to be achieved two developments had to happen simultaneously: there must be a conscious development of national strength, and favorable changes must take place in the international sphere. It is worth reminding ourselves how the National Democrats envisaged that this would happen.

The Polish nation was to attain political power in its own right. Side by side with the masses entering into the national life, there was to emerge a political elite which would assume leadership. The National Democrats, thus, strove to attain under foreign rule the nation's sovereignty through creating its own hierarchy of values, and its own social elites.[...] Unanimity among the entire society over the essential aspects of the "Polish question" was for Dmowski an indispensable precondition for the nation's becoming a power in its own right and, as such, a partner conducting its own policy in the international sphere. It was to be an "active policy" — gradual, flexible, yet systematic — where everything leading toward independence is good and everything leading away from it is wrong.[...] The national democratic concept of "active policy", thus, assumed the politicization of the broad masses of society and their acceptance of co-responsibility for the fate of the nation. During the partitions this was to be expressed by an intensified pressure upon foreign governments.[...]

In Poland's present situation the concept of "active policy" seems to be particularly useful. We are faced with a non-sovereign state which has at its disposal all the means of a totalitarian state. In these circumstances the advancement of national goals requires not only the activities of even the most mature and sophisticated elites, but also the active participation of the broad masses of society. Only the unity of the activities of the elites and the conscious efforts of the masses can effectively neutralize the destructive influence of the system, and create a sufficiently strong social pressure to throw the Communist state into retreat before the advancing nation.

* * *

The "active policy" was counterposed on the one hand to the policy of reconciliation with the foreign rulers, and on the other hand to the insurrectionist tactics. The National Democrats opposed the former especially before the revolution of 1905. They denounced the conciliators for abandoning the national aspirations and for condemning Poland to mere vegetation. [...] The conciliators, moreover, in renouncing the goal of independence and lowering the Polish national aspirations, had no successes. They failed to become genuine partners, with whom compromise should be sought, for the foreign rulers. [...] Dmowski branded the conciliators' political program as being tied to the existing socio-economic order, and its followers as representing the least worthy, purely opportunistic elements in the Polish society.

No less categorically did the National Democrats oppose the insurrectionist tactics which aimed to win Poland's independence through a single military upheaval. It is worth reminding ourselves of the arguments Dmowski used against the insurrectionist policy. "Our uprisings", he wrote, "were just armed protests against oppression, rather than real efforts to restore the Polish state.[...] As a result they brought about the rapid deterioration of Poland's position — the oppression was only intensified. And after the insurrections there followed a decline in the physical and moral strength of the nation, apathy and passivity, which only helped our enemies in their efforts to destroy Polishdom."[...]

"At the same time", added Dmowski, "the insurrectionist program was damaging in that it inspired an erroneous belief that the
struggle should be relegated into the future: that eventually there will
come a moment when an appropriate upheaval should be undertaken.
There are many people who, instead of pressing on with the incessant
revolution of today, wait for a revolution of tomorrow." This, however did not mean that Dmowski was opposed to military struggle
under any circumstances. But Dmowski regarded such tactics as just
one of the instruments available in advancing the Polish policy. He
was opposed to the view that this was the only road leading toward
independence, and that all other activities should be subordinated to it.

In Poland's present conditions the struggle of the Polish nation alone
is not enough to attain independence.[...] We should also carefully
watch for favorable developments in the international sphere and make
sure that our own efforts are carefully synchronized with them.[...]

This Dmowskian approach remains valid today. Polish policy should
follow the international developments closely, trying to anticipate,
and, wherever possible, to influence them in line with our interests.
Our attitudes to our neighbors should not be guided by emotions or
animosities, but should be rational. We should constantly keep in mind
that we are not just rebelling slaves, but a proud and a dignified nation.

Since Dmowski's days the map of Europe has much changed. In
the contemporary world the ideological conflicts have grown in importance, yet geopolitics still play a crucial role. And geopolitics could
be usefully learned from Dmowski. I believe that anyone who is
seriously interested in studying Poland's place in Europe and its policy,
should first read two of Dmowski's books: *Germany, Russia and the
Polish Question* and *The Polish Politics: The Reconstruction of the
State.*

\* \* \*

The problems with which Polish policy is faced today have changed.
Yet, Poland remains Poland. Thus, it is futile, and even impossible,
for each generation to start searching for ideas from scratch, as if
all before was a vacuum. The nation has long existed and searched
for the ways of its advancement in the past. There is no need, then,
for a Columbus, for the America has long been discovered. We have
the foundations of our political thought left to us by our predecessors.
And in approaching new problems we should not ignore these foundations.

The historic foundations, of course, have not been laid exclusively by the National Democrats. Yet, their contribution has been a major one. What has survived from their achievements? What has been accepted by all the Poles?

There continues, above all, the basic amalgam of ideas concerning the nature of the national community and its relationship to the state. Very many Poles, even those who have never heard of the National Democracy, think about the nation and the state in the categories developed by this political movement.

The Catholic Church has adopted many National Democratic concepts of the nation and the state as its own. It has deepened and elaborated on them — adding spiritual and religious aspects to the notion of national community. The Christian concept of the individual's personality developing through contact with other human beings has enriched our thinking about the ties linking the individual and the nation. [...] Primate Stefan Wyszynski and the Holy Father John Paul II have become great teachers of Polish patriotism.

Everyone who derives his concepts of the nation and the state from the National Democratic school could find them confirmed in the homilies which John Paul II delivered during his last pilgrimage to Poland. The grand synthesis of the Pope's thought on this subject was presented in Czestochowa on June 19, 1983: "The State is truly sovereign when it governs the society, but at the same time serves the common good of the society and permits the Nation to realize its own sovereignty and its own identity. This involves the establishment of appropriate conditions for development in the spheres of culture, the economy and other aspects of the life of the social community. The sovereignty of the State is inseparably linked to its ability to advance the freedom of the Nation; to create conditions which enable the Nation to express its entire historical and cultural identity, in other words to permit the Nation to be sovereign through its State".

It is this program of essential principles which cannot be abandoned. There is little hope that it will be implemented soon. At present, unfortunately, it also cannot be realized directly. What can be accomplished now, however, is the program of "internal sovereignty" of the nation. And this can be easily traced back to the National Democratic political thought.

The basic ideological concepts of the National Democracy are by now deeply ingrained in the Polish society; but this is not the case with its political methodology. Our national activities often take the form of sporadic upheavals, rather than that of systematic efforts; they are just protests, not a long range policy. Our attitudes toward our neighbors, and especially Russia, are predominantly emotional. Our analyses of the international situation and Poland's place in it are often characterized by naiveté and wishful thinking. And too often we measure ''our strength by our purposes'', and for political action we substitute mere gestures — believing, moreover, that this is what politics consists of.

The political lessons of the National Democracy, thus, still await re-discovery and popularization.

## ABOUT THE AUTHORS

ROMAN DMOWSKI (1864-1939). One of the founders and the most important leader of the National Democratic movement. A Polish delegate to the Paris Peace Conference; co-signed (with Ignacy Paderewski) the Treaty of Versailles on behalf of Poland.

STANISLAW STOMMA (1908-    ). Professor of Law at the Jagiellonian University. 1957-76 leader of the Catholic *Znak* Group in the Polish parliament. Since 1981 Chairman of the Primate's Advisory Council.

JAN SZCZEPANSKI (1913-    ). Professor of Sociology at the University of Lodz; since 1968 Director of the Institute of Philosophy and Sociology, and, subsequently, a Vice President of the Polish Academy of Sciences. 1978-82 Member of the State Council; 1982-84 Chairman of the Economic and Social Council.

STEFAN CARDINAL WYSZYNSKI (1901-1981). Primate of the Catholic Church in Poland 1948-81.

JANUSZ ZABLOCKI (1926-    ). From 1965 to 1985 a Catholic deputy in the parliament; and since 1967 Chairman of the Centre of Documentation and Social Studies. 1980-84 President of the Polish Social Catholic Association.

ANDRZEJ WALICKI (1930-    ). Professor of Philosophy and Social Thought at the Institute of Philosophy and Sociology of the Polish Academy of Science. Author of several works on Polish and Russian political thought in the 19th century. Presently at the Australian National University.

ALEKSANDER GELLA (1922-    ). Sociologist, author of several works, especially on the Polish intelligentsia. Since 1970 Professor of Sociology at the State University of New York at Buffalo.

ALEKSANDER HALL (1953-    ). Graduated in history from the University of Gdansk in 1977. Subsequently a leader of the Young Poland Movement, and in 1980-81 an advisor to Solidarity. 1981-83 a member of the underground Solidarity movement.

KAROL WOJTYLA (1920-    ) 1964-1977 Archbishop of Cracow. Since 1978 Pope John Paul II.

# INDEX

241